The Labour Markets of Emerging Economies

Advances in Labour Studies

Advances in Labour Studies is a wide-ranging series of research titles from the International Labour Office (ILO), offering in-depth analysis of labour issues from a global perspective. The series has an interdisciplinary flavour that reflects the unique nature of labour studies, where economics, law, social policy and labour relations combine. Bringing together work from researchers from around the world, the series contributes new and challenging research and ideas that aim both to stimulate debate and inform policy.

Published in the series:

THE LABOUR MARKETS OF EMERGING ECONOMIES: HAS GROWTH TRANSLATED INTO MORE AND BETTER JOBS? (by Sandrine Cazes and Sher Verick)

SHAPING GLOBAL INDUSTRIAL RELATIONS: THE IMPACT OF INTERNATIONAL FRAMEWORK AGREEMENTS (edited by Konstantinos Papadakis)

REGULATING FOR DECENT WORK: NEW DIRECTIONS IN LABOUR MARKET REGULATION (edited by Sangheon Lee and Deirdre McCann)

Forthcoming in this series:

WAGE-LED GROWTH: AN EQUITABLE STRATEGY FOR ECONOMIC RECOVERY (edited by Marc Lavoie and Engelbert Stockhammer)

TOWARDS BETTER WORK: UNDERSTANDING LABOUR IN APPAREL GLOBAL VALUE CHAINS (edited by Arianna Rossi, Amy Luinstra and John Pickles)

BEYOND MACROECONOMIC STABILITY: STRUCTURAL TRANSFORMATION AND INCLUSIVE DEVELOPMENT (edited by Iyanatul Islam and David Kucera)

CREATIVE LABOUR REGULATION: INDETERMINACY AND PROTECTION IN AN UNCERTAIN WORLD (edited by Deirdre McCann, Sangheon Lee, Patrick Belser, Colin Fenwick, John Howe and Malte Luebker)

The Labour Markets of Emerging Economies

Has Growth Translated into More and Better Jobs?

Sandrine Cazes and Sher Verick

First published 2013 by
PALGRAVE MACMILLAN and the INTERNATIONAL LABOUR OFFICE

Palgrave Macmillan in the UK is an imprint of Macmillan Publishers Limited, registered in England, company number 785998, of Houndmills, Basingstoke, Hampshire RG21 6XS.

Palgrave Macmillan in the US is a division of St Martin's Press LLC, 175 Fifth Avenue, New York, NY 10010.

Palgrave Macmillan is the global academic imprint of the above companies and has companies and representatives throughout the world.

Palgrave® and Macmillan® are registered trademarks in the United States, the United Kingdom, Europe and other countries.

ISBN 978–1–137–32534–1
ILO ISBN 978–92–2–124565–0

This book is printed on paper suitable for recycling and made from fully managed and sustained forest sources. Logging, pulping and manufacturing processes are expected to conform to the environmental regulations of the country of origin.

A catalogue record for this book is available from the British Library.

A catalog record for this book is available from the Library of Congress.

Contents

Figures

Tables

Box

Foreword

Over the past few decades, rapid economic growth in large middle-income countries has led to a fundamental shift in the global economy. In 1980, the share of developing countries in world GDP (in purchasing power parity terms) was less than a third. As this book is published, developing countries will account for more than half of the global economy. This economic transformation has been led by the rapid and sustained growth of China, but growth in other key economies such as Brazil, India, Indonesia and Turkey has also been a major contributor. The global financial crisis, which decimated jobs in advanced economies, inflicted less pain on these countries and their robust recovery has accelerated the increase in their share of the global economy.

Has this strong growth translated into increasing welfare and improved livelihoods for the people of these countries? Here the evidence is mixed. In some of the emerging economies poverty has been dramatically reduced, indicating a significant improvement in the well-being of the most vulnerable populations. In other countries poverty has been reduced only slowly. In most of the emerging economies inequality has increased, even where poverty declined.

Central to understanding how economic growth translates to the household level is the functioning of the labour market. Employment is the main path for individuals and their families to escape poverty and build a better life. However, it is not just any job that lifts people out of poverty: most poor people work but remain poor. Rather, employment that increases the productivity of the worker and provides adequate wages, rights at work and access to social protection is the only sustainable route to broadly shared prosperity and opportunity.

For these reasons, this book on the labour markets of emerging economies is timely and highly relevant. The volume provides a comparative view of labour market trends and describes the labour market policies and institutional environments in emerging economies. It looks broadly at all of the largest countries and provides in-depth case studies for four, namely Brazil, Indonesia, South Africa and Turkey.

The studies present a picture of mixed results. In several countries, rapid growth has led to job creation and extension of social protection to increasing shares of the population, while in others the creation of decent jobs in the formal economy has lagged. The global financial crisis did not change these patterns for most emerging economies, apart from such countries as South Africa, which was hit hard by the downturn.

The authors provide useful insights into how these countries have developed their labour market and social protection policies and institutions and how these decisions and structures have affected the outcomes. They look at both the long-term structural challenges the countries face as well as the performance of their labour markets in the face of shocks such as the global financial crisis. The book provides important lessons that can benefit other developing countries in their quest to deliver both economic progress and social inclusion for their people.

Sandra Polaski
Deputy Director-General for Policy
International Labour Office

Acknowledgements

Thanks go to the following researchers who provided statistical information and background country studies: Naercio Aquino Menezes Filho, Haroon Bhorat, Hakan Ercan and Meltem Dayioglu Tayfur; Fares Al-Hussami provided much assistance with data. The authors also benefited enormously from comments provided anonymously by three referees, as well as from discussions with a number of ILO colleagues on earlier drafts of individual chapters that appeared as ILO working papers.

Finally, thanks are due to Charlotte Beauchamp, Chris Edgar and Alison Irvine of ILO Publishing for their untiring support in getting the manuscript ready for publication.

Abbreviations

ADB	Asian Development Bank
AIDS	acquired immune deficiency syndrome
ALMP	active labour market policy
ANU	Australian National University
APE	average partial effects
AsgiSA	Accelerated and shared growth initiative for South Africa
BLK	Balai Latihan Kerja (vocational training centres)
BPC	Benefício de Prestação Continuada de Assistência Social
BPS	Badan Pusat Statistik (Statistics Indonesia)
BRIC	Brazil, Russian Federation, India and China
CB	collective bargaining
CCMA	Commission for Conciliation, Mediation and Arbitration
CCT	conditional cash transfers
CIG	Cassa Integrazione Guadagni
CPI	Consumer Price Index
CSG	child support grant
CTPS	Brazilian Labour and Social Security Booklet
CWP	Community Works Programme
DOL	Department of Labour
DPRU	Development Policy Research Unit
ECLAC	Economic Commission for Latin America and the Caribbean
EPL	employment protection legislation
EPWP	Expanded Public Works Programme
ESSA	Employment Services of South Africa
EU	European Union
EWI	Employing Workers Index
FAO	Food and Agriculture Organization
FAT	Fundo de Amparo ao Trabalhador
FDI	foreign direct investment
FGTS	Fundo de Garantia do Tempo de Serviço (Brazilian pension fund)
FGTS	Fundo de Garantia por Tempo de Serviço (Time of Service Guarantee Fund)

GDP	gross domestic product
GEAR	growth, employment and redistribution
GFC	global financial crisis
HIC	high-income countries
HLFS	Household Labour Force Survey
HSRC	Human Sciences Research Council
IFC	International Finance Corporation
ILLS	International Institute for Labour Studies
ILO	International Labour Organization
IMF	International Monetary Fund
INSS	Instituto Nacional de la Seguridad Social (National Institute of Social Security)
ISKUR	Turkish Employment Organization
ISSA	International Social Security Association
KHL	Kebutuhan Hidup Layak ('decent living standard')
KILM	Key Indicators of the Labour Market
LFPR	labour force participation rate
LIC	low-income countries
LMP	labour market policies
MGNREGA	Mahatma Gandhi National Rural Employment Guarantee Act
MIC	middle-income countries
MoMT	Ministry of Manpower and Transmigration
MPC	Monetary Policy Committee
MUV	World Bank Manufactures Unit Value Index
NATLEX	Database of national labour, social security and related human rights legislation
NEET	not-in-employment, education or training
NGP	New Growth Path
NSF	National Skills Foundation
OAP	old-age pension
OAW	own-account workers
OECD	Organization for Economic Co-operation and Development
PES	public employment services
PETI	Child Labour Eradication Programme
PME	Pesquisa Mensal de Emprego (Monthly Employment Survey)
PNAD	Pesquisa Nacional por Amostra de Domicílios (National Household Sampling Survey)

PNPE	Programa Nacional de Estímulo ao Primeiro Emprego (First Job Incentive National Programme)
PPP	public private partnership
QLFS	Quarterly Labour Force Survey (South Africa)
REPRO	Productive Recovery Program
SAHRC	South African Human Rights Commission
Sakernas	National Labour Force Survey (Indonesia)
SASSA	South African Social Security Agency
SETA	skills education training authorities
STATA	data analysis and statistical software
TLS	Training Layoff Scheme
UB	unemployment benefits schemes
UFW	unpaid contributing family workers
UI	unemployment insurance
UIF	unemployment insurance fund
UISA	individual capitalization accounts
UN	United Nations
UNICEF	United Nations International Children's Emergency Fund
USD	United States dollars
VAT	value-added tax
WBG	World Bank Group

1
Introduction

The process of development over the last two to three centuries has been built on the movement of people out of subsistence agriculture into more productive jobs in labour-intensive manufacturing. As captured by the writings of Arthur Lewis, Simon Kuznets and other development economists, this transition resulted in an increase in wages and household incomes, and subsequently, helped lift people out of poverty. This was the case in Western Europe in the 18th and 19th centuries, and was fundamental for the success stories of the latter half of the 20th century such as the Republic of Korea, Taiwan, Malaysia and Thailand. Therefore, central to the process of development is the functioning of the labour market, namely, the ability for an economy to create more productive and better jobs for a large share of the population.

With the economic and geo-political rise over the last couple of decades of large middle-income countries such as China, India, Brazil, Indonesia and Turkey, considerable attention has moved to this set of economies, which have to varying degrees embarked on a rapid path to economic development. For this reason, this group of nations are often referred to as 'emerging markets' or 'emerging economies'.[1] Whatever title is given to this grouping, the contribution of these countries to the transformation of the global economy over the last few decades is without dispute: in 1990, emerging economies and developing countries represented just 30.8 per cent of world gross domestic product (adjusted for purchasing power parity). By 2012, this share had reached 50 per cent, and will continue to grow over the coming years.[2]

During the past few decades, especially during the global boom years of the 2000s, these emerging economies expanded swiftly, with real GDP growing at well above the OECD average, and are indeed developing at far greater rates than witnessed in advanced economies during the

1

industrial revolution. This acceleration in growth was driven by sound macroeconomic policies, significant productivity gains and an increasing integration into the world economy, providing greater access to new technology, capital and financial markets. This trend has been most notable in Asia, particularly in China, and more recently in India. Other large emerging economies such as Brazil, Indonesia and Turkey have also made substantial economic progress in recent years, which represents a major departure from previous decades that were characterized by macroeconomic volatility, economic crises and unsustainable economic models. In this regard, although the global financial crisis that began in the United States in 2007 did impact emerging economies, especially through the collapse in world trade in 2009, these countries either proved to be relatively immune to the shock or recovered quickly in 2010 and 2011. South Africa is one of the few large middle-income countries where the effects of the crisis have been longer-lasting, though this reflects persistent structural challenges in the economy and labour market rather than the nature of this recent shock itself.

However, trends in GDP growth do not provide the full story in terms of how emerging economies have progressed in translating material progress into broader development outcomes. Once the situation in these countries has been delved into, it becomes clear that success in a multi-dimensional context has been less consistent and positive. In terms of poverty reduction, all countries have made some inroads into tackling deprivation, albeit it at different rates and not without hitting stumbling blocks and reversals. This was most notable in China where the poverty headcount ratio (at $2 a day, adjusted for purchasing-power parity) fell at an unprecedented rate from 84.6 per cent in 1990 to just 29.8 per cent in 2008. Experiencing a few setbacks (the East Asian Financial Crisis and the 2005 cut to fuel subsidies), poverty has fallen at a slower pace in Indonesia with the headcount ratio dropping from 84.6 per cent in 1990 to 46.1 per cent in 2010. In Brazil, the poverty rate decreased from 30.0 per cent in 1990 to 10.8 per cent in 2009, while poverty reduction has been slower in India and South Africa.

Though poverty has fallen, growth has mostly been accompanied by increasing inequality in a large number of emerging economies, especially in Asia (notably in China), reflecting that the benefits of newly gained prosperity have not been evenly shared in the population. While this is in line with predictions of Simon Kuznets (that is, the inverse U-shaped Kuznets curve capturing the non-linear relationship between inequality and per capita income), it represents major challenges in terms of the 'winners' and 'losers' in these countries. Indeed, in all emerging economies, there are segments of the population, such as specific racial and ethnic groups, that continue to miss out on the gains. Moreover, skills and spatial mismatches mean that individuals, especially youth, may have the wrong skills or live in the wrong places to be able to benefit from economic growth.

Ultimately, the key to understanding the relationship between economic growth and poverty/inequality in emerging economies is the centrality of the labour market in driving outcomes. In this regard, the labour market is the critical mechanism for lifting individuals and their families out of poverty. However, given that formal-sector job creation has been weak, informality, working poverty and vulnerable employment, all different indicators of decent-work deficits, continue to be the norm for most people in emerging economies. Moreover, women, youth and other segments of the population face barriers to accessing the few good jobs in the formal economy. Overall, promoting better outcomes in the labour market represents one the greatest challenges to emerging economies.

For this reason, the main themes of this book centre on the labour market situation, trends and regulations in emerging economies. While there is a wide range of publications providing a macroeconomic perspective or a focus on poverty and inequality (for example, OECD 2010), far less has been written on the labour markets of these countries. Moreover, in order to learn from the global financial crisis, it is crucial to reflect and compare different experiences and policy responses at the country level. This book attempts to fill this gap by addressing both short-term issues, particularly in relation to the global financial crisis, and longer-term challenges that stem not only from economic conditions, but also historical legacies and social factors.

Although this volume focuses on emerging economies (or large middle-income countries), the goal is not to provide sweeping generalizations about this group of countries. After all, the diversity in their labour markets is far more important than their commonalities. In this regard, the common trends witnessed in the worldwide boom years of 2002–2007 were more of a global phenomenon than one that was specific to these nations. At the same time, the increasing geo-political role of emerging economies means that a greater understanding of their labour markets is important, not only as an abstract academic exercise, but also as a means to raise a more general awareness of the situation in these countries. In addition to exploring the great diversity in the labour markets of emerging economies, this book focuses in more detail on four countries: Brazil, Indonesia, South Africa and Turkey, which provide useful case studies given their country-specific challenges.

Brazil was once an economy prone to overheating and crises, which was driven by lax macroeconomic policy. In recent years, however, the government, starting with former President Luiz Inacio 'Lula' da Silva, adopted both a prudent macroeconomic policy approach and a social policy that has successfully brought down poverty and inequality. Indeed, Brazil is one of the few countries to have created a significant number of jobs in the formal sector in recent years.

Indonesia used to belong to the group of the East Asian 'tigers', along with Thailand and Malaysia. However, the East Asian Financial Crisis of 1997–1999 hit Indonesia much harder and resulted in a massive economic contraction, a commensurate rise in poverty and, ultimately, the fall of the Soeharto regime. Over the last seven years or so, Indonesia has managed to 're-invent' itself through progress towards democratization and decentralization. Since 2005, the Indonesian economy has performed strongly thanks to its large domestic market and exports of commodities.

In contrast to the other three countries, South Africa has been burdened by the legacies of Apartheid, which resulted in some of the highest unemployment rates in the world. Despite being a commodity exporter, Africa's largest economy has been unable to take advantage of the global commodity boom, and remains in a weak economic state that continues to be reflected by high unemployment rates.

Turkey is another country that has emerged from decades of crises and economic mismanagement to present itself as a modern, secular economy, which has grown strongly in recent years and been accompanied by robust job creation.

Therefore, while these four countries are different in terms of size and weight in the world economy, they have all experienced both periods of sustained growth and episodes of crisis. Though these countries are not the largest emerging economies, they are diverse in terms of their longer-term structural labour market challenges, which also reflect their very different historical contexts. These challenges have been tackled by governments through a range of interventions despite limited public services provision, low coverage of social insurance schemes and the high incidence of informality. More recently, policymakers in the four countries have all sought to mitigate the impact of the global financial crisis through stimulus packages, but with emphasis on different policies and areas of intervention.

By focusing on Brazil, Indonesia, South Africa and Turkey, this volume, therefore, contributes to broadening the debate and discussion on the rise of emerging economies, which is usually limited to China and India (or the BRICs, that is, Brazil, the Russian Federation, India and China). All four countries chosen are already strategic players in their respective regions as reflected by not only their economic importance, but also their role as political players at the regional and global level. With respect to the latter, these countries are all members of the G20 grouping, and have actively sought to improve global governance in such areas as financial regulation and policy coordination. Moreover, to ensure broader relevance, findings are presented, mostly in chapters 2 and 3, on the most prominent and largest emerging economies, China and India,[3] and other middle-income countries such as Argentina, Mexico and the Russian Federation.

Relevant to a wider discourse on labour market policies and institutions, the book addresses much debated themes such as the role of employment protection legislation and minimum wages in these countries. However, the volume goes beyond the normally narrow debate on their detrimental effect on labour market outcomes by providing a comprehensive coverage of how labour market policies, such as training and public employment programmes, have been utilized in these countries over recent years, especially during the global financial crisis.

In summary, there are three key and interrelated themes woven throughout this book:

A mixed picture on labour market outcomes: Despite strong economic growth, the labour market in most emerging economies continues to be characterized by informality and the lack of better jobs in the formal economy. Moreover, many jobs that are created tend to be precarious, which is indeed linked to their increased integration in the global economy. In terms of micro-level factors, one of the main drivers of labour market outcomes is education. Indeed, the challenge is not only the lack of education and training, but the phenomenon of a mismatch between the supply of skills and those demanded by employers. Against this longer-term context, the global financial crisis did not fundamentally change the overall trends in the labour market of these large middle-income countries.

Increasing use of labour market policies to address structural challenges and crises: In contrast to earlier decades, emerging economies are increasingly developing and implementing labour market policies to address both structural and demand-related unemployment and underemployment such as public employment programmes, entrepreneurship incentives, and training, often targeting women and youth.

Labour market institutions can play a positive role but their effectiveness remains a challenge: While there has been a strong tendency around the world towards deregulating labour markets, emerging economies are showing that regulations such as minimum wages can be used effectively to address poverty and inequality, without hampering formal-sector job creation. Institutions also have an important role to play during crises because they provide protection to workers. At the same time, many regulations in these countries are not adequately enforced, which needs to be addressed with respect to improving job quality and efficiency.

As illustrated in Figure 1.1, these three themes are interrelated. Firstly, the longer-term structural problems/trends in emerging countries have been a key determinant of the impact of the global financial crisis. For example, in South Africa, the high level of unemployment and weak attachment to the labour market among the African population left this group vulnerable to the global financial crisis, which hit the country in 2009. At the same time, the danger of any crisis is that the fall in aggregate demand results in more permanent damage to the labour market such that a short-term economic downturn leads to a worsening

Figure 1.1 The structure of the book – linkages between long-term structural challenges in the labour market, the impact of the global financial crisis, and labour market regulations (policies and institutions)

of (structural) unemployment, underemployment and other outcomes. This well-known lag in the labour market following a crisis has been described in IMF (2010) and Reinhart and Rogoff (2008). That said, the resilience of many emerging economies to the impact of the global financial crisis is testimony to an increasing robustness of the labour market, at least in quantitative terms.

Structural unemployment is typically associated with the problem of a skills mismatch or the impact of labour market regulations. In terms of the latter issue, there has been a long-running and highly controversial debate on the effect of such institutions as employment protection legislation and minimum wages on unemployment; indeed, it was seen by many economists as a major reason why unemployment was higher in Europe than in the United States. In emerging economies, the relationship between regulations and labour market outcomes is more complex because the majority of workers are located either in the agricultural sector or the urban informal economy. Moreover, enforcement of regulations is weak due to such factors as insufficient labour inspection and corruption. At the same time, it is often argued by economists that these labour market regulations are a driver of informality: enterprises would rather remain unlicensed and unregistered to avoid punitive labour laws that would require them to adhere to such conditions as the minimum wage and severance pay.

During the global financial crisis, labour market regulations have received new interest among certain commentators (such as the International Labour Organization) in terms of their role in mitigating the shock emanating from the trade collapse and credit crunch. For example, in many European countries, protection from dismissal (and the associated severance pay and other indirect costs) encouraged employers to adjust to the shock through internal mechanisms, namely working hours, before firing workers, which was the main channel of adjustment in countries with weak protection such as the United States. In emerging economies, there has been a stronger focus on the role of minimum wages in protecting the incomes of the poor during the global financial crisis; in this respect, Brazil raised the minimum wage over recent years, helping reduce poverty and inequality despite the adverse economic downturn in 2009. In terms of the policy environment, the country chapters also discuss the role of social policies such as Bolsa Família in Brazil and the Child Support Grant in South Africa, because these (conditional and unconditional) transfers have become priority areas of intervention in emerging economies, and ultimately, have an impact on the labour market.

The framework presented in Figure 1.1, which stresses the inter-linkages between longer-term labour market challenges, the impact of the global financial crisis and the role of labour market regulations, therefore, forms the overriding storyline for this book. The discussion and insights are strengthened by an in-depth examination of the aggregate trends (also disaggregated by gender, education and other factors) and micro-econometric analysis utilizing unit-level data, which allows for the identification of the role of specific factors, such as education, in driving labour market outcomes.

The remainder of this book centres on two segments: Part I provides a comparative perspective on labour market trends (Chapter 2) and labour market policies and institutions (Chapter 3), which allows for an overview of these issues across a number of emerging economies. Part II consists of the four country chapters on Brazil (Chapter 4), Indonesia (Chapter 5), South Africa (Chapter 6) and Turkey (Chapter 7), which all address the troika displayed in Figure 1.1 to varying degrees. It should be stressed that the emphasis in these country chapters is not the same; rather, the aim is to highlight the diversity in the labour markets of these emerging economies, though building from a common framework. In order to find more robust and deeper insights on these relationships, all of the country chapters turn to the unit-level data to estimate simple but highly relevant micro-econometric models that supplement the analysis of aggregate data in the comparative chapters.

Chapter highlights

Part I

Chapter 2: Labour Market Trends in Emerging Economies: Resilience versus Decent Work Deficits

While there is wide acceptance that consistently strong economic growth is a necessary condition to make major inroads into reducing poverty, less thought has been given to how this expansion in economic activity has translated into labour market outcomes in emerging economies. In this regard, high rates of economic growth have been witnessed in Indonesia and Brazil (prior to the 2000s). China has more recently emerged as the leading growth centre of the world, while India has begun to stake a claim at being part of this elite group of countries. Countries like Turkey have shown a new era of resilience in the face of the crisis and strong economic prospects. However, despite robust economic progress in emerging economies, and in most cases, falling rates of poverty, the labour markets of these countries have not always benefited to the same extent. In particular, informality, working poverty and vulnerable employment continue to be the norm for most workers. At the same time, women, youth and other segments of the population face hurdles to accessing the few good jobs in the formal economy.

For this reason, unemployment is typically not the best indicator of slack and distress in these labour markets. More importantly, the labour markets in emerging economies continue to be characterized by strong segmentation between a small formal sector and large informal sector. Many people continue to live in rural areas and rely on small household plots and subsistence farming, while an increasing number have left for urban areas and to seek their fortunes in other countries. Another common feature is the presence of gender disparities as reflected by low female labour force participation in some countries (notably in India and Turkey), under-representation in industry and overrepresentation in informal employment in most economies. Other labour market inequalities exist for such groups as youth, as noted above, and some segments of society that have been excluded from benefiting from economic gains such as the black African population in South Africa and Brazil and the scheduled castes and tribals in India.

Altogether, the global financial crisis had a diverse impact on emerging economies with more severe outcomes in Central and Eastern Europe and the Commonwealth of Independent States (such as the Russian Federation) and milder effects in Asia (such as in Indonesia) and Latin America (to a lesser extent). However, even for the harder-hit countries, economic recovery in emerging economies was mostly strong in 2010 and has subsequently led to a fall in unemployment. Overall, these countries have demonstrated considerable resilience to the downturn of 2009, which contrasts with their experience in earlier periods of crisis. The milder impact on employment and wage outcomes in these emerging economies can be explained by a combination of factors including the continuing growth of China and its subsequent impact on commodity exporters, large domestic markets, lack of exposure to the financial calamities that hit the United States and Europe, large foreign currency reserves, low levels of debt, and better policymaking. In terms of the last, the country chapters present specific examples of how policymakers responded to the downturn through stimulus packages and labour market policies.

Despite the apparent resilience in these countries, the trends presented in this chapter confirm, nonetheless, that many challenges remain in the labour markets of emerging economies, namely the failure to create more and better jobs in the formal economy and the persisting gender, spatial and other inequalities, especially those facing young people in these countries. These issues are investigated in much more depth in this volume, particularly in the following country chapters.

Chapter 3: Labour Market Regulations for Development: Enhancing Labour Market Institutions and Policies in Emerging Economies

Taking a similar comparative perspective, this chapter provides an overview of the main theoretical and empirical arguments surrounding the complex and controversial issue of labour market regulations and their effect on economic and employment outcomes. Given that the empirical findings, in particular cross-country ones, are far from robust, it is not surprising that the debate on these effects is still unsettled. The chapter then presents the main features and characteristics of existing labour market policies and institutions in emerging economies, with particular emphasis on employment protection legislation, minimum wages, trade unions and collective bargaining, as well as unemployment benefits schemes. As in Chapter 2, special reference is also made to China, India and other emerging economies not covered in Part II of the book. Each of these institutions is examined and characterized by a set of various parameters. This cross-country overview reveals, on the one hand, the important heterogeneity amongst emerging countries in terms of the labour market institutional setting, in particular, regarding employment protection legislation and minimum wage schemes. On the other hand, it underlines the low coverage rates of social insurance schemes (such as unemployment protection) that characterizes all these countries.

In a second part, the chapter reviews the main labour market programmes that have been put in place in emerging economies such as the public employment programmes in India (Mahatma Gandhi National Rural Employment Guarantee Scheme [MGNREGS]) and South Africa (Expanded Public Works Programme [EPWP]), and conditional cash transfers (for example, Bolsa Família). While these latter schemes are not, strictly speaking, labour market policies, they nonetheless have important implications for labour force participation. Finally, the chapter considers how emerging economies have utilized labour market policies during the recent global financial crisis to help mitigate the impact of the shock.

Part II

Chapter 4: Transitions out of Informality and Falling Unemployment: The Transformation of the Brazilian Labour Market since the 2000s

Following decades of extreme inequality and poverty along with bouts of high inflation and crises, the performance of the Brazilian economy and labour market over the last decade is rather remarkable. This achievement is the outcome of not only strong economic growth and macroeconomic stability, but also effective government interventions in the area of taxation and social policies. Notably, the government under President Luiz Inacio 'Lula' da Silva facilitated the rise in minimum wages (and thus pensions) along with increasing spending on the famous Bolsa Família scheme that provides conditional cash transfers to poor households. With also important implications for pensions, the government raised minimum wages, which had been stagnant or falling during the 1990s and early 2000s. In a stark departure from previous crises, Brazil responded effectively to the global financial crisis through a stimulus package and social protection measures. Thanks also to strong external demand, the recovery in Brazil in 2010, like many other countries around the globe, was swift.

Turning to the labour market, the positive growth story and effective implementation of policies have resulted in a fall in the unemployment rate from 11.5 per cent in 2004 to 5.2 per cent at the end of 2011. This was driven by the robust creation of jobs in the formal economy: the Brazilian economy created 15.3 million formal jobs from 2003 to 2010, which continued even during the recession of 2009. Increased formalization in Brazil resulted from both a supportive macroeconomic environment, stronger incentives for formalization through the taxation and social security system, improved labour inspection, reduced demographic pressures and increased educational attainment.

That said, the results from the econometric analysis show that the inequalities in accessing formal sector jobs remain, particularly as a result of low levels of education. Indeed, there is an urgent need to improve education to diminish the not-in-employment, education or training (NEET) rate of youth and to enhance the skills of future Brazilian workers. It is particularly important to improve the job prospects of the poorest fraction of young Brazilians. For these reasons,

Brazil needs to further expand education in terms of promoting transitions from high school to college education and vocational training.

Chapter 5: The Tale of Two Labour Markets: The Resilience of the Indonesian Labour Market to the Global Financial Crisis versus Increasing Casualization of Jobs

As one of the star performers of the Asia region, Indonesia had grown rapidly during the 1980s and 1990s, resulting in a significant fall in poverty. However, when the East Asian financial crisis hit in 1997–1998, the country suffered a major blow to this economic and social progress. When the global financial crisis spread in late 2008 to emerging economies like Indonesia, it was expected that these countries would be severely affected. However, in contrast to previous crisis episodes, Indonesia proved to be rather resilient despite the fact that exports collapsed in 2009.

The findings presented in the chapter both confirm the findings of previous studies and show that much of the recent developments in the Indonesian labour market seem to have been part of a longer-term trend since the mid-2000s, particularly regarding the increasing casualization of the workforce. The findings of the chapter also point towards the underlying changes in the relationship between educational attainment and employment states in the late 2000s.

Despite the apparent resilience of Indonesia to the impact of the global financial crisis, the country, however, continues to face a number of substantial challenges. In particular, the Indonesian economy has failed in recent years to generate sufficient regular formal-sector jobs, notably in the manufacturing sector. Ultimately, the Indonesian government should aim to develop more effective labour market regulations and an unemployment benefit system that provide adequate income and employment protection to workers. A broader approach to social protection than currently exists would ensure that the burden of unemployment and underemployment is shared between the government and social partners.

Chapter 6: The South African Labour Market: Long-term Structural Problems Exacerbated by the Global Financial Crisis

Since the end of Apartheid in 1994, South Africa has been plagued by some of the highest unemployment rates and lowest employment-population ratios in the world. During the global boom years of 2002–2007, unemployment began to finally fall as economic conditions further improved. Owing to its strong trade and financials links, South

Africa was, however, hit hard by the global financial crisis, which has exacerbated the longer-term structural problems in the economy and labour market.

In spite of the fiscal stimulus package and the loosening of monetary policy, the ensuing recession of 2008–2009 devastated the South African labour market, as reflected by the fall in employment (both formal and informal) and an increase in the number of discouraged individuals. As a result, there has been a strong rise in discouraged workers. Looking at changes from the 2008 to 2009–2010, the chapter presents evidence that the probability of being unemployed and discouraged increased the most during the crisis for black Africans, the poorly educated and individuals in the most-affected provinces. Departing from longer-term gender disparities, searching and non-searching unemployment increased more during the recession for poorly educated African men than for women with similar characteristics, which stems from the sectoral impact of the crisis. The results also show that the likelihood of job search among the unemployed is linked to the search status of their spouse; that is, couples tend to be jointly discouraged.

The response of policymakers to the first post-Apartheid recession indicates that the South African government is placing considerable emphasis on existing schemes such as the Expanded Public Works Programme (EPWP), while experimenting with innovative measures such as the Training Layoff Fund. However, most policies did not specifically target the issue of discouragement and job search. In 2010, the South African government announced the latest policy initiative, the 'New Growth Path', which focuses on how and where to create jobs. Though addressing insufficient labour demand is indeed a critical issue, this needs to be supplemented with policies that tackle the supply side, namely the problems of inadequate skills, work experience and spatial inequalities.

Chapter 7: Strengthening the Turkish Labour Market through More Efficient Labour Regulations

Based on both aggregate labour market statistics and labour force survey micro-data, this chapter provides an in-depth review of the Turkish labour market over the decade 2001–2010. Labour market policies and institutions are also examined in light of the key labour market challenges of the country, which are all facets of the process of transition for this middle-income country: the ongoing rural–urban migration; low levels of education; and the very low labour force participation rate of women. The upshot is that Turkey had its ongoing structural labour market problems when the effects of the global financial crisis were felt in 2008–2009. This chapter argues, however, that although the global financial crisis hit Turkey hard, the country proved to be far more resilient than expected. In particular, though the unemployment rate increased quickly in 2009, reaching around 7 per cent, it fell rapidly in 2010 and almost reached its pre-crisis level.

During the crisis period in Turkey, agricultural employment has risen, reflecting that the sector has acted as a buffer to job losses in the formal sector. A more negative development was the increase in discouraged workers, like South Africa covered in Chapter 6. However, the results from the micro-econometric analysis indicate that the crisis of 2009 did not change much in the labour market, and the longer-term issues are still very much evident, such as the disparities in access to formal sector jobs for individuals with low levels of educational attainment. This chapter also underscores that, beyond the short-time working scheme, most labour market institutions and policies do not appear to be effective or widespread in Turkey. So, major challenges remain in the Turkish labour market, such as the low level of social security coverage and inadequate female labour force participation. The long-term policy agenda for the country should, therefore, focus on establishing and promoting efficient labour market regulations, such as a set of policies and institutions, which will ensure more and better jobs. In particular, Turkey must improve education standards to equip its labour force with better skills, extend social security coverage and review possibly costly segments of the labour market institutions, such as social contributions or high severance pay. At the same time, it should also provide enough resources to support labour market policies. Moreover, given the serious gender gap identified throughout the analysis, policies promoting equality of opportunities and social inclusion with a focus on women and young people are crucial for supporting the transition of the informal economy to a formal one.

Chapter 8: Conclusion

Covering the interlinked themes of longer-term labour market trends, the impact of the global financial crisis and the role of labour market regulations, this book documents both common issues and the diversity in emerging economies. These insights reveal that despite high levels of economic growth, decent-work deficits continue to characterize the labour markets of these large middle-income countries. More specifically, the norm for most workers in these labour markets continues to be informal employment: in lower-middle countries like India and Indonesia, agriculture still plays an important role. In contrast, Brazil has been more successful at both tackling unemployment and creating jobs in the formal sector. The problem of skills mismatches means that unfilled jobs exist alongside a large pool of unskilled or poorly educated workers.

Education is a central factor in driving specific outcomes in the four emerging economies studied in-depth in this book. Indeed, uneducated workers are less likely to make the transition from informality into formality (Brazil) and have a higher probability of being in casual jobs (Indonesia). They also are more likely to give up job searches and become discouraged (South Africa) and have a greater likelihood of being informally employed or discouraged (Turkey).

At the same time, emerging economies proved to be more resilient to the global financial crisis than previous episodes due to better policymaking, large domestic economies and less exposure to the housing and financial markets of the United States. The labour market of South Africa, however, was badly affected and failed to rebound in 2010 along with other countries that were hit by the fall in world trade in 2009.

The comparative and detailed country-specific insights on labour market policies and institutions indicate that policymakers in emerging economies are increasingly turning to these interventions to shape and improve labour market outcomes. With regard to policies, countries are utilizing a range of measures to improve the match between labour demand and supply, while also trying to protect and create jobs, most notably during the global financial crisis.

This book covers a number of contentious labour market issues, namely employment-protection legislation and minimum wages. The Indonesian Manpower Law of 2003 (and the severance payments covered by this law) has been a highly controversial piece of legislation, but there is little evidence that it is a major hindrance to job creation in the country. Moreover, rather than showing a negative impact on employment in the formal sector, minimum wages appear to, in fact, have positive spill-over effects on wages in the economy. Also known in the literature as the 'lighthouse effect', minimum wages help improve workers' bargaining power in the informal sector and thus can make a contribution to poverty alleviation and a reduction in inequality, as is evident in the case of Brazil.

The challenge for emerging economies, therefore, continues to be how to promote a more inclusive growth pattern that is driven and accompanied by the creation of better jobs that provide not only sufficient income to lift people out of poverty, but also greater protection.

To achieve this goal, policymakers need to ensure that labour market policies and institutions play a supportive role in terms of both protecting workers during crises and tackling structural problems related to poverty and inequality. Together with representatives of trade unions and employer organizations, policymakers need to specifically consider:

- Promoting the formalization of enterprises and workers through both stronger incentives (progressive taxation, access to social security, etc.) and improved labour inspection;

- Enhancing enforcement and relevance of labour market regulations such as employment protection legislation and minimum wages in order to increase protection to workers, while not unduly hindering flexibility of employers – here, the important issue is that governments and tripartite partners should strive to cultivate both flexibility and security, which in turn reinforces positive outcomes in the labour market and economy as a whole;

- Expanding coverage of social protection (in line with the recommendations of the ILO-initiated and now widely accepted Social Protection Floor) to improve income security of workers and their families to help further reduce poverty and inequality, while supporting labour market participation;

- Improving access to and the quality of education and training, especially with the involvement of employers to reduce the phenomenon of skills mismatch; and

- Enhancing (active) labour market policies that address both long-term structural problems and mitigate the impact of economic and natural shocks through both targeted interventions (such as for youth and women) and universal schemes (such as public employment programmes).

Notes

1. The term 'emerging economies' is a variation on the catchphrase 'emerging markets' introduced by former World Bank economist, Antoine van Agtmael, in 1981. Beforehand, these countries had been referred to as 'developing countries' or the 'third world'. In this context, van Agtmael wanted to highlight the business and investment opportunities in these economies rather than seeing them more negatively as just countries with backward and poor populations. In 2001, Jim O'Neil of Goldman Sachs coined the acronym 'BRICs', a grouping

of Brazil, the Russian Federation, India and China. O'Neil predicted that the BRICs would overtake the six largest advanced economies by 2041 (which has since been revised downwards). The grouping has been more recently expanded to include South Africa, Africa's largest economy (hence, the group is now referred to as 'BRICS').

2. Share of GDP in world total based on purchase-power-parity, IMF World Economic Outlook Database, April 2012; accessed 28 June 2012.

3. Relevant micro-data is, unfortunately, not available for China and India.

Part I

2
Labour Market Trends in Emerging Economies: Decent Work Deficits Persist Despite Growth and Resilience to the Crisis

2.1 Introduction

Rapid and sustained economic growth has become the hallmark of successfully developing countries in recent times. Some of these countries have been able to grow at 8 per cent per annum or more over a long period, resulting in a doubling of the economy every decade. Though such high growth rates have become a benchmark for all aspiring developing countries, history shows that only a relatively small sample of countries has been able to sustain such high levels of growth over an extended time-frame. In this respect, the Growth Commission noted in its 2008 report that only 13 countries have managed to achieve a growth rate of 7 per cent or more over a period of at least 25 years (Growth Commission 2008).[1] Nonetheless, growth rates in many developing countries are far greater than witnessed during the Industrial Revolution: for example, Crafts (1985) estimates that the British economy grew on average by only 2.5 per cent per annum between 1831 and 1860.

As a consequence, these modern fast-growing developing countries have, in most cases, been able to reduce poverty. China stands out here insofar as it has been able cut the poverty rate from 60.2 per cent in 1990 to just 16.3 per cent in 2005 (US$1.25 per day adjusted for purchasing power parity), representing a fall in the number of extreme poor by over 500 million over this decade and a half period.[2] Over the past two decades, Indonesia has also been able to drastically reduce poverty by more than half from 100 million extreme poor in 1990 to 43 million in 2010. At the same time, countries like India (until more recently) and

21

South Africa have been less successful at making progress on reducing material deprivation.

While there is wide acceptance that consistently strong economic growth is a necessary condition to make major inroads into reducing poverty (though not a sufficient one – resource-rich countries are examples of such cases), less thought has been given to how this expansion in economic activity has translated into labour market outcomes in emerging economies. Gross domestic product (GDP) is the single indicator that is typically focused on in terms of economic growth, which renders a comparison across time and countries more straightforward (although there is the issue of converting nominal changes into real ones and accounting for difference in purchasing power parity). In contrast, understanding the health of a country's labour market requires reviewing and tracking a range of indicators.[3] In the majority of advanced economies, most of the focus is on the unemployment rate as evidenced by the discourse of politicians, international organizations, academics and the media in Europe, North America and other OECD countries. In some cases, the unemployment rate plays a more central role even in macroeconomic policymaking: for instance, in the United States, the Federal Reserve has a dual mandate (price stability and full employment) and, therefore, the unemployment rate is closely monitored, especially by the markets in terms of pre-empting the Federal Reserve's policy response.

However, as stressed in the introduction and elsewhere in this book, the unemployment rate, though relevant in a number of middle-income countries, a range of other dimensions are far more important in terms of documenting decent work deficits. It is crucial to not only understand which part of the labour force is unemployed, but also highlight whether productive jobs are being created in the formal economy that promote transitions in the labour market. These transitions, in turn, should result in higher wages to lift workers and their families out of poverty, provide access to social and employment protection and promote enforcement and protection of workers' rights. The reality for most developing countries, in spite of economic growth, is unfortunately far from this stylized picture of a well-functioning developing country labour market.

Moving to the specific situation of the emerging economies covered in this book, high rates of economic growth have been witnessed in Indonesia and Brazil (prior to the 2000s). China has more recently emerged as the leading growth centre of the world, while India has begun to stake a claim at being part of this elite group of countries.

Countries such as Turkey have shown a new era of resilience in the face of the crisis and strong economic prospects. However, despite robust economic progress in emerging economies and, in most cases, falling rates of poverty, the labour markets of these countries have not always benefited to the same extent. In particular, informality, working poverty and vulnerable employment[4] continue to be the norm for most workers. At the same time, women, youth and other segments of the population face hurdles in accessing the few good jobs in the formal economy. That said, there is a great deal of diversity and evidence of both positive and negative trends in the labour markets of emerging economies.

This chapter delves into both the macroeconomic and labour market situation among a key set of emerging economies (Argentina, Brazil, China, India, Indonesia, Mexico, the Russian Federation, South Africa and Turkey). The data shows both common trends and divergences among these countries. In addition, there is an in-depth coverage of the impact of the global financial crisis on these middle-income countries, comparing outcomes to previous crisis episodes that had hit these economies much harder.

Against this background, the remainder of this chapter is structured as follows. Section 2.2 presents macroeconomic and labour market trends. The section addresses not only differences in the unemployment rate, which only provide a limited insight into the labour market in such economies, but also informality, employment status, wages and differences across the population. Section 2.3 presents the impact of the global financial crisis on this set of emerging economies, taking a comparative view across countries and with respect to previous crises. Finally, section 2.4 concludes.

2.2   A macro view on emerging economics

Before analysing trends and characteristics of the labour market in emerging economies, it is useful to briefly review economic growth in nine of these countries over the last two decades. China has grown rapidly since 1990 with the economy expanding by more than 600 per cent, which far outweighs other middle-income countries. Figure 2.1 illustrates the rapid growth in China. As a consequence of this acceleration in growth, this set of emerging economies has increased their share in world GDP from 11 per cent in 1990 to 17 per cent in 2009. However, a considerable proportion of this convergence is due to China. Indeed, excluding China shows that the share in world GDP of the eight

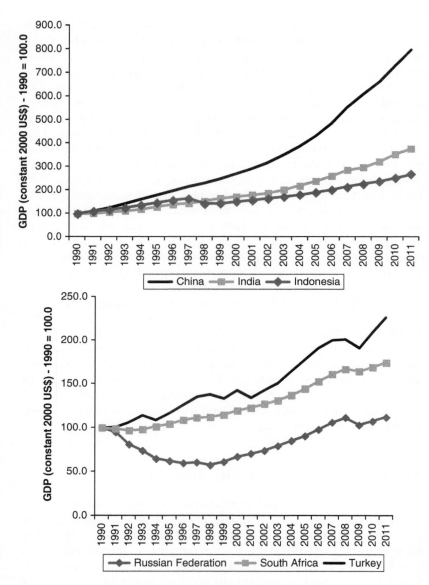

Figure 2.1   Growth in GDP since 1990 (rebased 1990 = 100.0)

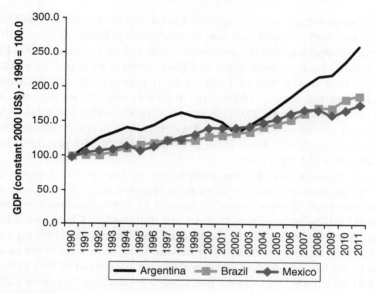

Figure 2.1 (Continued)
Notes: GDP in 2000 constant prices (US$) has been converted into an index with 1990 as the
base (1990 = 100.0).
Source: World Development Indicators database, authors' calculations.

other economies has only marginally increased over this period from 9
to 10 per cent.

Figure 2.1 illustrates the rapid growth in China since 1990, with the
economy increasing by almost 700 per cent by 2011. In comparison,
India's economy has grown by around 270 per cent since 1990, accelerating during the global boom years in the 2000s, while Indonesia
has expanded by less than 170 per cent over this period, which was
disrupted by the East Asian financial crisis of 1997–1998. Though the
overall trends have been positive in Latin America, the economies of
Argentina, Brazil and Mexico have been more volatile. Turkey has similarly suffered a number of crises since 1990, but has recently grown
strongly with more than a doubling of the economy over this period
and a robust recovery in 2010 and 2011 (see below for a further discussion on the impact and recovery from the global financial crisis). South
Africa has struggled more over the past few decades, while the Russian
Federation suffered an extended period of contraction until the end of
the 1990s, but has expanded rapidly in the 2000s, largely due to the
commodity boom.

In fast-growing countries, notably China and India, growth has been associated with a rapid increase in productivity. From 2002 to 2010, labour productivity (GDP per person employed in constant 1990 PPP-adjusted $) more than doubled in China, while it increased by almost 60 per cent in the case of India.[5] Labour productivity also increased strongly in the Russian Federation, Indonesia and Turkey (by over 30 per cent from 2002 to 2010). In contrast, productivity was more sluggish over this nine-year period in Argentina (23.6 per cent total growth from 2002 to 2010), Brazil (11.6 per cent), Mexico (3.9 per cent) and South Africa (12.3 per cent).

As a consequence of these growth trends, the relative weights in the global economy and rankings have changed. Out of this group of nine countries, the five largest economies in 1990 were Brazil (around US$502 billion in constant 2005 dollars), followed by China ($445 billion), Mexico ($413 billion), the Russian Federation ($386 billion) and India ($275 billion). As of 2011, China and India have risen in the rankings to the first and second places with an annual output of $3.5 trillion and $1.04 trillion, respectively (constant 2005 dollars). The three Latin American countries follow: Brazil ($945 billion), Mexico ($720 billion) and Argentina ($473 billion).

2.2.1   Poverty falling but has been accompanied by rising inequality in many countries

As stressed by Amartya Sen and other development economists, growth is only a means to promoting human and social progress and not an end in itself (for example, Sen 1999). For this reason, it is important to reflect on changes in poverty and inequality juxtaposed against this period of robust economic growth. The main constraint to looking at these dimensions is the lack of data, particularly insufficient points over time to have a good idea about trends in the level and distribution of income. Available data (PovCalNet from the World Bank or national sources) suggests that while poverty decreased during the 2000s (prior to the impact of the global financial crisis) in the majority of emerging economies, trends in income inequality are less favourable (Figure 2.2 (b)).

For example, the proportion of the population living on US$2 per day or less (adjusted for purchasing power parity) has been starkly reduced in China from 73.8 per cent on average in the 1990s to 39.3 per cent in the following decade (reaching a low of 29.8 per cent in 2008). At the same time, however, inequality has risen sharply with the Gini Index increasing from 35.7 (1990s average) to 42.5 in the 2000s (2005 figure). Though rising inequality along with rapid growth and falling poverty is not surprising, the challenge for such countries is to ensure that the benefits of growth go to the poor to ensure an even more rapid reduction in poverty and to avoid social unrest. In the case of India,

(a)   Poverty headcount ratio at $2 a day (PPP) (% of population) (1990s versus 2000s)

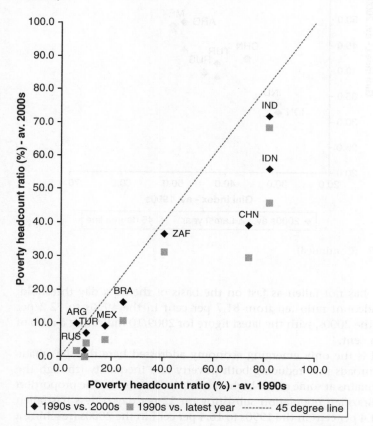

Figure 2.2 Poverty and inequality in emerging economies (1990s versus 2000s)
Notes: Latest year for poverty headcount ratio: Argentina (2010); the Russian Federation (2009); Turkey (2008); Mexico (2008); Brazil (2009); South Africa (2009); China (2008); India (2010); Indonesia (2010). Latest year for Gini Index: Indonesia (2005); India (2005); China (2005); Turkey (2008); the Russian Federation (2009); Argentina (2010); Mexico (2008); South Africa (2009); Brazil (2009).
Source: World Bank World Development Indicators online database, accessed 7 August 2012.

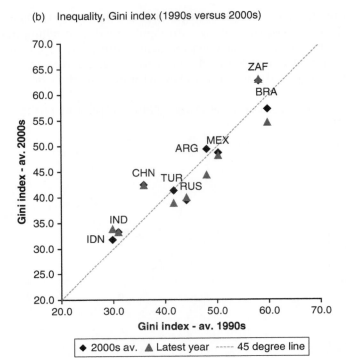

(b)   Inequality, Gini index (1990s versus 2000s)

Figure 2.2   (Continued)

poverty has not fallen as fast on the basis of the $2 a day threshold: the headcount ratio fell from 81.7 per cent in the 1990s to 72.2 per cent in the 2000s, with the latest figure for 2009/10 indicating a ratio of 68.7 per cent.

Brazil is the only emerging economy addressed here that has made major inroads into reducing both poverty and inequality (though the latter remains at some of the highest levels in the world). The proportion of the Brazilian population subsisting on $2 per day or less has fallen from 24.4 per cent in the 1990s to 16.4 per cent in the 2000s (reaching a low of 10.8 per cent in 2009), while inequality as measured by the Gini index declined from 59.7 in the 1990s to 57.2 in the next decade. The Gini index for Brazil has since fallen to 54.2 in 2009. In Argentina, the picture is slightly more mixed, though increasingly positive: the poverty headcount ratio increased from the 1990s average of 6.0 per cent to 10.0 per cent, which was driven by the debt crisis in 2001. The ratio subsequently dropped to 1.9 per cent in 2010. Similarly, the average Gini index rose from 47.9 in the 1990s to 49.5 in the following decade, but subsequently dropped to 44.5 in 2010.

After increasing in the wake of the East Asian financial crisis of 1997–1998, poverty fell again in Indonesia in the latter half of the 2000s: the headcount ratio, using the $2-a-day threshold, declined rapidly from 81.9 per cent on average in the 1990s (at a similar level to India during the same period) to 56.2 per cent in the 2000s. The latest figure for 2010 reveals a ratio of 46.1 per cent. Therefore, there is no evidence that the global financial crisis has negatively impacted poverty in Indonesia (the ratio stood at 56.6 per cent in 2007), though it had deteriorated following cuts in fuel subsidies in 2005. Poverty figures using the national poverty line confirm the same trends (BPS 2010). Inequality, however, as measured by the Gini index, increased from 29.7 in the 1990s to 31.9 in the 2000s, reaching 34.0 in 2005.

2.3 Labour market challenges in emerging economies

Moving from the macroeconomic view to the situation in the labour market, there is great diversity in outcomes in emerging economies with characteristics of decent work deficits from both developing and advanced economies. Some countries, notably South Africa, struggle with very high rates of unemployment, which is most notable among youth who experience much greater jobless rates. In many countries, such as India, the unemployment rate is higher among the more educated because they can afford to remain without a job. In contrast, most people cannot afford to live without a job, and hence seek employment in the informal sector.

For this reason, unemployment is typically not the best indicator of distress in the labour market. More importantly, the labour markets in emerging economies continue to be characterized by strong segmentation between the formal and informal sectors, though the relative predominance of informal employment varies considerably across countries with higher rates of informality in low-income countries such as Indonesia and India. Many people continue to live in rural areas and rely on small household plots and subsistence farming, while an increasing number have left for urban areas or to seek their fortunes in other countries. Another common feature is the presence of gender disparities as reflected by low female labour force participation in some countries (notably in India) and overrepresentation in informal employment in all economies. Other labour market inequalities exist for such groups as youth, as noted above, and some segments of society that have been excluded from benefiting from economic gains, such as the African population in South Africa and Brazil, and the scheduled castes in India.

Apart from these stylized facts, it is important to recognize that, alongside the monumental economic changes, the labour market has been in the throes of considerable changes. For this reason, this section focuses on different dimensions to the challenge of creating more and better jobs in emerging economies in terms of both cross-sectional variation (that is, differences across countries) and trends over recent years.

2.3.1   Emerging economies at different stages of the demographic transition

In contrast to low-income countries, emerging economies have in general moved further along the demographic transition as a result of falling birth rates and rising life expectancy. Population growth rates (2010 figures) vary from stagnation/decline in the Russian Federation and 0.5 per cent per annum in China to 1.4 per cent in India and South Africa.[6] Overall, countries such as China (due to its one-child policy) and the Russian Federation are more similar to richer economies: the median age in these countries is 34.5 and 37.9 (2010), respectively. In comparison, the median age is only 25.1 in India and 24.9 in South Africa.[7]

Looking at the potential for reaping the benefits of a demographic dividend reveals that countries like India still have the prospect of taking advantage of its youth bulge. The dependency ratio in India was 55 as of 2010 (the ratio of individuals aged 0–14 and 65+ to those aged 15–64); however, as young people enter the labour market over the coming years, this ratio will continue to fall until it reaches 46 in 2040 (United Nations Population Division projections).[8] In comparison, the ratio reached a low of 38 in China in 2010; since the number of young people joining the labour market are much lower, the ratio will soon rise, spelling an end to the era of unlimited labour (which is already reflected in the fast rate of wage growth witnessed in China over recent years).

As a consequence of this demographic situation, countries are either facing the challenge of how to benefit from a demographic dividend over the coming decade or so (such as India and Indonesia) or prepare for a rapidly ageing society (the likes of China and the Russian Federation). In the first case, the economy needs to create enough jobs to absorb young labour market entrants who, in turn, require the right set of skills demanded in a fast-changing environment. In the latter countries, great efforts are needed to improve labour productivity, while ensuring that social protection schemes are established (on a sustainable basis) that will help protect the old-aged from falling into poverty. This constitutes a major challenge to not only emerging economies but to developing countries in general: though growth rates can be accelerated to unprecedented levels due to demographics and high rates of investment, this is being accompanied by a similarly rapid ageing process. Therefore, the window for a demographic dividend is much smaller than witnessed during the Industrial Revolution.

2.3.2 The complex phenomenon of rural–urban and international migration of workers from and to emerging economies

Given that most emerging economies (at least in terms of those considered in this chapter) have large populations, ranging from around 40 million in Argentina to over 1 billion in India and China, it is not surprising that the labour markets in these countries also exhibit considerable spatial heterogeneity. The main dichotomy evident in emerging economy labour markets is between rural and urban areas. In this case, the former is still dominated by the agricultural sector and, consequently, many rural households suffer from underemployment (due to the seasonal nature of the sector). As a result, many households send one or more members in search of wage (usually casual) employment in urban areas. In countries like India, many rural migrants have ended up in recent years working in the booming construction sector, while such migrants have been the cornerstone of the success of factories in urban areas in coastal regions of China, despite the controls that have been placed on internal migration. Rather than a simple transition as encapsulated in the Lewis model, rural–urban migration is a complex phenomenon – it is often temporary until households are able to establish a permanent urban residence.

Overall, urbanization, a key feature of the process of industrialization and economic modernization, has occurred at a rapid rate in emerging economies. In 1950, less than a third of the world's population resided in urban areas (29.4 per cent); however, due to different colonial legacies and development trajectories, a number of these large middle-income countries already had a relatively urbanized population in that year. In this respect, a number of countries (mainly in Latin America) had an urbanization rate exceeding the global average: Argentina (65.3 per cent), Brazil (36.2 per cent), Mexico (42.7 per cent), Russian Federation (44.1 per cet), and South Africa (42.2 per cent). In comparison, China, India, Indonesia and Turkey had rates below 25 per cent. By 2010, the fast pace of urbanization had increased the share of the population in urban areas across all countries, most notably in Brazil (an increase from 36.2 per cent in 1950 to 84.3 per cent in 2010), China (from 11.8 per cent to 49.2 per cent), Indonesia (from 12.4 per cent to 49.9 per cent) and Turkey (from 24.8 per cent to 70.5 per cent). In contrast, the rate went up by just 13.9 percentage points in India over this six-decade period (from 17.0 per cent to 30.9 per cent).

In addition to the process of rural–urban migration, emerging economies both receive international migrants (in the context of their own region; for example, Nepalese in India and Zimbabweans in South Africa) and send migrant workers, particularly skilled ones, to advanced economies (for example, Indians in Silicon Valley). In 2010, the top three sending nations of legal permanent migrants to the United States were Mexico (13.3 per cent), China (6.8 per cent) and India (6.6 per cent).[9] In Australia, the top sending countries in 2010 were the United Kingdom (19.9 per cent), New Zealand (9.1 per cent), followed by China (6.3 per cent) and India (5.7 per cent).[10]

Over the period 2005–2010, all of these emerging economies were net sending countries, except for the Russian Federation and South Africa. Net migration during this five-year period (2005–2010) exceeded –1 million (the negative value indicating emigration was greater than immigration) in: Indonesia (–1.3 million), Mexico (–1.8 million), China (–1.9 million) and India (–3.0 million), where the last has the highest net migration figure in the world (but not as a percentage of the population).[11]

2.3.3   Unemployment rate: less relevant but high in some countries

Despite the limitations in focusing on unemployment, it is a useful starting point because it remains relevant in some countries and it is possible to make a comparison across emerging economies and over time. Firstly, in terms of cross-country variation, the average unemployment rate for 2004–2008 (that is, before the global financial crisis hit these economies) ranged from under 5 per cent in Mexico, China and India (countries where the indicator is clearly less relevant to describing poor labour market outcomes) to over 23 per cent in the case of South Africa (Figure 2.3 (a)). In the case of the other economies, the average unemployment rate is clustered around 10 per cent.

In terms of trends in unemployment rates (Figure 2.3 (b)), there had been considerable improvements in most of these emerging economies prior to the global financial crisis, notably in Argentina, Brazil and

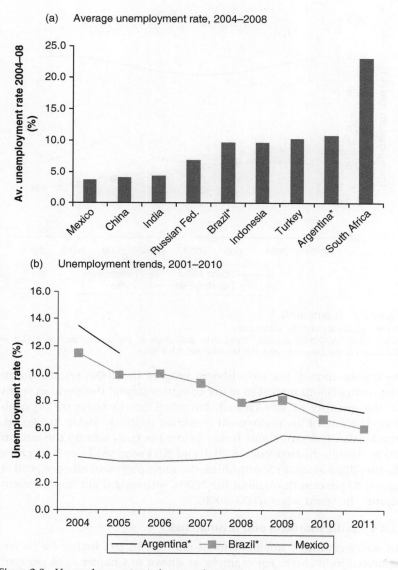

Figure 2.3 Unemployment rate in emerging economies

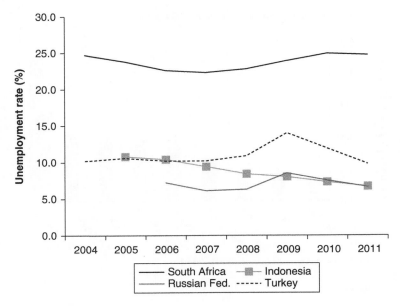

Figure 2.3   (Continued)

Notes: * figures are only for urban areas.

Source: ILO LABORSTA database Short-term indicators of the labour market; ILO Key Indicators of the Labour Market (KILM) database, 7th Edition.

Indonesia. Indeed, the global boom years of the 2000s resulted in an improving labour market in many countries around the world in terms of the quantity of jobs created (but often not in terms of job quality). The rate of unemployment remained relatively stable in Mexico, the Russian Federation and Turkey before the crisis sent up the rates in 2009, though the recoveries in 2010 and 2011 were swift (see below for a further discussion). In South Africa, the unemployment rate persisted at above 20 per cent throughout the 2000s, with only slight improvement during the 'good' years (2002–2008).

2.3.4   Skills shortages and mismatches

In many countries, unemployment rates are in fact higher for better-educated individuals. For example, as shown in Chapter 7, 14 per cent of Turkish individuals with a senior high school education were unemployed in 2008, while the rate was 'only' 7 per cent for those without any schooling. Behind this problem is the type of skills imparted to young people in these countries. In this respect, too many young people in emerging economies finish their schooling or tertiary education without skills that are demanded in the labour market, leading to a phenomenon known as skills mismatch. This is a long-term challenge for policymakers as it reflects differences between the skills provided through education and training (or rather, the lack of appropriate education and training) and the demands of employers, which, in a globalized world, is constantly changing in response to changes in demand and technological adoption. As a consequence of skills mismatch, labour markets are characterized by both vacancies and unemployed/underemployed.[12]

The phenomenon of skills mismatch (and related to this, a spatial mismatch) exists in most emerging economies and developing countries, despite the coexistence of a large pool of unskilled and willing workers. For example, the Manpower Group's Talent Shortage Survey Results 2011 report cited reveals that 67 per cent of Indian employers reported difficulties in filling jobs compared to a global average of 34 per cent, the second highest share in the sample covered by this study (exceeded only by Japan with 80 per cent). This figure for India is up from just 16 per cent in 2010. In Brazil, 57 per cent of employers cited in 2011 such difficulties, while in Argentina and Turkey the shares are 51 and 48 per cent, respectively. In comparison to these countries, only 24 per cent of Chinese and 14 per cent of South African employers indicated difficulties in filling jobs.

Skills mismatches and the associated shortages have resulted in wage rises in a number of countries. Overall, this phenomenon has become a major bottleneck for emerging economies, and governments are increasingly trying to rectify the situation through the alignment of education and training with the demands of employers (see, for example, the Nationals Skills Policy of India 2009).

2.3.5 Low female labour force participation rates in some emerging economies

Overall, labour force participation is high in developing countries, particularly as a result of the inadequate coverage of social protection systems that support individuals out of employment. However, in most of these labour markets, female participation is considerably lower than for males, which is partly a reflection of cultural norms about the role of women in the workplace. As presented in Figure 2.4, this disparity is most noticeable in Turkey (see Chapter 7) and India, where the rate for females is just 28.1 and 29.0 per cent, respectively, in comparison to rates of 71.4 and 80.7 per cent for males in these two countries. Three countries have female participation rates that exceed the OECD

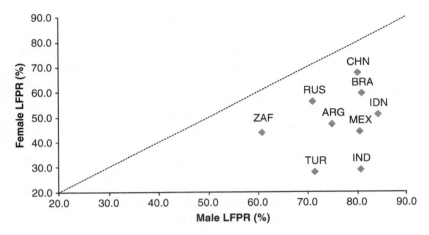

Figure 2.4   Disparity in female labour force participation rates
Notes: Argentina = ARG,   Brazil = Brazil,   China = CHN,   India = IND,   Indonesia = IDN,
Mexico = MEX, the Russian Federation = RUS, South Africa = ZAF, Turkey = TUR.
Source: ILO Key Indicators of Labour Market (KILM), 7th Edition.

average: Russian Federation (57.1 per cent), Brazil (59.9 per cent) and China (67.5 per cent).

In the literature, there has been considerable discussion about the relationship between the female labour force participation rate and the level of development (see, for example, World Bank 2011). Indeed, this correlation appears to be U-shaped: participation rates are highest in low-income countries where most working-age women are engaged in subsistence agriculture and other informal economy activities. As the economy grows, women can afford to withdraw since their spouses have moved into better-paid jobs. At the same time, educational attainment increases among women, which eventually leads to greater participation in the labour force (because of later age of marriage and declining fertility rate). In more mature economies, women are also able to find jobs that provide better protection and are more family-friendly (particularly in terms of allowing for part-time and flexible work arrangements).

This is evident in the cross-sectional scatter plot of the female labour force participation rate and the log of GDP per capita for 2010, as shown in Figure 2.5. Using a polynomial trend line, there is evidence of a U-shaped relationship between the two variables, though this trend explains only 17 per cent of variation in the data. Looking more specifically at the nine emerging economies covered in more detail in this

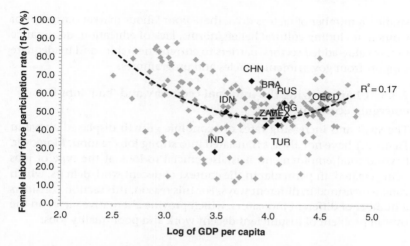

Figure 2.5 U-shaped relationship between female labour force participation rate and economic development (2010)

Notes: Sample of 170 low, middle and high-income countries with data for both the female labour force participation rate and GDP adjusted for purchasing power parity in constant 2005 international dollars.

Source: World Bank World Development Indicators online database.

chapter, India and Turkey are clearly outliers due to the very low rates of female labour force participation, which reflects cultural and social norms about women in the world of work. Contrasting with these countries, China and the Russian Federation have much higher rates of participation than the trend line. The other countries along with the OECD average are very close to the trend line. Despite this generalized empirical finding based on cross-sectional data, individual countries do not necessarily display such a relationship between economic development and female labour force participation over time.

Beyond the labour force participation gaps noted above and highlighted in Figure 2.4, gender inequalities in the labour markets of emerging economies continue to be present in terms of the under-representation in the formal economy and hence their over-representation in most forms of informal and insecure employment. Moreover, the gender wage gap is well-documented and cannot be accounted for alone by differences in characteristics. Another major issue is that labour force survey data do not accurately capture women's activities, notably because much of women's work is invisible since it is home-based. As discussed in the World Bank (2011) and other studies, a number of factors drive these poor labour market outcomes of women, including cultural beliefs/norms, lack of education, dominance in low value-added sectors, barriers to entrepreneurship, and inadequate support from government policies and programmes.

2.3.6   Characterizing the informal economy and 'bad' jobs in emerging economies

The swift and increasing rates of economic growth displayed above in Figure 2.1 have not always translated into strong job creation. Moreover, beyond total employment, it is also crucial to look at the type of jobs being created, in particular in the context of decent work deficits, which can be measured in different ways. For this reason, this section considers a number of different indicators, which provide alternative views on the overall problem of insufficient decent work and poor quality jobs:

1. Distribution of employment by sector;
2. Informal sector and employment shares;
3. Working poverty; and
4. Employment status.

As a starting point, it is instructive to reflect on the sectoral composition of employment. One of the most discussed topics in development economics is structural transformation and how employment should move from the subsistence sector (agriculture) to the capitalist sector (manufacturing). As espoused in the Lewis model, economic growth should translate into a shift of employment out of agriculture without leading to an increase in real wages in the formal manufacturing sector (until the surplus has been exhausted) (Fields 2004). In this regard, the share of employment in agriculture has fallen rapidly in nearly all emerging economies, especially in China, Indonesia and Turkey (though it increased in the latter during the global financial crisis; see Chapter 7). The greatest challenge and puzzle is that this fall in the share of employment in agriculture has increasingly been accompanied not by a rise in manufacturing employment but rather in the service sectoral share.

Turning to sectoral employment shares in more detail, Figure 2.6 shows that women are under-represented in industry (in terms of employment share). In the cases of Argentina, Brazil, Indonesia, Mexico, the Russian Federation and South Africa, women are more likely to be in the service sector than men, while in India and Turkey women have a greater employment share in the agricultural sector. The share

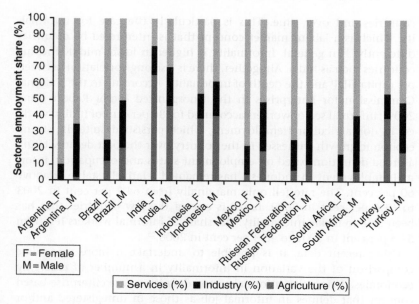

Figure 2.6 Distribution of employment by sector, by sex (%)
Notes: Latest year: Argentina (2009); Brazil (2009); India (2010); Indonesia (2009); Mexico (2010); Russian Federation (2008); South Africa (2009); Turkey (2011).
Source: ILO Key Indicators of Labour Market (KILM), 7th Edition; accessed 9 August 2012.

of women employed in the non-agricultural sector (as a percentage of total employment) is an indicator under Millennium Development Goal (MDG) 3 on gender equality with the reasoning that better jobs are found outside agriculture. In line with the numbers presented in Figure 2.6, there is considerable variation in this share among the nine emerging economies. The share of women in non-agriculture employment is relatively high in Latin America (Argentina (42.7 per cent), Brazil (45.1 per cent), Mexico (41.5 per cent), Russian Federation (50.1 per cent) and South Africa (45.3 per cent).[13] In contrast, the share is very low in India (18.2 per cent) and Turkey (23.1 per cent), which is due to the cultural/social norms that keep women out of the wider labour market in these countries (as also revealed in Figure 2.4). In general, these shares are rising in these countries, though it is often at a slow pace.

Secondly, though the lack of decent employment constitutes the greatest challenge in emerging economies, difficulties in measuring this dimension render it more problematic to make comparisons across countries and over time. This is particularly the case for informality, which is a labour market concept that is interpreted by countries differently.[14] In general, informality is higher in lower-middle-income countries such as India. Altogether, there is a strong correlation between per capita GDP and the depth of informality. According to the National Commission for Enterprises in the Unorganized Sector Report (June 2009), informal sector workers accounted for 86 per cent of Indian workers in non-agricultural employment, which persists despite the strong economic growth witnessed in the country over the past decade. Using a broad definition based on employment status and occupation, informal employment in Indonesia has remained relatively stable at above 60 per cent. The rate fell only marginally from 64.7 per cent in 2003 to 61.6 per cent in 2009. Brazil is one of the few countries that has been able to tackle informality: the share of informal workers fell from 52.4 per cent in 2001 to 46.3 per cent in 2008.[15]

Using recent data, it is possible to undertake a more up-to-date comparison of the variation in informality in a number of emerging economies. Using the informal-sector definition (an enterprise-based concept that defines an informal job as those in unregistered and/or small unincorporated private enterprises), the share of informal workers (as a percentage of non-agricultural employment) ranges from 12.1 per cent in the Russian Federation (2010 figure) to 60.2 per cent in Indonesia and 67.5 per cent in India (2010) (Figure 2.7).[16] Moving to the broader definition of informal employment (a job-based concept that includes workers who lack basic social or legal protection or employment benefits and may be found in the formal sector) unsurprisingly results in a higher proportion of informal workers. As displayed in Figure 2.8, this share reaches 72.5 per cent in Indonesia and 83.6 per cent in India, while it is around 30 per cent in the cases of Turkey and South Africa (30.6 and 32.7 per cent, respectively).

With respect to gender disparities in informal sector/employment, in countries where comparable disaggregated data is available (Mexico, the Russian Federation, South Africa and Turkey), women have higher shares in informal employment, while men tend to have higher shares in employment in the informal sector (which is a narrower definition). For example, in Mexico, 57.8 per cent of women in non-agricultural employment were informally employed in 2009 compared to 50.8 per cent of men. In South Africa, the difference is 36.8 per cent versus 30.1 per cent (2010 figure). Using the enterprise definition for informal sector employment, men in this small sample of emerging economies have higher shares than women. For instance, the share of men in

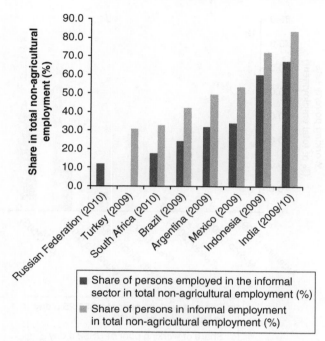

Figure 2.7   Informal sector versus informal employment, latest year available

Notes: Persons in informal employment (a job-based concept) represents the sum of informal jobs in formal enterprises, informal sector enterprises, and households producing goods for own consumption or hiring paid domestic workers. Persons employed in the informal sector (an enterprise-based concept) include the informal jobs in informal enterprises plus formal jobs in informal sector enterprises. Persons employed in informal employment outside the informal sector include those employed in the formal sector and households producing goods for own use or employing paid domestic workers.

Source: ILO Key Indicators of Labour Market (KILM), 7th Edition.

informal sector employment in Mexico stood at 35.7 per cent in 2009, while it was 31.8 per cent for women. A similar gap is found in the Russian Federation and South Africa. This finding indicates that women's informal employment reflects their engagement in not only informal enterprises, but also in unprotected/informal jobs in the formal sector and home-based work.

Another approach to looking at the lack of decent work in emerging economies is to highlight the relationship between employment and poverty. More specifically, the concept of working poverty, an indicator under the Millennium Development Goal 1b, shows that a job is often not enough to ensure that an individual and his/her family can

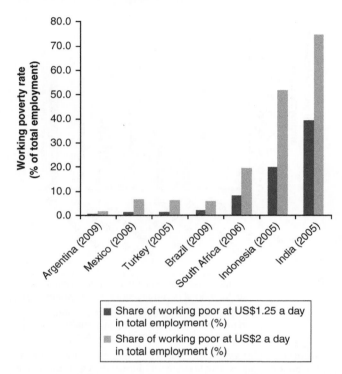

Figure 2.8 Working poverty is higher in lower-middle-income emerging economies, various years (based on national household data)

Notes: These national estimates of working poverty are generated using micro-data from national household income/expenditure surveys. Poverty status is determined at the household level, with poor households defined as those with per capita expenditure below the given poverty line. In order to maximize comparability across countries, international poverty lines are used, whereby prices in local currencies are converted using purchasing power parity exchange rates and adjusting for inflation. Employment status is determined at the individual level. In order to be classified as working poor, a person must be both employed and living in a household with per capita expenditure below the poverty line.

Source: ILO Key Indicators of Labour Market (KILM), 7th Edition.

escape material deprivation. In this regard, working poverty based on household data shows considerable variation across the countries investigated in this book. Though the data points are for different years, the statistics presented in Figure 2.8 show that the highest rates of working poverty are found in lower-middle-income countries such as India and Indonesia. The working poverty rate using the US$1.25 per day (adjusted for PPP) threshold ranges from under three per cent for Argentina (0.6 per cent), Turkey (1.4 per cent), Mexico (1.3 per cent) and Brazil

(2.0 per cent), to 19.8 per cent in Indonesia and 39.2 per cent in India (Figure 2.8). The extreme working poverty rate in South Africa is 8.3 per cent, which is relatively high considering the country's per capita income level. The rate using the US$2 per day threshold reveals a similar variation across countries but a much higher degree of working poverty (up to 52.0 per cent for Indonesia and 74.5 per cent for India).

A fourth way of highlighting disparities among individuals with jobs is to look at employment status. Generally, employment status consists of three categories: 1) wage and salaried workers (or employees); 2) self-employed workers, which includes the self-employed with employees (employers) and those without any workers (own-account workers (OAW)); and 3) unpaid contributing family workers (UFW). Vulnerable employment, which is an indicator under MDG 1B, is defined as the sum of own-account workers and unpaid contributing family workers. This is closely aligned with the notion of informal employment since workers in these two categories typically do not have access to social protection.

Moving beyond aggregate figures on employment reveals considerable diversity in the labour markets of emerging economies, particularly in terms of employment status. Wage and salaried workers account for only 34 per cent of employment in Indonesia. In comparison, the share of employees in the Russian Federation and South Africa reaches 92.7 per cent and 82.4 per cent, respectively. The converse of this situation is the high proportion of own-account workers and unpaid contributing family workers in those countries with a low share of employees. In Indonesia, these two categories (OAW and UFW) represent 45.8 per cent and 17.3 per cent respectively, while in Turkey they account for 21.5 and 13.9 per cent.

Looking at gender differences in employment status indicates some interesting characteristics of these labour markets (Figure 2.9). Firstly, wage and salaried workers actually account for a greater share of employed women in Argentina, Brazil, the Russian Federation and South Africa, while it is larger for men in India, Indonesia, Mexico and Turkey. Unsurprisingly, working men are much more likely to be employers than women in all countries. The share of employed men undertaking own-account work (which largely takes place in the informal sector) is higher than for women in Argentina, Brazil, India, Indonesia, the Russian Federation and Turkey. As expected, women are much more likely to be contributing family workers. In the case of India and Indonesia, 35.7 and 32.4 per cent of employed women have this status.

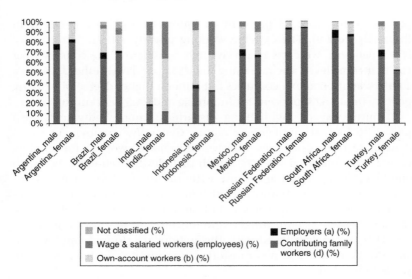

Figure 2.9   Employment status in emerging economies by sex, various years (%)
Notes: Latest year: Argentina (2009); Brazil (2009); India (2005); Indonesia (2009); Mexico (2008); the Russian Federation (2008); South Africa (2009); Turkey (2011).
Source: Key Indicators of Labour Market (KILM), 6th Edition; national sources.

Employment status as defined above is not without its limitations, primarily because it is not a perfect measure of job quality. In this respect, the category of wage and salaried workers does not equate to formal employment because this grouping includes casual workers and those who do not have a contract or access to social protection. The phenomenon of rising casualization is evident around the world as employers have sought to reduce labour costs and coverage under labour market regulations. Though comparable data is not available for most emerging economies, OECD data suggest that the incidence of temporary employment varies from 8.5 per cent in the Russian Federation (2011 figure) and 12.3 per cent in Turkey (2011), which is near the OECD average, to 20.3 per cent in Mexico (2004).[17] The issue of casual or temporary employment is also investigated further in Chapter 5 on Indonesia.

2.3.7   Youth are more vulnerable to poor outcomes in the labour market

Youth unemployment and underemployment is prevalent around the world because of not only demand-side deficits (inadequate job opportunities), but also because they lack skills, work experience, job search abilities and the financial resources to find employment.[18] As a result, youth unemployment rates tend to be two to three times higher than for adults. Furthermore, as highlighted below, youth have been hit harder during the global financial crisis due to the sectors they tend to work in and their vulnerabilities to layoffs. According to global figures generated by the ILO, almost 75 million young people aged 15 to 24 are unemployed as of 2012, reflecting an unemployment rate of 12.7 per cent (ILO 2012). It is, therefore, a major concern for governments around the world, including the emerging economies considered in this chapter.

Turning to the sample of emerging economies considered in this chapter, like the overall unemployment rate, there is considerable diversity in the youth unemployment rate (Figure 2.10). The rate ranges from around 10 per cent in Mexico and India to over 50 per cent in South Africa. As found around the world, young women tend to have higher unemployment rates than their male counterparts; this phenomenon is most notable in Brazil, Argentina and South Africa where the difference reaches 5.3, 3.5 and 5.2 percentage points, respectively. As also witnessed globally, the youth unemployment rates in these countries are much higher than those found in the adult population. In this regard, the ratio of youth to adult unemployment rate varies: in Mexico, the

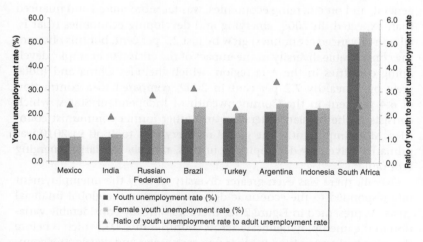

Figure 2.10 Youth unemployment rate in emerging economies, latest year
Note: Latest year: Mexico (2011); India (2010); Russian Federation (2011); Brazil (2009); Turkey (2011); Argentina (2009); Indonesia (2009); South Africa (2011).
Source: ILO Key Indicators of Labour Market (KILM), 7th Edition, accessed 8 August 2012.

Russian Federation, Turkey and South Africa the ratio is between two and three times. However, in the case of Indonesia it is almost five times the adult unemployment rate.

2.4   Diversity and resilience during the global financial crisis

Though the global financial crisis started in the United States in 2007, its effects reverberated around the world, particularly after the collapse of Lehman Brothers in September 2008. At this point, the financial system connecting countries and firms was brought to a standstill as liquidity quickly dried up. This translated into a massive trade shock that saw a record fall in global exports over the following 12 months. At this stage of the crisis, it was widely expected that developing countries would also be hit hard due to their dependency on commodities. The Chief Economist of the World Bank, Justin Lin, said in a speech to the Korean Development Institute on 31 October 2008 that 'There is a distinct danger that emerging markets could go through crises of their own, for example if their own domestic asset-market bubbles burst (or even if fair-market values collapse) and weaken their own banking sector.'[19]

In 2009, the world economy shrunk by 0.5 per cent, the first time in more than 60 years. However, the impact on developing countries in general, and on emerging economies, was far more muted and nuanced than expected. In 2009, emerging and developing economies (that is, all non-advanced economies) grew by just 2.7 per cent, but this obscures the considerable diversity in the impact of the crisis. For example, developing countries in the Asia region, which includes China and India, grew by a healthy 7.2 per cent in 2009, compared to a contraction of 6.4 per cent in the Commonwealth of Independent States, which consists of the Russian Federation and other former communist countries. More importantly, the global recovery that took off in 2010 was primarily driven by developing countries, notably the large emerging economies.

Overall, there was even greater diversity in how the unemployment rate responded to the economic downturn during the global financial crisis. As presented in Figure 2.12, there was already considerable variation in the unemployment rate across countries in 2008, which is before the crisis had transmitted to emerging economies and developing countries. The rate ranged from just 3.3 per cent in Thailand to 22.8 per cent in South Africa, which has one of the highest levels of unemployment in the world.

Following the impact of the global financial crisis, the unemployment rate increased in 2009 in all of the countries in this selected sample apart from Morocco and Indonesia, where it fell by 0.4 percentage points in both countries (Figure 2.11). The increase was the highest in Central and Eastern Europe and the Commonwealth of Independent States. In the Russian Federation and Turkey, the increase was 2.2 and 3.1 percentage points, respectively. In Latin America, Chile and Mexico were most severely affected (1.9 and 1.5 percentage points, respectively). For the African region, it is more difficult to have a full picture because of the lack of data. The available labour force surveys show that South Africa was hardest hit with an increase of 1.1 percentage points, though as will be noted in Chapter 4, the impact was noticeable in terms of an increase in the number of discouraged workers. The unemployment rate also increased in

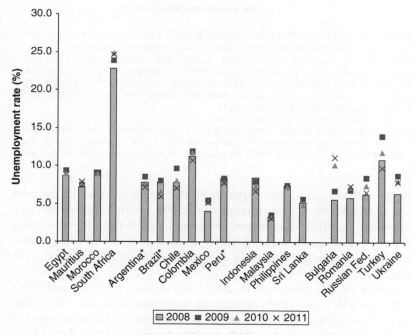

Figure 2.11 Change in the unemployment rate from 2008 to 2011 in selected emerging economies and other middle-income countries

Note: * = urban areas only.

Source: ILO LABORSTA database, Short-term indicators of the Labour Market, accessed 8 August 2012.

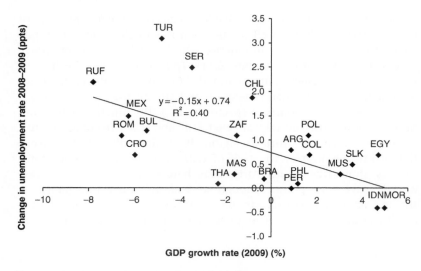

Figure 2.12   Relationship between output in 2009 and change in unemployment rate, 2008–2009 (annual averages), selected middle-income countries

Notes: Country codes: Argentina* = ARG; Brazil* = BRA; Bulgaria = BUL; Chile = CHL; Colombia = COL;   Croatia = CRO;   Egypt = EGY;   Indonesia = IDN;   Malaysia = MAS; Mauritius = MUS;   Mexico = MEX;   Morocco = MOR;   Peru* = PER;   Philippines = PHL; Poland = POL; Romania = ROM; Russian Fed.= RUF; Serbia = SER; South Africa = ZAF; Sri Lanka = SLK; Thailand = THA; Turkey = TUR.

* = unemployment rate is for urban areas only.

Source: GDP growth rate 2009 is from IMF World Economic Outlook April 2011 database, www.imf.org/external/pubs/ft/weo/2011/01/weodata/index.aspx;   unemployment   rate 2008–2009 is from the ILO LABORSTA database, Short-term indicators of the labour market.

Egypt and Mauritius. Asia experienced the mildest impact in terms of the unemployment rate (though the effects of the crisis could have appeared in other dimensions, this does not appear to have been the case; see, for example, Chapter 4 on Indonesia). In this region, the unemployment rate barely moved in 2009 or fell in the case of Indonesia.

Following the downturn in 2009, the recovery in 2010 and 2011 was varied in terms of changes in the unemployment rate. The statistics presented in Figure 2.11 reveal that the unemployment rate fell in the majority of these middle-income countries. In Turkey, Chile, Brazil and the Russian Federation, the subsequent decrease in the rate of unemployment in 2010 was quite substantial (by 2.1, 1.6, 1.4 and 1.0 percentage points, respectively), reflecting a robust recovery for these economies. Struggling with a weak economy and structural labour market deficits, the unemployment rate continued to rise in South Africa before falling slightly in 2011. Eastern European countries such as Bulgaria have been badly hit and, as a result, the unemployment rate has continued to increase.

It is also interesting to view the relationship between economic growth in 2009 and the change in the unemployment rate. Known as Okun's Law, this empirical correlation provides an insight into how shocks are transmitted to the labour market (though it is only a partial story given that the unemployment rate is not the best indicator of labour market distress in these countries). This relationship is presented in Figure 2.12, which shows considerable diversity in the GDP growth rate in 2009 and the associated change in the unemployment rate from 2008 to 2009. Overall, the correlation is positive, as expected (that is, a contraction in the economy is accompanied by an increase in the unemployment rate), and the change in the unemployment rate explains around 40 per cent of the variation in the GDP growth rate in 2009. Behind this statistical relationship there are a number of complex interrelated factors such as trade openness, size of domestic market, population, and links to financial markets (Islam and Verick 2011).

The Russian Federation, Turkey and Mexico were among the hardest-hit countries, suffering both large contractions in output and a rise in unemployment. Even though growth in a number of countries remained positive, the slowdown in 2009 translated into an increase in the unemployment rate, notably in Poland, Argentina, Colombia and Egypt. In Brazil, the mild contraction resulted in only a small increase in the rate of unemployment (similarly in Malaysia and Thailand). Figure 2.12 also displays a number of countries that continued to grow in 2009. Growth in Indonesia and Morocco surpassed 4 per cent and these countries also experienced a decline in the unemployment rate. The fact that other countries grew in 2009 but nonetheless witnessed a rise in unemployment is a reflection that growth, though positive, was not fast enough to generate jobs in line with the expansion in the population.

In addition to analysing the elasticity of the unemployment rate with respect to growth, it is perhaps more useful to look at the elasticity of employment (also w.r.t. growth). Figure 2.13 presents changes in employment elasticities during the global financial crisis, which show that employment was growing prior to the onset of the crisis, notably in 2008. The largest elasticities are found for Turkey, which reached 2.9 in 2008, which reflects the combination of low GDP growth in

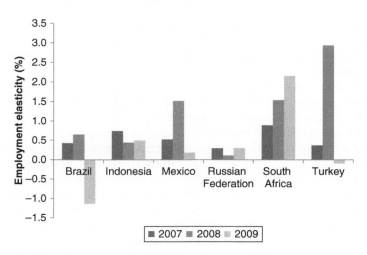

Figure 2.13 Employment elasticities during the global financial crisis, 2007–2009

Sources: International Monetary Fund, World Economic Outlook Database, April 2011; ILO LABORSTA database, Short-term indicators of the labour market. Statistics Indonesia BPS; Statistics South Africa.

that year (0.7 per cent) and high employment growth (1.9 per cent). In the midst of the downturn in 2009, the employment elasticities in these six emerging economies diverged considerably. Employment fell only in Mexico, the Russian Federation, and particularly in South Africa. In contrast, employment continued to grow in Indonesia (along with positive but slower GDP growth), while it grew in Brazil and Turkey despite the economic contraction in these countries (–0.6 and –4.7 per cent, respectively, in 2009). Reflecting longer-term trends, the employment elasticity decreased in China over recent decades (from an average of 0.102 for 1990–1999 to 0.083 for 2000–2009).[20] Using the National Sample Survey data, the employment elasticity for India on the basis of figures for 2004–2005 and 2009–2010 fell to just 0.01 per cent (reflecting a stagnant level of employment, which increased from just 457.5 million in 2004–2005 to 460.2 million in 2009–2010).

Looking at trends in employment status with available data doesn't reveal much in terms of recent changes in the share of wage employees and other categories during the global financial crisis. As witnessed earlier in the 2000s, this proportion continues to be much lower in

Indonesia than the other emerging economies such as the Russian Federation and South Africa. As explained in Chapter 5, the situation in South Africa is rather unique; in particular, the low share of own-account workers in the country is a legacy of the Apartheid regime, which had actively discouraged entrepreneurship.

Turning to recent wage trends in the larger emerging economies, there has been considerable attention paid to the wage situation in China in particular. Real wages in China have grown by more than 10 per cent per annum since 2000, leading many commentators to suggest that China's days as a location of cheap labour will soon be over.[21] Based on data from the National Sample Survey rounds of 2004–2005 and 2009–2010, the average daily real wage rate in India increased for both regular and casual workers. Moreover, there has been a rise for women and men, leading to a small decrease in the gender wage gap.[22]

2.5 Is this time different? Comparison of labour market outcomes to previous crises

Emerging economies have experienced many economic and financial crises throughout the last century. In fact, the period leading up to the global financial crisis was noted for the fall in macroeconomic volatility (which has been referred to as the 'Great Moderation'), even in developing countries. These global boom years were unique in the sense that most economies were growing strongly. This synchronicity was expected to continue during the crisis of 2008–2009; rather, as discussed further below, large middle-income countries came out looking far stronger than expected. In general, this resilience in the latest of a series of crises came, in some ways, as a surprise and is in stark contrast to the experience of the crises of previous decades, especially the debt and currency crises of the 1980s and 1990s.

As documented in Fallon and Lucas (2002), Reinhart and Rogoff (2009) and others, emerging economies have long been accustomed to crises. For example, Brazil has had 10 banking crises since 1890 (Reinhart and Rogoff 2009). The 1980s was a notable period for debt crises in these countries, particularly in Latin America, which resulted in an interconnected wave of sovereign default, high and persistent inflation and severe banking collapses. The 1990s continued with a series of systemic crises that involved a number of countries. In 1994–1995, the devaluation of the peso and the subsequent outflow of capital decimated the Mexican economy. The East Asian financial crisis started in Thailand in 1997 as a result of a speculation that the baht could no longer be supported, and quickly spread to Korea, Malaysia and Indonesia (Fallon and Lucas 2002). As shown in Chapter 4, Indonesia was severely impacted by that crisis, resulting in a 13 per cent contraction of the economy in 1998. In 1998, the Russian Federation defaulted on its domestic debt and ceased to pay foreign creditors, which hit confidence in the Brazilian economy (which, in turn, led to an IMF bailout and devaluation of the real). Turkey also experienced a currency and banking crisis in 2000–2001, while an insolvent Argentina famously defaulted on its sovereign debt in 2001. Therefore, clearly for 'many emerging markets, the Great Moderation was a fleeting event' (Reinhart and Rogoff 2009: 256), reflecting that the period of 2002–2007 was not only one of strong growth but also unusual because of the absence of crises in such countries.

The issue of interest for this chapter is how these previous crises impacted the labour markets of emerging economies, and whether the impact was similar during the global financial crisis. To investigate this point, the experiences of Indonesia and Mexico are explored further in this section. The focus here is on unemployment rates, though it should be clearly acknowledged that adjustment in such labour markets often is captured by other indicators (as highlighted in the case of Indonesia).

The Indonesian success story of rapid economic and social development was interrupted by the East Asian financial crisis of 1997–1998, which began in Thailand in July 1997 and led to an unexpectedly severe downturn in Indonesia. As captured by Figure 2.14 (a), the economy contracted by over 13 per cent in 1998, by 14 per cent in per capita terms. Following an emergency loan from the International Monetary Fund (IMF), the government of Indonesia reined in government spending – though the crisis was largely driven by unsustainable external lending to the private sector – and let the rupiah (Rp.) float. Consequently, the rupiah fell from Rp. 2450/US$ in June 1997 to Rp. 14,900/US$ a year later, while interest rates were ratcheted up to defend the currency (from 19 per cent in June 1997 to 36 per cent in September 1998). In addition, external capital flows swiftly reversed, leaving businesses facing a severe credit crunch. Government debt rose from negligible levels prior to the crisis to US$72 billion (Dhanani et al. 2009; Islam and Chowdhury 2009). The crisis also triggered a political crisis, which resulted in the end of the 33-year Soeharto era.

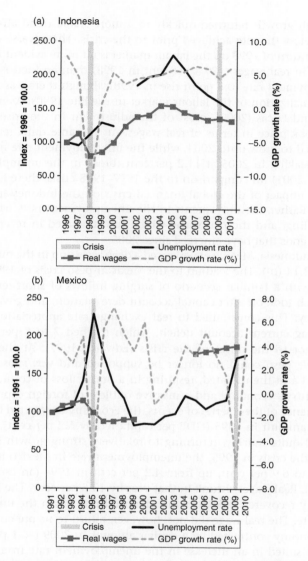

Figure 2.14 Comparison of unemployment rates and real wages during crises – Indonesia and Mexico

Notes: Real wage and unemployment rate converted into an index with a base of 100.0 (1996 for Indonesia and 1991 for Mexico). The break in the series represents changes in definitions and samples. The grey bar denotes the respective crisis periods: 1995 Peso Crisis (Mexico); Asian Financial Crisis 1997 (Indonesia); and Global Financial Crisis 2009 (both countries). *Sources*: ILO Key Indicators of the Labour Market; ILO Global Wage Database; IMF World Economic Outlook; OECD Labour Force Statistics.

Though growth returned quickly to a more stable trend after 2000, it was below the rate achieved prior to the crisis. The adverse effect of the downturn of 1998 on the labour market is far more evident in terms of a fall in real wages (–29.3 per cent in 1998) than an increase in the unemployment rate (0.8 point rise in 1998), though there was increase in informalization of the labour market in the late 1990s. As noted by Fallon and Lucas (2002), most of the adjustment in the crises of the 1990s took place in terms of real wages. At the same time, real wages continued to grow until 2004, while the unemployment rate increased before peaking in 2005 at 11.2 per cent (break in the unemployment series in 2001). In comparison to the 1997–1998 crisis, there is no discernible impact of the global financial crisis on the Indonesian labour market. Rather, the movements in the unemployment rate, which has been falling, and the real wage, which has stagnated in recent years, reflect trends that have emerged since 2005.

Like Indonesia, Mexico experienced a deep recession in the mid-1990s (Figure 2.14 (b)). The lead-up to the Mexican peso crisis of 1994–1995 started with a familiar scenario of surging inflows of short-term capital, which took off after capital account deregulation, and government profligacy. This contributed to real exchange rate appreciation and a worsening current account deficit, which reached 7 to 8 per cent of GDP prior to the onset of the crisis (Edwards 1997). At the end of 1994, the peso could no longer be supported and was subsequently devalued and then floated, resulting in a drastic loss of confidence in the country's economy and a massive outflow of foreign capital. As a consequence of these series of events, the economy contracted by a substantial amount in 1995 (GDP per capita fell by 6.2 per cent), only to rebound quite quickly, returning to relatively strong growth in 1996. During the crisis in 1995, the unemployment rate in Mexico increased quickly to 6.9 per cent, up from 4.2 per cent in 1994 (an estimate of the rate). Real wages shrunk in that year by 13.6 per cent. The Mexican economy recovered quickly, which helped bring down the unemployment rate. The real wage did not, however, return to its pre-crisis level. The economy contracted by a similar amount in 2009 (–6.1 per cent), which resulted in an increase in the unemployment rate from 3.5 per cent in 2008 to 5.2 per cent in 2009. There does not appear to be a clear negative impact on the real wage during this most recent crisis period.

Another insight into the difference between previous crises and the most recent episode in five emerging economies (Argentina, Brazil, Indonesia, Mexico and Turkey) is provided by the figures in Table 2.1.

Table 2.1 Comparison of change in unemployment rates, real wages and GDP in earlier crises in the 1990s/2000s versus the global financial crisis (2008–2009)

Country	Change in unemployment rate (ppts)		Change in real wage (%)		GDP growth rate (%)	
	Crisis in 90s/00s	GFC	Crisis in 90s/00s	GFC	Crisis in 90s/00s	GFC
Argentina (2000, 2008)	3.6	0.8	n.a.	11.7	−4.4	0.8
Brazil (1999, 2008)	0.7	0.2	−3.6	2.3	0.3	−0.6
Indonesia (1997, 2008)	0.8	−0.5	−29.3	1.6	−13.1	4.6
Mexico (1995, 2008)	2.7	1.7	−13.6	0.7	−6.2	−6.1
Turkey (2000, 2008)	1.9	3.0	35.3	9.9	−5.7	−4.7

Source: ILO Key Indicators of the Labour Market; OECD Labour Force Statistics; ILO Global Wage Database; IMF World Economic Outlook database.

These numbers relating to the change in the unemployment rate, real wage and GDP show considerable differences, though a few generalized remarks can be made. Firstly, in terms of output, all countries contracted in the early crisis, except for Brazil, which experienced a milder slowdown in 1999. As noted above, Indonesia suffered a depression-like fall in output of 13.1 per cent in 1998 in the midst of the East Asian financial crisis, which is in stark contrast to the positive but slower rate of growth in 2009 (4.6 per cent). Similarly, the Argentinean economy contracted during the 2000 sovereign debt crisis by 4.4 per cent, while it continued to grow, albeit slowly, in the wake of the global financial crisis. In comparison, both Mexico and Turkey witnessed similar falls in economic output in both crisis periods.

Secondly, turning to the labour market, these figures show that the unemployment rate increased more in the previous crisis in the case of all countries apart from Turkey. In Indonesia, the unemployment rate did not increase by much in 1998, while it in fact fell in 2009 (by 0.5 percentage points). In the case of Brazil, the unemployment rate increased by 0.7 points from 1998 to 1999, while the rise from 2008 to 2009 was just 0.2 points (before falling by 1.4 points from 2009 to 2010). Like Brazil, Turkey experienced an increase in the rate of unemployment during the global financial crisis (by 3.0 percentage points from 2008 to 2009) followed by a rapid fall over the subsequent year (by 2.5 points). This is in contrast to the Turkish situation just one decade ago: the unemployment rate increased by 1.9 percentage points from

2000 to 2001, and then there was a further increase of 2 points from 2001 to 2002.

However, it must be again underscored that the unemployment rate is not the best indicator of the labour market impact of such downturns. As noted above, Fallon and Lucas (2002) point out that the effect of previous crises has been more evident in changes to real wages. In this respect, the data presented in Table 2.1 reveals that real wages (though using different definitions) contracted in previous crises, except in Turkey. As highlighted above, the fall in real wages was most notable in Indonesia (29.3 per cent in 1998) and Mexico (13.6 per cent in 1995). In comparison, real wages increased in 2009 in all five countries, particularly in Argentina (11.7 per cent) and Turkey (9.9 per cent).

What can explain the improved resilience to external shocks in emerging economies as illustrated by the differences between the crises of the 1990s and early 2000s and the global financial crisis? In general, it is possible to highlight a number of differences between this latest crisis and previous shocks. Firstly, governments of emerging economies had much lower levels of debt and primary budget surpluses, which provided the fiscal space to implement stimulus packages. In the case of such countries as Indonesia, in earlier episodes governments were forced to enact austerity measures as part of IMF loan agreements. Moreover, better revenue collection and the allocation of expenditure on social sectors has led to the development of far more effective social protection schemes (for example, Brazil's Bolsa Família, South Africa's old age pension and child support grants, India's Mahatma Gandhi National Rural Employment Guarantee Scheme), which helped buffer the poor from the worst fallout of the global downturn in 2009.

Secondly, inflation was far more subdued prior to the onset of the global financial crisis. As pointed out by Reinhart and Rogoff (2009: 180), 'If serial default is the norm for a country passing through the emerging market state of development, the tendency to lapse into periods of high and extremely high inflation is an even more striking common denominator.' This study also stresses that inflation and crises resulting from domestic and external debt defaults are very much interrelated: governments used to rely on printing money to finance deficits. Moreover, once countries were forced to devalue their currencies in the face of a shock and an outflow of capital (as witnessed in Mexico in 1994–1995, Indonesia in 1997–1998 and other emerging economies), inflation spikes as a consequence of a rapid depreciation of the currency (which led to higher import prices). Inflation is an important indicator of an impact of crisis because of its implications for the real wage: the

Table 2.2 Inflation (consumer prices) in selected emerging economies, percentage change

Country	Av. 1990–99	Av. 2000–09	2009
Argentina	253.7	8.6	6.3
Brazil	854.8	6.9	4.9
China	7.8	1.9	−0.7
India	9.6	5.5	10.9
Indonesia	14.6	8.5	4.8
Mexico	20.4	5.2	5.3
Russia	222.2	14.0	11.7
South Africa	9.9	6.1	7.1
Turkey	77.2	23.2	6.3

Source: IMF World Economic Outlook database, April 2012; accessed 2 September 2012.

decline in real wages evident in Indonesia in 1998 (Table 2.1) was due to a spike in inflation rather than a cut to nominal wages.

In general, inflation has fallen across the world in recent decades (described as part of the 'Great Moderation' phenomenon by some commentators). Thus, as displayed in Table 2.2, the average rate of consumer price inflation in emerging economies decreased considerably from the 1990s to the 2000s, displaying remarkable convergence at single-digit figures. Argentina, Brazil and the Russian Federation experienced inflation rates in the hundreds in the 1990s but reached a rate below 10 per cent in the following decade (though the Russian Federation was still at 14 per cent). Spikes in the inflation rate are evident for Mexico in 1995, Indonesia in 1998 and Argentina in 2002. In Indonesia, inflation went from under 10 per cent in the early 1990s to 58.4 per cent in 1998 as result of the floating and subsequent depreciation of the rupiah. In Argentina, prices fell from 1999 to 2001 before increasing by 25.9 per cent in 2002.

Most importantly, inflation has in fact fallen in the wake of the global financial crisis, which has played an important part in ameliorating the impact of the downturn on emerging economies (though high prices did benefit commodity exporters such as Brazil and Indonesia prior to the crisis and during the recovery in prices since 2010). Prior to the crisis, inflation had been rapidly increasing as a consequence of rising food prices. According to the FAO annual Food Price Index, real food prices reached a peak in 2008, 64.5 per cent higher than the average of 2002–2004. Following the collapse of Lehman Brothers in September 2008, prices fell, and in 2009, the Food Price Index stood 18 per cent lower (in real terms) than the previous year. Unfortunately for developing countries around the world, prices resumed the rising trend of the pre-crisis period and have since reached new highs in 2011.[23]

In addition to inflation, it is worth mentioning the issue of decoupling: emerging economies, though highly integrated in the global economy, are increasingly dependent of south–south trade, notably with China. For example, the share of Brazilian exports destined for China rose from 8 per cent in 2008 to 14 per cent in 2009, more than making up for the fall in exports to the United States in that year. Bilateral trade between Brazil and China increased from just $2 billion in 2000 to $56.2 billion in 2010, while China became Brazil's largest source of FDI (which reached $17 billion in 2010).[24]

2.6   Summary of labour market trends over the past two decades

Rapid and sustained economic growth has become the hallmark of successfully developing countries in recent times. While there is wide acceptance that consistently strong economic growth is a necessary condition to make major inroads into reducing poverty, less thought has been given to how this expansion in economic activity has translated into labour market outcomes in emerging economies.

In this regard, in emerging economies, it is crucial to understand not only the unemployment situation, but also to highlight whether productive jobs are being created in the formal economy, which promote transitions in the labour market. These transitions, in turn, should result in higher wages to lift workers and their families out of poverty, provide access to social and employment protection and promote enforcement and protection of workers' rights. The reality for most developing countries, in spite of economic growth, is unfortunately far from this stylized picture of a well-functioning developing country labour market.

Moving to the specific situation of the emerging economies covered in this book, high rates of economic growth have been witnessed in Indonesia and Brazil (prior to the 2000s). China has more recently emerged as the leading growth centre of the world, while India has begun to stake a claim at being part of this elite group of countries. Countries such as Turkey have undergone a new era of resilience in the face of the crisis and strong economic prospects. However, despite robust economic progress in emerging economies, and in most cases, falling rates of poverty, the labour markets of these countries have not always benefited to the same extent. In particular, informality, working poverty and vulnerable employment continue to be the norm for most workers. At the same time, women, youth and other segments of the population face hurdles to accessing the few good jobs in the formal economy.

For this reason, unemployment is typically not the best indicator of distress in the labour market. More importantly, the labour markets in emerging economies continue to be characterized by strong segmentation between a small formal sector and large informal sector. Many people continue to live in rural areas and rely on small household plots and subsistence farming, while an increasing number have left for urban areas or to seek their fortunes in other countries. Another common feature is the presence of gender disparities as reflected by low female labour force participation in some countries (notably in India), under-representation in industry and over-representation in informal employment in most economies. Other labour market inequalities exist for such groups as youth, as noted above, and some segments of society that have been excluded from benefiting from economic gains such as the African population in South Africa and Brazil and the scheduled castes in India.

Altogether, the global financial crisis had a diverse impact on emerging economies with more severe outcomes in Central and Eastern Europe and the Commonwealth of Independent States (such as the Russian Federation) and milder effects in Asia (for example, Indonesia). However, even for the harder-hit countries, economic recovery in emerging economies was strong in 2010 and has subsequently led to a fall in unemployment. Overall, these countries have demonstrated considerable resilience to the downturn of 2009, which contrasts with their experience in earlier periods of crisis. The milder impact on employment and wage outcomes in these emerging economies can be explained by a combination of factors including the continuing growth of China and its subsequent impact on commodity exporters, large domestic markets, lack of exposure to the financial calamities that hit the United States and Europe, and better policymaking. In terms of the latter, the country chapters in this volume present specific examples of how policymakers responded to the downturn through stimulus packages and labour market policies.

Despite this apparent resilience in these countries, the trends presented in this chapter confirm, nonetheless, that many challenges remain in the labour markets of emerging economies, namely the failure to create more and better jobs in the formal economy and persisting gender, spatial and other inequalities, especially those facing young people in these countries. These issues are investigated in much more depth in throughout this book, particularly in the following country chapters.

Notes

1. The countries are: Botswana; Brazil; China; Hong Kong, China; Indonesia; Japan; the Republic of Korea; Malaysia; Malta; Oman; Singapore; Taiwan, China; and Thailand (Commission on Growth and Development 2008).
2. Source: World Bank's World Development Indicators online database, accessed on 6 August 2012.
3. See, for example, the ILO Key Indicators of the Labour Market (18 indicators); www.ilo.org/kilm.
4. Vulnerable employment is defined as including own account and unpaid family workers, who tend to be unprotected, and hence vulnerable to falling into poverty. See http://kilm.ilo.org/2011/download/kilm03EN.pdf.
5. Source: ILO Key Indicators of the Labour Market.
6. World Bank's World Development Indicators online database; accessed 6 August 2012.
7. United Nations Population Division, World Population Prospects, the 2010 Revision, online database; accessed 6 August 2012.
8. United Nations Population Division, World Population Prospects, the 2010 Revision, online database; accessed 6 August 2012.
9. Source: Department of Homeland Security, Office of Immigration Statistics, Yearbook of Immigration Statistics. Available at www.dhs.gov/files/statistics/publications/yearbook.shtm.
10. Source: Department of Immigration and Citizenship (Australian Government) (2012) Population flows: Immigration aspects, 2010–11 edition (Canberra: Commonwealth of Australia).
11. Source: World Bank's World Development Indicators online database, accessed 10 August 2012. Net migration is the net total of migrants during the period, that is, the total number of immigrants less the annual number of emigrants, including both citizens and noncitizens. Data are five-year estimates.
12. The empirical relationship between these indicators is known as the Beveridge curve (attributed to the British economist, William Beveridge).
13. Source: ILO Key Indicators of the Labour Market, 7th Edition; accessed 10 August 2012.
14. According to the 15th International Conference of Labour Statistics (ICLS), the informal sector is defined as units of production within unincorporated enterprises owned by households.
15. A similar trend is likely to be the case for China since the 1990s but the lack of data does not allow a proper comparison. The definition of informality includes employees without a labour record booklet, domestic maids, self-employed workers producing for their own consumption and unpaid workers.

16. See ILO Department of Statistics, Statistical Update on Employment in the Informal Economy; www.ilo.org/global/statistics-and-databases/WCMS_157467/lang–en/index.htm
17. See www.oecd.org/els/employmentpoliciesanddata/onlineoecdemployment database.htm
18. International Labour Office (ILO) (2006) *Global Employment Trends for Youth* (Geneva: ILO).
19. See p. 11, at: http://siteresources.worldbank.org/DEC/Resources/Oct_31_JustinLin_KDI_remarks.pdf
20. ILO background paper on China.
21. ILO background paper on China.
22. See Chowdhury (2011).
23. See: www.fao.org/worldfoodsituation/wfs-home/foodpricesindex/en/. All indices have been deflated using the World Bank Maanufactures Unit Value Index (MUV) rebased from 1990=100 to 2002–2004=100.
24. Source: International Monetary Fund, Direction of Trade Statistics.

References

BPS (Badan Pusat Statistik/Statistics Indonesia) (2010) *BPS Strategic Data* (Jakarta: BPS-Statistics Indonesia).

Chowdhury, S. (2011) 'Employment in India: What Does the Latest Data Show?', *Economic and Political Weekly*, Vol. XLVI, No. 32, pp. 23–26.

Crafts, N. F. R. (1985) *British Economic Growth during the Industrial Revolution* (Oxford: Oxford University Press).

Dhanani, S. et al. (2009) *The Indonesian Labour Market; Changes and Challenges* (London: Routledge).

Edwards, S. (1997) 'The Mexican Peso Crisis? How Much Did We Know? When Did We Know It?', NBER Working Paper No. 6334 (Cambridge, MA: NBER).

Fallon, P. R. and R. E. B. Lucas (2002) 'The Impact of Financial Crises on Labor Markets, Household Incomes, and Poverty: A Review of Evidence', *World Bank Research Observer*, Vol. 17, No. 1, pp. 21–45.

Fields, G. S. (2004) 'Dualism in the Labor Market: A Perspective on the Lewis Model after Half a Century', *The Manchester School*, Vol. 72, No. 6, pp. 724–735.

Growth Commission (2008) *The Growth Report: Strategies for Sustained Growth and Inclusive Development. Commission on Growth and Development* (Washington, DC: International Bank for Reconstruction and Development/World Bank).

Islam, I. and A. Chowdhury (2009) *Growth, Employment and Poverty Reduction in Indonesia* (Geneva: ILO).

Islam, I. and S. Verick (2011) *From the Great Recession to Labour Market Recovery: Issues, Evidence and Policy Options* (Basingstoke and Geneva: Palgrave Macmillan and ILO).

ILO (International Labour Office) (2012) *Global Employment Trends 2012* (Geneva: ILO).

Leibbrandt, M., I. Woolard, A. Finn and J. Argent (2010) 'Trends in South African Income Distribution and Poverty since the Fall of Apartheid', OECD Social, Employment and Migration Working Papers, No. 101 (Paris: OECD).

OECD (Organisation for Economic Co-operation and Development) (2010) *Tackling Inequalities in Brazil, China, India and South Africa: The Role of Labour Market and Social Policies* (Paris: OECD Publishing), at: http://dx.doi.org/10. 1787/9789264088368-en.

Reinhart, C. M. and K. S. Rogoff (2009) *This Time is Different: Eight Centuries of Financial Folly* (Princeton and Oxford: Princeton University Press).

Sen, A. (1999) *Development as Freedom* (Oxford: Oxford University Press).

World Bank (2011) *World Development Report 2012: Gender Equality and Development* (Washington, DC: World Bank).

3
Labour Market Regulations for Development: Enhancing Institutions and Policies in Emerging Economies

3.1 Introduction

The discipline of economics has become increasingly concerned with the understanding of labour markets' adjustment in response to economic and structural changes and, in particular, the role of labour market regulations (institutions and policies) in influencing that process. The global financial crisis has recently revealed the extent to which the policy and institutional mix had been able to provide fair adjustments protecting workers and promoting employment outcomes. Assessing the impact of labour market regulation is, however, one of the most complex areas since they both constitute a warranty of fair employment conditions, but may at the same time be an obstacle to (formal) employment growth (see Freeman 2005). Therefore, while regulations' first objective is to correct market failures and improve workers' welfare, it can lead to adverse outcomes, even for the same workers that regulations want to protect. The perspective of this section is to articulate these two aspects and focus on the 'economics' of labour market regulations. As stated before, some of the regulations have to do with the welfare state, as they provide income guarantees; when considered 'too generous', they are accused of creating unemployment through two mechanisms: work disincentives and wage behaviour. Others may influence the wage structure and/or labour costs.

All countries, irrespective of their level of economic development, have labour market regulations. The distinction between countries lies in the degree to which regulations are embedded in law, whether the law is enforced, and the extent to which government policies are

63

..iently developed to pursue certain objectives. Labour market regulations encompass a wide range of both institutions[1] and policies, all of which affect the functioning of the labour market. Labour market institutions tend to rather refer to long-term horizons that are considered by the economic agent as given when making their own decision; institutions are often established by laws and often embodied in a country's labour code, but they can also be regulated by social norms or conventions. Their origin reflects balanced ambitions of different stakeholders in the labour market, mostly rights of workers as well as the demands of business according to their production needs. Labour laws are sometimes a 'formalization' of what already exists informally, though most often they are a remedy to correct that which exists: most fundamentally, the bargaining power disadvantage that workers have *vis à vis* employers. Labour market policies (LMP) on the other hand, refer to short-term horizons. They are government policy choices that influence the interaction between labour supply and labour demand. They comprise all kinds of regulative policies that provide income replacement (usually called passive labour market policies) as well as labour market integration measures available to the unemployed or those threatened by unemployment (usually labelled as active labour market policies).

This chapter concentrates on four aspects of labour market regulations, namely: employment protection legislation (EPL);[2] minimum wages; the role of trade unions; and collective bargaining and unemployment compensation schemes. It first highlights the main findings of existing literature and the debate on the effects of labour market regulations on labour market outcomes, based largely on OECD countries; it then reviews the existing policies and institutions in place in the main emerging economies and discusses possible lessons that can be learned in that different context given the characteristics of labour markets, the lack of fiscal space and inadequate administrative capacity. Finally, the chapter provides some insights into the policy responses to the global financial crisis, more specifically how emerging economies have utilized labour market policies to help mitigate the impact of the shock. In doing so, the chapter does not systematically distinguish between active and passive labour market policies since this terminology may not be relevant for the emerging countries context,[3] but will generally refer to labour market policies and concentrate on the social and employment protection policy in place in the country.

The chapter opens with an overview of the main theoretical and empirical arguments about the issue of labour market regulations and their effect on economic outcomes. It then provides a presentation of the main features and characteristics of existing labour market policies and institutions for a group of nine emerging countries: Argentina, Brazil, China, India, Indonesia, Mexico, the Russian Federation, South Africa and Turkey. Amongst the institutions reviewed, more emphasis is given to employment protection legislation since new indicators have been produced following the methodology used by the OECD. This makes it possible to compare the labour market institutions of the emerging economies with those of the OECD countries, but also to analyse them within emerging economies. In a third part, the chapter reviews the main labour market programmes that have been put in place in the different emerging economies. Finally, the chapter considers how emerging economies have used labour market policies during the recent global financial crisis to help mitigate the impact of the shock.

3.2 The role of labour market regulations: theoretical and empirical background

3.2.1 Employment protection legislation

Employment protection legislation (EPL) refers to hiring and firing rules which are designed to 'protect' the welfare of workers and provide some support in case of workers' dismissals. It consists of both norms and administrative procedures that have to be followed in case of individual and collective dismissals. In most countries around the world, rules exist to, at least, provide some cash payments to workers who involuntarily separate from their employers. Such severance pay schemes are usually related to the number of years worked with the last employer, and linked to the last salary in the job. From the point of view of economic analysis, attention has been most often focused on those severance payments programmes since they were said to be the most 'costly' element of EPL and the easiest to measure. Moreover, and particularly for middle-income and low-income countries severance pay programmes are often the main (and sole) form of workers' protection and compensation in the case of job loss, at least in the formal economy.

The level of the employment protection legislation may affect both employers' and employees' decisions: the main argument for employment protection relates to employees' security at work, in employment and income, and the advantage of a stable employment relationship that encourages investment in human capital and thereby upgrades the productivity of the worker. Another argument in favour of EPL refers to the willingness of workers to accept technological change and internal job mobility, with a potential increase of productivity.

At a macroeconomic level, EPL may also be seen as a 'stabilizer', in smoothing labour market adjustment to adverse macroeconomic shocks. The main argument against employment protection is that it constrains firms' behaviour by raising labour costs in case of stricter EPL as layoffs are combined with severance pay and other obligations in favour of redundant workers (e.g. assistance in re-employment, funding of labour market training, etc.). Moreover, due to more lengthy administrative procedures (advance notice, negotiations with workers' representative bodies and/or labour market institutions) the firm has to keep redundant workers on payroll for a certain period, which again implies significant additional costs. Therefore, the 'stricter' the EPL, the more cautious firms may be in recruiting workers for regular jobs. The main theoretical arguments are summarized below and developed in Cazes and Verick (2012). In a nutshell, EPL generates a number of effects on labour costs, employment and productivity, some favourable and some unfavourable. The net impact of these effects seems likely to vary by size of firm, type of activity and according to the economic conditions. But theoretical models suggest rather clearly that employment should be more stable and individual employment relationships more durable when EPL is higher.

To the extent that firing costs prevent dissolution of existing employment relationships, sharp employment reduction is less likely in countries with stringent job security provisions. At times when employment would increase in the absence of EPL, however, employers are less inclined to hire when they fear that future firing costs shall make it difficult to reverse current decisions. Hence, EPL reduces job creation as well as job destruction, and results in smoother employment dynamics. More subdued turnover implies that individuals who – like new entrants to the labour market – happen to be unemployed at any given point in time are less likely to exit into employment, and more likely to experience long-term unemployment.

Since EPL has contrasting effects on employers' propensity to hire and fire, its net effect on longer-run relationships between wage and employment levels is a priori ambiguous. It may increase or decrease average employment, depending on such subtle features of formal models as the functional form of labour demand functions, the persistence of labour demand fluctuations, and the size of discount and attrition rates. A general insight holds true: since higher turnover costs reduce both hiring and firing, their effect on average employment levels over periods when both hiring and firing occur is an order of magnitude lower than that on hiring and firing separately. Such issues are studied in some detail by

EPL = Employment Protection Legislation.

Bentolila and Bertola (1990), who find that average employment effects are indeed small and of ambiguous sign in reasonable parameterizations of dynamic labour-demand problems.

Empirical work has explored these implications using the above-mentioned overall EPL indicators, and a variety of cross-sectional indicators of labour market performances such as employment, unemployment, stocks and flows. Most studies on the effects of EPL take a cross-country approach. The evidence is generally quite weak, and not conclusive: a few studies identified a negative correlation between EPL and employment in OECD countries (for example, Lazear 1990), while Heckman and Pagès' studies (2000), covering Latin American, Caribbean and industrialized countries showed a large negative – but not statistically significant – impact of EPL on employment rates. Estimates also point to increases in informal employment, partially offsetting formal employment loss. Cross-country evidence of effects on job flows, however, is slightly more robust. More recent studies have been developed with a wider coverage, including developing countries as well. The evidence is rather strong and shows that firing costs reduce turnover of jobs and workers in the labour market. Important cross-country studies are Micco and Pagès (2006), Lafontaine and Sivadasan (2009), Haltiwanger et al. (2010) and Martin and Scarpetta (2011). Micco and Pagès (2006) have a worldwide coverage and use industry-level cross-country panel data; they test and find supportive evidence for the theoretical finding that EPL stabilizes industries that are more volatile in terms of demand and supply shocks. Martin and Scarpetta found that employment protection had a sizeable effect on labour market flows, and those flows, in turn, have significant impact on productivity growth.

In recent years, work exploring the effects of EPL within single countries, using panel data on individuals or firms, has flourished. In general, increased interest in the role of EPL and better data availability have generated a greater focus on the effects of labour legislation in developing countries, especially in Latin America and India (for example, Kugler 1999 for Colombia, Besley and Burgess 2004 for India; Montenegro and Pagés 2003 for Chile; Boeri and Jimeno 2005 for Italy; Almeida and Carneiro 2008 for Brazil). Generally, these within-country studies found small but qualitatively consistent correlations with the predictions of economic theory.

3.2.2 Minimum wages

In OECD countries, much attention has been devoted to the effects of minimum wages on employment and unemployment. However, it is important to recall that minimum wages have been introduced to contribute to the reduction of poverty and inequality, notably in developing countries.[4] As for the employment effects of the minimum wages, they vary according to the economic models considered. In the case of a competitive labour market, theory provides clear predictions: if set above the market clearing level, the minimum wage will reduce employment and increase the equilibrium wage level. However, departing from the perfectly competitive framework (for example, introducing some distortions in the labour market) makes the effects of the minimum wages much more complex to assess: in the case of a monopsony (when employers face a labour supply curve that is not perfectly elastic and therefore sets wages), for example or, in the case of a dual labour market where the minimum wage actually does not apply to the secondary market or informal labour market, results may dramatically change. So, generally, those effects will depend crucially on a series of institutional variables, including the degree of compliance, enforcement, sanction for non-compliance, structure of minimum wages and the existence of uncovered sectors. Overall, even if the common understanding from economic theory is that the existence of a minimum wage tends to reduce employment, a number of market imperfections do exist, that make the minimum wages' effects not that clear-cut.[5]

The lack of conclusive theoretical findings, as in the case of EPL, generated a extensive amount of empirical research assessing the economic effects of minimum wages. In OECD countries, many studies have investigated the impact of the minimum wage on employment (for example, Dolado et al. 1996; OECD 1998, 2006; also Card and Krueger 1995 for the US). Those studies found some, albeit small, negative effects of the minimum wage on employment, notably for young workers. A growing literature has also tested the effects of minimum wages for developing countries, especially Latin America, on two outcomes: wages (such as those of the formal economy) and employment (in both the formal and informal sectors). Table 3.1 below provides an overview of the main empirical studies in developing countries. In some cases, the level of the minimum wage could be set so low that it is not binding. This is what Bell (1997) found for Mexico, for example. Several papers find that compliance with the minimum wage laws is related to some workers' or employers' characteristics: Andalon and Pagès (2008), for instance, find that in Kenya minimum wages are better enforced in the non-agriculture urban sector. Gindling and Terrel (2007) for Costa Rica, and Maloney and Nunez Mendez (2004) for Colombia, find that minimum wages are most likely to affect the wages of the bottom of the wage

Table 3.1 Effects of a 10 per cent increase in minimum wage on wages and employment, selected countries

Country	MW/average wage	Effect on average wage	Effect on employment	Comments
Indonesia (Rama 1997)	0.34	10%	2% decline	Larger negative effects in small firms
Colombia (Maloney and Nunez Mendez 2004)	0.4	6.4%	1.5% decline	Larger wage and employment effects for workers with lower wages
Brazil (Lemos 2004)	0.27	1.37%	No effect	Larger wage effects for workers with lower wages
Mexico and Colombia (Bell 1997)	0.3–0.4 (Mexico) 0.46–0.52 (Colombia)	n/a	No effects in Mexico; but 2–12% decline in Colombia	Larger effects for low-skilled
Costa Rica (Gindling and Terrel 2007)	0.5–0.7	n/a	10.9% decline in employment; 6% in hours	Larger effects for low-skilled workers
Kenya (Andalon and Pagès, 2008)	0.17 (2004)	n/a	1.1–5.5 pp decline in formal employment and 2.7–5.9 pp increase in self-employment	Higher compliance in occupations other than agriculture

Notes: pp = percentage points; n/a = not available.
Sources: Authors' compilation.

distribution, but also actually affect the entire distribution. Another important result of this study relates to the so-called 'lighthouse effect', that is, the fact that the minimum wage is used as a reference point for setting wages even in the informal economy. When an effect of the minimum wage is detected on wages in general, the next question is whether this will impact negatively on employment levels ('disemployment'). Here, the empirical literature provides mixed results. As indicated in the last columns of Table 3.1, when negative effects of the minimum wages are found, they tend to affect certain categories of the workforce. Other studies identify effects on: youth (Montenegro and Pagès 2004 in Chile); females (Feliciano 1998 in Mexico); and blue-collar workers (Suryahadi et al. 2003 in Indonesia).

Finally, an important aspect of minimum wages' impact in developing countries relates to the possible incentives for firms and workers to work in the informal economy and avoid minimum wage laws. Most studies that looked at the impact of the minimum wage on wages and in the informal economy found mixed evidence: Maloney and Nunez Mendez (2004) find that a higher minimum wage had a positive impact on employment for full-time self-employed males in Colombia. Gindling and Terrel (2007) find no effect of the minimum wage on informal employment[6] in Costa Rica. Fajnzylber (2001) finds positive effects of the minimum wage and negative employment effects for salaried informal workers[7] as well as for the self-employed in Brazil. The mixed results provided here are not very surprising given the difficulty of defining concepts such as 'informal employment' and 'informal economy'.

3.2.3   Trade unions and collective bargaining

The trade unions are also an important institutional variable to consider. Clearly, in countries where unions have strong bargaining power, employers have to go through a more lengthy process to dismiss workers (particularly for collective dismissals). Unions, and more generally industrial relations systems, also play a crucial role in determining wage flexibility in response to economic shocks. The finding that trade unions matter in things related to wages appears to be consistent with the large body of country-specific literature. In effect, the 'wage mark-up' (the difference in the average wages of workers with and without union support) lies at the very heart of the existence of trade unions. The largest literature covers the United States and the United Kingdom, where the average 'mark-up' indicates that workers with union support earn on average about 10 to 15 per cent more than other workers with similar individual and workplace characteristics. Limited country-level evidence suggests that the 'mark-up' might be even higher in low- and middle-income countries. In South Africa, for example, a series of estimates indicate that unions possibly increase the wages of black blue-collar workers by one quarter compared to non-unionized workers. Some authors consider that these high 'mark-ups' in developing countries discourage investment and are only possible because of the relatively small size of the covered sector and, therefore, the limited adverse effect that such high mark-ups may have on a country's macroeconomic performance; when most workers are covered by collective agreements, such high mark-ups might be unsustainable (Tzannatos 2008).

Overall, the strength of the trade unions will depend on coverage, but chiefly on coordination, which is a particularly important aspect of ensuring consensus in bargaining on macroeconomic objectives. However, unions may also set employment goals and accept wage restraint, trading wage moderation against additional employment creation (or preservation of employment during a crisis). Ultimately, trade union policy will be a key variable influencing labour market outcomes.

3.2.4 Unemployment insurance schemes

Within the labour market package, the unemployment benefit schemes (contributory and non-contributory) aim at maintaining income levels after losing a job, providing insurance to maintain consumption levels and time to search for a new job. They are part of the labour market regulations that, it has been argued, drive cross-country differences in labour market outcomes (in particular unemployment patterns). Unemployment compensation systems do vary quite dramatically between countries and features with respect to the level of unemployment benefits, their duration and the conditions of eligibility, which may impact both firms' decisions to hire and fire workers in response to changing economic circumstances and employees' decisions to stay in or leave their current jobs. According to theoretical arguments, unemployment benefit schemes provide good income protection to formal sector workers and can help reduce poverty; but such insurance schemes also suffer from two potential shortcomings: they leave out informal sector workers, and can create moral hazard that increases work disincentives and imposes efficiency costs.[8] As for labour supply effects, standard search theory suggests that increasing the 'generosity' of income support (either in terms of the level of the benefits or their duration), as well as extending its coverage, leads to an increase in the unemployment rate. This happens because getting benefits acts as a disincentive to undertaking job search or even to taking job offers (by increasing the reservation wage of unemployment and reducing the 'fear' of unemployment, hence increasing the upward pressure on wages from employees [Pissarides 1979]). Despite the disincentive effect of unemployment insurance on unemployment duration, unemployment benefit generosity may also increase job match quality by allowing individuals to wait for better job offers.

There exists a large empirical body of literature that analyses the impact of unemployment insurance schemes on the duration of unemployment in OECD countries and former 'transition' economies. For example, van Ours and Vodopivec (2008) advocated that, in Slovenia, the shortening of the potential duration of unemployment insurance benefits reduced substantially the length of the unemployment spell of recipients (see also Nickell 1997; Vodopivec 2004, 2005; Layard et al. 2005). This literature suggests that high and long-term unemployment benefits generate long-term unemployment and potentially affect unemployment rates, though this has been more recently disputed (Boeri et al. 2008). The positive association between the 'generosity' of unemployment insurance and unemployment duration is interpreted as a labour supply disincentive effect or a moral hazard, as described earlier. Many studies have also identified another type of impact on unemployment duration: they showed that the exit rate from the unemployment pool typically exhibits a spike around the time benefits finishes (Feldstein 2005). This finding may not be as important as suggested (Card et al. 2007). Moreover, in developing countries (Cazes and Scarpetta 1998), moral hazard effects due to unemployment insurance are likely to be different in the context of widespread informality and weak enforcement capacity. Hence, one may expect such impact of unemployment insurance on work incentives to be weaker in those countries, but very few empirical studies have investigated this topic in the case of developing countries. Another relatively poorly researched subject relates to the association between unemployment benefit schemes and labour market flows. One attempt has been made by Boeri and Garibaldi (2008), who found that less generous unemployment benefits in Europe contributed over the last fifteen years to increased labour market mobility, measured either in terms of unemployment turnover, mobility indices for transition matrices or job-to-job flows.[9]

3.3   A cross-country overview of existing labour market institutions

This section concentrates on the four main labour market institutions just presented. Each of these provisions is examined and characterized by a set of various parameters. While quantitative measures can be readily computed for some aspects of these institutions – such as the level of severance payment or the percentage of persons covered by unemployment benefit schemes – others are more difficult to measure, notably in the field of workers' protection legislation; for example, the interpretation of the notion of 'just cause' for employment termination (see Bertola et al. 2000). Bearing the caveats in mind, it is still possible to consider a set of parameters and compare various countries on the basis of several indicators characterizing the system.

3.3.1 Employment protection legislation

This section sets out several aspects of employment protection as well as different ways of capturing it: summary indicators of EPL based on standardized methodology;[10] severance pay and more subjective indicators based on employers' perceptions. Figure 3.1(a) and (b) below presents, for example, synthetic EPL indicators ranging from (0 to 6) following the OECD methodology.[11] These indicators are based on very detailed normative information, which is coded and aggregated according to a weighting scheme. The first level of aggregation covers twenty-two items, some readily available in quantitative form (for example, advance notice periods or severance payments), and some obtained from qualitative information (procedural obligation or the definition of unfair dismissals). All of these EPL indexes are de jure indicators, based on the provision of legislation in place, such as labour codes, employment protection acts and other types of laws.

Two facts are noteworthy. First, there are marked differences across countries so emerging economies do not constitute a homogeneous group: when the OECD index is compared, the de jure degree of employment protection legislation ranges from just 0.3 in Georgia to 3.9 in Nepal. Moreover, Malaysia, South Africa and the Russian Federation are amongst the less protective countries and below the OECD average of 2.23, while Turkey, Mexico and Indonesia are amongst the most protective ones (Figure 3.1. (a)). Most of the low- and middle-income countries, however, provide de jure greater employment protection than OECD countries: thirteen out of the twenty-one countries for which data are available have employment protection legislation that results in greater protection than the OECD average; however, this covers only formal employment.

Secondly, it is crucial to decompose the index and examine separately the legislation governing regular versus non-standard forms of employment, as well as individual versus collective dismissals, since the diversity identified before is very much due to the heterogeneity of

(a)   EPL Index in selected developing and emerging countries (2008)

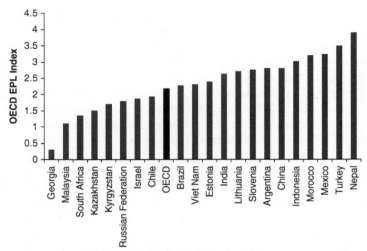

Note: Data for the Overall EPL Index is for 2008. The overall summary measure of EPL relies on three main components related to protection of regular workers against (individual) dismissal, specific requirements for collective dismissals and regulation of temporary forms of employment. The scale is from 0 (least restrictions) to 6 (most restrictions).
Source: OECD Employment Protection database and ILO figures. OECD (2012); ILO calculations based on OECD methodology (www.oecd.org/employmentprotection and the ILO EPLex database).

(b)   Decomposition of the EPL Index in selected countries

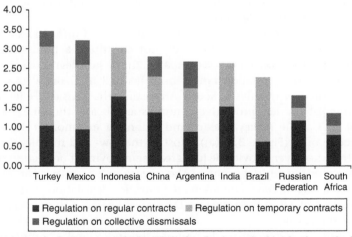

Source: Authors' calculations and OECD (2010). See also Appendix 3A.1 for the methodology and details.

Figure 3.1   EPL indexes in emerging countries

employment legislation applying to temporary contracts. Hence, if only the regulations applying to regular contracts are considered (the dark grey bar of Figure 3.1. (b)), then Brazil, South Africa and Argentina are amongst the most flexible countries of the selected group, while India and Indonesia are amongst the most restrictive ones. Finally, it is also important to note that three of those countries have no regulation at all on collective dismissals (Indonesia, India and Brazil).

Another way of capturing the employment protection level relates to severance pay programmes for formal economy work according to different years of service; as said before, this represents an important (if not the only) part of income support to the worker made redundant, in particular in emerging and developing countries where unemployment benefits schemes (if such schemes exist, see next section) are unlikely to provide any protection to job losers (OECD 2010). Table 3.2 below presents the level of the mandated severance payment for no-fault dismissals for workers after nine months, four years and twenty years of service, as well as the maximum severance pay a worker could receive. But clearly, the percentage of workers with twenty years of job tenure is likely to be extremely low in emerging economies and certainly not representative of any standard worker in those countries (Berg and Cazes 2008).[12] So figures are provided to show the wide range of years of service and highlight the fact that attention should not be focused precisely on long-tenure workers – non-representative cases – especially in emerging economies.[13] Indeed, while diversity across countries seems to prevail again, focusing on workers with long tenure tends to amplify this heterogeneity (for example, between Argentina, Turkey, and Uruguay at the top and South Africa providing the lowest severance pay with 2.5 months for 20 years of service) and overestimates the 'cost burden' of severance pay programmes.

Another way of assessing employment protection is to look at more subjective measures of labour regulations, such as the firms' perceptions of major constraints for investing. Evidence from the World Bank Group's surveys indicates, for example, that firms operating in the formal sector do not perceive hiring and firing rules as one of the main constraints (Figure 3.2 below); in fact, the shortage of skills/educated workforce is perceived as a far greater obstacle in all countries.

Actually, matching previous quantitative assessments (such as the EPL Index) with more subjective measures (such as enterprises' perceptions) shows no correlation between the two (Figure 3.3). This illustrates the complexity of capturing the multidimensional aspect of employment protection and in particular the fact that available indicators measure,

Table 3.2   Severance payment by years of service (by tenure)

Country	Year	Severance Pay (months of salary)			
		Maximum	9 months	4 years	20 years
Argentina	2005	40	1.125	4	30
Brazil[a]		No limit specified	0.288	1.536	7.68
Costa Rica	2005	8	0.667	4	8
Egypt	2003	12.5	0	2	6.25
India	2005	10	0	2	10
Indonesia[b]	2005	9	1	4	9
Mexico	2005	16.3	3	5.6	16.3
Philippines	2005	20	0.75	3	15
Peru[c]	2005	12	0	6	12
South Africa	2005	5	0	0.5	2.5
Thailand	2005	6	1	6	6
Turkey[d]	2005	No limit specified	0	4	20
Uruguay	2005	20	0	4	20
Venezuela[e]	2005	3	1	3	3

Notes:
a. For dismissal without cost and redundancy. Compensation for unfair dismissal is 40% of the updated value of deposits in the FGTS account. According to the 'Fundo de Garantia por Tempo de Serviço' (FGTS), every month the employer is required to deposit 8% of the employee's monthly salary into an account managed by the Federal Savings Bank ('Caixa Econômica Federal') on behalf of the employee.
b. For dismissal without a cause and redundancy. Severance pay amounts to one month's wages for a length of service from 6-12 months; two months' wages for years of employment up to one year or more but less than two years; four months' wages for years of employment up to three years or more but less than four years; nine months' wages for years of employment up to eight years or more (Art. 156 Manpower Law (25.03.2003)).
c. For dismissal without a cause. The severance pay is equivalent to 1.5 months of wages for each complete year of service. This has an upper limit of 12 months of wages. (Art. 34 & 38 of the Competitiveness and Labour Productivity Law (27.03.1997)).
d. For dismissal and redundancy. Severance pay entitles 30 days' wages for each complete year of service or in proportion for any fraction thereof, effective from the date of employment and for the entire duration of the contract (Labour Act of 2003 No. 4857 that does not modify the art. 14 Labour Act No. 1475).
e. For dismissal without a cause. Severance pay is equivalent to 10 days' wages for length of service between 3 and 6 months; 30 days' wages for length of service between 6 and 12 months; 30 days' wages per year of service up to 150 days' wage (Art. 125-126 OLL).
Source: Aleksynska and Schindler (2011).

at best, de jure legislation; it also reveals the high level of informality, as well as the lack of capacity of labour inspectorates to enforce labour laws. Hence, the 'paradox' of Indonesia, for example, (very high EPL Index but not perceived by a high percentage of firms as a major obstacle) could reflect low levels of enforcement that render the legislation ineffective. Moreover, the majority of workers in developing

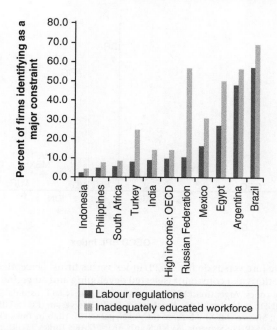

Figure 3.2 Perceptions of constraints among enterprises in selected countries: percentage of firms reporting labour regulations versus skills as a major obstacle (various years)

Notes: Percentage of firms reporting labour regulations and skills as major obstacles. Year reported: Indonesia (2009); Philippines (2009); South Africa (2007); Turkey (2008); India (2006); Russian Federation (2009); Mexico (2010); Egypt (2008); Argentina (2010); and Brazil (2009).

Source: Enterprise Surveys (www.enterprisesurveys.org), World Bank.

countries are located in the informal economy and hence beyond the scope of regulations, implying that employers are not directly affected by the impact of rigidities arising from labour laws.[14] Another puzzling case is Brazil, where hiring and firing rules are seen as important binding constraints by firms, while more objective measures provide a different assessment. This issue is detailed in the country chapter devoted to Brazil (Chapter 4).

Most emerging and developing economies provide protection to workers chiefly through legislation, which is inadequate because it merely covers the small formal economy. Moreover, the lack of enforcement implies that even those formal workers are afforded little protection in practice. This gap in worker protection remains one of the key challenges to policymakers in developing countries and emerging economies.

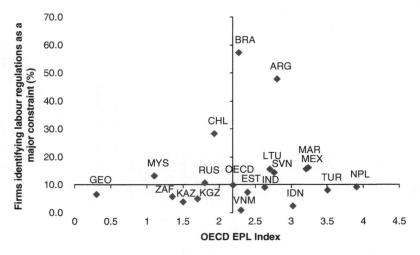

Figure 3.3   De jure versus de facto: EPL index versus firms' perceptions of labour market regulations as a constraint (selected developing and emerging economies)
Notes: Country codes: Argentina (ARG); Brazil (BRA); Chile (CHL); Estonia (EST); Georgia (GEO); India (IND); Indonesia (IDN); Kazakhstan (KAZ); Kyrgyzstan (KGZ); Lithuania (LTU); Malaysia (MYS); Mexico (MEX); Morocco (MAR); Nepal (NPL); High income: OECD (OECD); Russian Federation (RUS); Slovenia (SVN); South Africa (ZAF); Turkey (TUR); and Viet Nam (VNM).
Sources: See Figures 3.1 and 3.2.

3.3.2   Minimum wages

The minimum wage is another key labour market institution existing in most of the countries reviewed in this chapter.[15] It is an important aspect of regulation as it sets a wage floor that establishes a lower boundary to the wage paid to individual workers. Therefore, it will mostly affect the low end of the wage distribution, while the other wage-setting institutions (such as trade unions and collective bargaining) will affect the whole distribution. In emerging and developing countries, given the limited coverage of collective bargaining and the challenges facing trade unions to organize low-paid workers, the minimum wage can play an important role protecting the purchasing power of low-paid workers. Moreover, it is often used as a reference for other workers' benefits but also by informal workers and employers (the 'lighthouse effects').

In order to do some cross-country comparisons, attention usually concentrates on key statistics on minimum wage systems like the ratio of the minimum wage to the average wage, the percentage of workers at or near the minimum wage and the frequency of adjustment, as well as some more qualitative information describing the wage-setting mechanisms. The ILO, the OECD and the IMF, for example, provide such information. Figure 3.4 displays the ratio of the minimum wage to the average wage in a large number of developing countries and emerging economies, which is a standard statistic often used in international comparisons. In principle, using the median rather than the average wage as a denominator would be better as median wages are less sensitive to outliers and thus may better measure earnings distribution.[16]

Figure 3.4 illustrates the huge diversity across countries with the ratio of the minimum wage to the average wage ranging from 1.8 per cent in Uganda to 81.2 per cent in Pakistan. In terms of emerging economies, the ratio varies from 17.8 per cent in South Africa to 63.2 per cent in Indonesia. India, Brazil and China are in the middle of this distribution with ratios of 41.4, 35.1 and 34.3 per cent, respectively. By comparison, the minimum wage relative to average wage of full-time workers in the OECD ranges between 27 per cent in the United States and 52 per cent in New Zealand, while the OECD average was at 37.9 per cent (2008) (not shown in Figure 3.4). It is important to recall that this ratio is mainly presented here to illustrate the diversity of the minimum wages situation among countries; indeed, other drawbacks of this measure include the fact that it does not include the large informal labour market in which minimum wage legislation does not apply or is not enforced; in many developing countries, there are sometimes multiple minimum wages,[17] varying across occupations, industries and/or geographical region; and, finally, the existence of high and volatile inflation, which generates wide fluctuations in real wages in such countries.

3.3.3 Trade unions and collective bargaining

In most countries, trade unions play a major role in the collective bargaining process and are, therefore, likely to influence wage formation and labour costs. Providing a cross-country comparison of the influence of trade unions is not an easy task. Three aspects of the role of trade unions are usually – at least for the OECD countries – considered and captured by comparable measures: they include the union density or rate of unionization (the fraction of workers registered with some trade unions); the coverage of collective bargaining rate (the percentage of the workforce whose contract is regulated by the

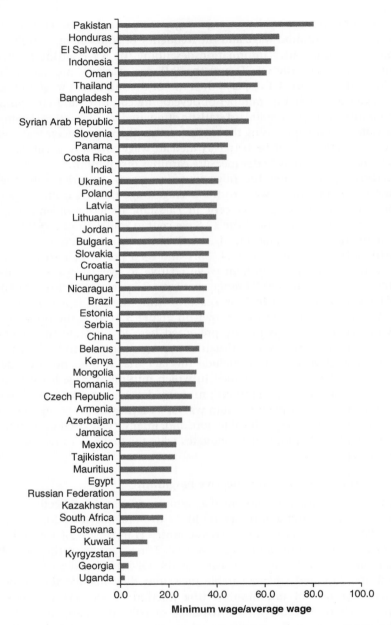

Figure 3.4 Minimum wage to average wage (%) in developing countries and emerging economies
Sources: ILO Global Wage 2012 database (www.ilo.org/wage12).

collective agreements signed by the union) and the degree of coordination (the extent to which trade unions manage to coordinate their wage-setting activities together with employers' organizations). Government involvement in the negotiation process is another relevant aspect (not explored here). Finally, centralization is another important aspect which may be distinguished from coordination and which refers to the level at which bargaining takes place (company, industry, sectoral or national). Highly coordinated bargaining is not necessarily centralized, as it is in Germany or Denmark, for example. While empirical research has generated datasets on unions and employers' organizations for OECD countries (see Calmfors and Driffill 1988; Layard et al. 2005; and Traxler and Kittel 1997) few data are available for emerging countries.

As a matter of fact, the rate of unionization and the coverage of collective bargaining in emerging countries are usually quite low. In advanced European countries, coverage of collective bargaining reaches 70 per cent or more of employees in a majority of countries. In developing regions, the rate of coverage is typically much lower. In Asian countries, it is usually below 15 per cent and often below 5 per cent of employees. In both Latin America and Africa, trade unions appear to have been weakened by years of structural adjustment policies. Table 3.3 summarizes the key features of the trade unions in a sample of selected emerging economies. According to the available data, the percentage of trade union membership ranges from about 90 per cent in China to 2 per cent in Thailand. However, if China is excluded from the sample (the percentage for China is from 2000 and reflects more the situation of 'transition' economies with union density rates close to 100 per cent, reflecting a centralized wage-setting system), the situation is less heterogeneous and shows three groups of countries: one with relatively high union density, comparable with those of OECD countries (Turkey, South Africa and Argentina at around 40 per cent and above); another group with very low rates (below 10 per cent; Indonesia and Thailand[18]) and finally a mid-range group with union density rates around 15 to 25 per cent (most Latin/South American countries and Egypt).

Table 3.3 also shows that collective bargaining coverage (defined here as the proportion of wage and salary earners, unionized or not, who have their pay and working conditions determined by collective agreements in the enterprise sector) also differs dramatically among emerging countries. However, none of those countries has a coverage rate above 70 per cent;[19] coverage rates range between extremely low values in the

Table 3.3 Trade unions and collective bargaining in selected countries, mid-2000s

Country	Union density (a) %	Collective bargaining coverage (b) %
Argentina	37.6	60.0
Brazil	20.9	60.0
Chile	12.5	9.6
China	90.3	15.1
Egypt	26.1	3.4
El Salvador	11.9	4.1
Guatemala	12.9	n.a.
India	6.3	n.a.
Indonesia	3.4	14.0
Mexico	17.0	10.5
Philippines	26.8	2.2
South Africa	39.8	27.3
Thailand	2.1	26.7
Turkey	59.0	*n.a.*
Uruguay	19.0	21.6

Notes: For China: 2000 for column (a) and 1995 for column (b); for India: 2002; for Indonesia: 1995 for column (a) and 2005 for column (b).
Sources: ILO (1997/1998); Trade Union Statistics (ILO 2001); Hayter and Stoevska (2011); for India, Ahn (2010).

Philippines, Egypt or El Salvador to 60 per cent (both in Argentina and Brazil, in 2006). In both Latin America and Africa, trade unions appear to have been weakened by years of structural adjustment policies. In Peru, for example, collective bargaining has reached a historically low level, with less than 8 per cent coverage and a decrease in the number of collective agreements from 2000 in the early 1980s to 300 in 2007. In Tanzania, too, coverage declined when a centralized wage policy was replaced by wage bargaining at the enterprise level (Belser 2012).

In the context of emerging economies, the limited influence of trade unions, as suggested by both low density and coverage rates, is more likely to reflect the challenges facing trade unions to organize low-paid workers as well as reaching informal workers. A study by Rani and Belser (2011) shows that being part of a trade union in India considerably reduces the probability of low pay for both salaried and casual workers. Unfortunately, the overall collective bargaining coverage in India remains relatively limited, with an estimated 24.9 million unionized workers in 2002, representing a union density of just 6.3 per cent (Ahn 2010). Generally, it also remains a challenge for trade unions in those countries to develop inclusive systems and organize low-paid workers.

Indeed, few low-paid workers are union members and the low partici-pation of women in workers' organizations compounds this challenge. In the Republic of Korea, the overall union membership fell to 12.2 per cent in 2009 and only 2.2 per cent of low-paid workers are union mem-bers. Even in South Africa, where about 31 per cent of wage earners were estimated to belong to trade unions in 2007, union membership among low-paid workers was only 13.3 per cent.

Generally, social dialogue can also be weak in developing and emerg-ing economies because of a lack of trust amongst stakeholders and the lack of capacity of social partners. Moreover, because the majority of workers are in the informal economy, unions would only be repre-senting a small minority. At the same time, there are other types of organizations that are relevant to those outside the formal economy including entrepreneurs' associations and cooperatives.

3.3.4 Unemployment protection systems

Income support for the unemployed is another key element of social protection. Unemployment compensation can be provided by insurance or assistance schemes. In most OECD countries (except Australia and New Zealand), unemployed people get benefits through unemployment insurance schemes, which provide at least partial income replacement and maintain a certain standard of living during the transition period until a new job is available. Such unemployment benefits are typically funded by contributory schemes for employees in the formal economy, and offer unemployment compensation related to the previous earnings of the beneficiary after a qualifying period, mostly for a limited period of time. Unemployment benefits schemes can play an important role in cushioning the social impacts of an economic recession and serve as an important automatic stabilizer during a slowdown. In addition to this, public unemployment assistance systems exist in a number of countries (especially high income ones), but play only a residual role in closing relatively small coverage gaps. These are usually not based on prior earnings but are flat-rate non-contributory cash transfers to those who are still unemployed, either once their entitlements to unem-ployment benefits have expired, or when they have never been entitled. Income support to the long-term unemployed and their families is often taken over by general means-tested social assistance schemes.

As said before, the absence of unemployment insurance or other statu-tory income support programmes for the unemployed in most low and middle-income countries[20] has often made mandated severance payments the only available protection in the case of job loss and has led to higher employment protection legislation, at least de jure, and for those workers in the formal economy. However, while both severance payments and unemployment insurance do provide income compensation to job losers, they are different instruments with different approaches: unemployment insurance schemes are worker-oriented (linked to the individual status of being unemployed), while severance payment schemes are job-oriented (linked to the specificity of job matches and the value of seniority). Moreover, there are also differences related to their financing and level of security provided. Severance pay is based on employers' liability, while unemployment insurance is financed from contributions paid by workers and employers and pooled. The latter does not entail any additional financial pressure on ailing enterprises (unlike severance payments, which in practice are often not delivered to workers) and tends to also provide protection for workers with shorter periods of job tenure and lower wage levels. Moreover, severance pay is a lump sum, while unemployment insurance provides periodical benefits, usually for a prescribed duration. Finally, severance pay tends to be more strongly related to the wage level and job tenure in a specific enterprise than unemployment benefits, which affects the level of protection and labour mobility.

Several countries – typically in Central and Latin America – have introduced hybrid systems to combine these two approaches: various reforms took place in that region during the 2000s to allow individual savings accounts or experience-rated unemployment insurance which combines layoff taxes paid by firms (a form of employment protection) with collective unemployment insurance (for example, in Chile [2002–2005] and the Bolivarian Republic of Venezuela [2002–2005],[21] see Robalino et al. 2009). Those private schemes often provide complementary supports, such as the Chilean unemployment insurance system which combines individual capitalization accounts (UISA, from which the accumulated – by the worker – contributions are paid out on job separation) and a subsidized solidarity fund for those dismissed for economic reasons (to which the employer and the State contribute). Again, it is important to highlight the fact that UISA, unemployment insurance and severance pay are not alternative forms of income support and each instrument has its own features and limits. UISA schemes are based on mandatory individual savings. They are usually characterized by extremely low take-up, both for workers and employers, even for those workers in the informal economy with relatively good contributory capacities, and more so for those with low contributory capacities and those who face disadvantages in the labour market (often women, and various vulnerable groups). Further challenges linked to private individualized savings options relate to possible regressive effects, low coverage and high administrative costs.

Table 3.4 presents some stylized characteristics of unemployment protection systems for selected emerging economies reviewed in this chapter, such as the type of programmes, the level of unemployment benefits, which captures the 'generosity' of the unemployment benefit system and is measured by the initial replacement rate (that is, the ratio of unemployment benefits a worker in a formal job receives relative to his last earnings); and the number of unemployment benefit recipients (that is, the number of individuals who are receiving the unemployment benefits as a percentage of the unemployed (the coverage rate index)). These two latter indicators are useful for capturing key aspects of unemployment insurance systems, but are subject to some caveats, in particular for cross-country comparison (see Aleksynska and Schindler 2011).

As expected, the situation differs quite dramatically between countries and emerging economies display great diversity: in some countries there are no unemployment protection schemes at all (Indonesia, the Philippines and Mexico, for example). As mentioned before, in some cases, there exist legal provisions (usually included in the labour code) obliging employers to pay a lump sum equivalent to several months' salary to workers who are laid off; the entitlements and amounts of such severance payments normally depend on job tenure.[22] And in those countries that have an unemployment protection scheme, entitlements to unemployment benefits tend to be restricted to those in formal employment, limiting the number of beneficiaries, such as India where less than 1 per cent of workers are covered (Table 3.4).

The effective level of coverage by unemployment protection schemes is often substantially lower than legal coverage. But in the case of those emerging countries reviewed here, the wedge between the two may be particularly high with a dramatically low effective coverage in those countries. This low coverage can be explained by different factors, such as eligibility rules, the obligation for beneficiaries to have some work experience (in insurance schemes) or some administrative obligations. In South Africa, for example, a large share of the unemployed is either long-term unemployed or without any work experience and thus are not entitled to unemployment benefits (see also Chapter 6). In Turkey, eligibility conditions are very strict as workers should have contributed for twenty months to the unemployment insurance scheme in the last

Table 3.4 Unemployment protection systems for formal sector job losers in selected emerging countries, latest available year

Country	Type of programme	Unemployed receiving benefits (%)	Initial replacement rate	Duration of benefits
Argentina	Social insurance	5.7 (2010)	50% of the highest wage in the 6 months before unemployment. Extended UB: 70% of the first UB paid	2 months for 6–11 months of contributions; 4 months for 12–23 months; 8 months for 24–35 months; 12 months for 36 months +.
Brazil	Social insurance; social assistance	7.8 (2010)	From 50% to 80% of previous earnings, decreasing with the earning level	3 months for 6–11 months of prior employment; 4 months for 12–23 months; 5 months for 24 months +; The benefit may be extended for 2 months under special conditions.
Chile	Mandatory private insurance; social assistance	22.4 (2011)	50% (open-ended contracts) then decreasing; 35% (fixed-term contracts) then decreasing.	5 months (open-ended contracts and age); 2 months benefits (fixed-term contracts).
China	Social insurance	11.3 (2010)	Lump sum from 60% to 70% of the minimum wage, as determined by local governments	Up to 12 months if contributions are less than 5 years; up to 18 months if above 5 years but less than 10 years; up to 24 months if it is above 10 years
Egypt	Social insurance	n.a.	60% of the insured's last monthly wage	4 months; can be extended up to 7 months if the individual contributed for the last 24 months prior to unemployment

Indonesia	No provision	n.a.		n.a.
India	Social insurance	n.a.	50% of average wage	Up to 6 months/up to one year (ISSA)
Russian Federation	Social insurance; social assistance	24.1 (2010)	75% of previous earnings for the first 3 months; 60% for the next 4 months and 45% for the last 5 months.	12 months; then unemployment assistance
South Africa	Social insurance	12.7 (2010)	38% to 58% of average earnings over the previous 6 months depending on the length of contribution	Up to 8 months depending on contribution records (one day of benefit for every 6 days of contribution)
Thailand	Social insurance	22.4 (2010)	50% of average wage if involuntary unemployment; 30% of average wage if voluntary unemployment	Up to 6 months if involuntary unemployment; up to 3 months if voluntary unemployment
Turkey	Social insurance	11.4 (2011)	50% of average net wage over the last 4 months	6–10 months according to contribution period
Viet Nam	Social insurance	9.1 (2010)	60% of the average monthly earnings	12 months for contributions of 12 years or more; 9 months for 6–12 years; 6 months for 3–6 years; 3 months for 1–3 years

Sources: ILO (2012/2013); ISSA (2011); ILO Statistics (2011).

three years (see Chapter 7); these rules are also relatively strict in China and cover only urban enterprises and their employees. Finally, and more generally, the low coverage may be due to the fact that a significant share of the workers is not affiliated to the social security schemes, such as in Brazil, China and Turkey.

Besides the eligibility rules, the key features of the unemployment scheme can be also captured by the evolution of the level and the duration of the benefit. The last two columns of Table 3.4 show the maximum duration of the benefits and the initial replacement rates – that is, the share of income which is replaced by the unemployment benefit. Generally, replacement rates are relatively low in emerging countries, in particular compared to the OECD average; but there is substantial cross-country diversity. Initial replacement rates (the ratio of initial highest benefits to previous earning wages) in the countries reviewed in Table 3.4 range from 50 to 70 per cent, with the exception of two extreme cases: South Africa (38 per cent) and Brazil (up to 80 per cent). The duration of benefits also differ across countries, but are also generally lower than in most OECD countries (12 to 24 months). For instance, the maximum duration ranges from three months in Brazil to twelve months in China or the Russian Federation.[23]

Finally, those differences are also reflected in the share of expenditure on unemployment benefits as a proportion of GDP, although this percentage will also depend on the level of unemployment. According to the OECD, it is, in the selected countries, highest in Brazil (0.5 per cent) and lowest in China (0.01 per cent), with Turkey and the Russian Federation at, respectively, 0.06 per cent and 0.04 per cent of GDP. In Chile, unemployment benefits amounted to 0.1 per cent of GDP in 2008, out of which less than 4 per cent came from the Solidarity Fund. By comparison, OECD countries spent about 0.6 per cent of their GDP on average in 2007 (OECD 2009, 2010). Generally, these figures are still lower than those of EU countries which devote, on average, 1.7 per cent of their GDP to unemployment benefits.

3.4   The labour market policy response to the global financial crisis 2008–2009

3.4.1   Why use labour market policies?

As defined above, labour market policies comprise all kinds of regulative policies that influence labour demand and supply, and the interaction between the two. Cazes et al. (2010) provide a typology of those labour market programmes that go beyond the OECD terminology and identify six categories (job search assistance, training schemes, job/wages subsidies, public employment programmes, entrepreneurship incentives, income replacement). But, beyond categorizing labour market policies, it is crucial to understand why governments need to resort to such policy interventions. Theoretically, it is possible to provide a number of arguments for utilizing these policies. Firstly, as well acknowledged throughout the world, labour markets are not competitive, and, therefore, do not clear, resulting in (involuntary) unemployment.[24] This can arise due to skills mismatch, search costs or rigidities (though this last factor is controversial and not nearly as straightforward as many commentators suggest).

A second theoretical argument supports the need for government interventions in training. There is an incentive problem in the sense that employers will underinvest in firm-specific human capital because they cannot prevent trained workers from leaving, which would allow other companies to take advantage of the training without having to pay for it (this could be achieved by offering a higher wage).

3.4.2 Evidence from the global financial crisis

Different labour market policies have been used, on top of fiscal stimulus packages and monetary ('quantitative') easing. These measures have centred on four main areas:

1) the support of labour demand by keeping people in jobs to prevent unemployment and working poverty (for example, help employers avoid laying off workers through measures to reduce labour costs such as a reduction in working hours); but also by creating new jobs to lift people out of unemployment/underemployment (such as hiring subsidies or public work programmes);
2) the prevention of human capital deterioration, long-term unemployment and drop-outs from the labour market by increasing employability;
3) the provision of income support to job losers and low-income earners to smooth consumption and prevent poverty;
4) the targeting of the most vulnerable segments of society such as youth, older persons, persons with disability, and refugees and migrants, which is a cross-cutting goal relevant to those listed above.

Though it is difficult to gather full information on labour market policies across the globe, available studies and responses reported by governments (Table 3.5 and Figure 3.5 provide some important insights into the main tools adopted by governments). The responses reported here

Table 3.5 Coverage of selected active labour market policies (ALMPs) during the global financial crisis, 2008–2010

Country	Name of ALMP	No. of beneficiaries
Work-sharing		
Germany	Kurzarbeit	1.43 million workers (June 2009)
Italy	Cassa Integrazione Guadagni (CIG)	716.8 million hours compensated in Jan–Oct 2009
Netherlands	Deeltijd WW	36,000 workers (third quarter 2009)
Turkey	Short-pay scheme	508,000 beneficiaries in 2009
South Africa	Training layoff scheme	7,676 workers (June 2010)
Wage subsidies		
Argentina	Productive Recovery Program (REPRO)	By September 2009, coverage had extended to 2,317 enterprises and 123,444 workers
Training		
Indonesia	Vocational Training Centres (BLK)	50,000 jobseekers received training
Republic of Korea	Youth internship programme	90,000 interns employed at administrative agencies, public institutions and SMEs
Russian Federation	Vocational training	107,000 workers threatened with lay-off
Public works programmes		
India	National Rural Employment Guarantee Scheme	1.77 million person days generated in 2009/10 financial year (five months)
Spain	State Fund for Local Investment	400,000 jobs created
South Africa	Expanded Public Works Programme	568,224 beneficiaries (2008/09)

Source: Islam and Verick (2011).

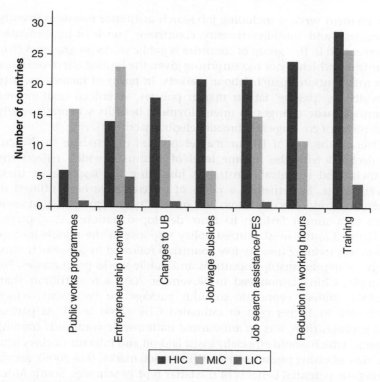

Figure 3.5 National labour market policy responses to the global financial crisis, 2008–2009

Notes: HIC = high-income countries; MIC = middle-income countries; LIC = low-income countries, which are grouped according to the World Bank's classification of countries, see http://go.worldbank.org/D7SN0B8YU0. UB = unemployment benefits schemes.
Source: Cazes et al. (2010).

draw from various studies that assess policy decisions in seventy-nine OECD and non-OECD countries from Europe, North America, Latin America, Asia, Oceania, the Middle East and Africa.[25] It should be stressed that this information is by no means complete.

As illustrated in Figure 3.5, a large number of high-income (mostly OECD) countries have considered policy measures that address all four types considered in this chapter. The most commonly used intervention durung the GFC in high-income countries was training for both those threatened by layoffs and the unemployed (including work experience and apprenticeship initiatives) (twenty-seven countries), followed by work sharing (twenty-four countries), increased resources for public employment services including job search assistance measures (twenty countries), and subsidies (twenty countries). The least-implemented intervention in this group of countries is public works programmes (five countries), which is not too surprising given the limited effectiveness of this intervention in such labour markets. In terms of income security provided by 'passive' labour market policies, seventeen high-income countries made changes to unemployment benefits schemes (usually extensions of coverage and broader eligibility criteria).

Overall, the use of labour market policies in response to the crisis declined with the income level of countries, which reflects the financial and technical constraints hindering the response of these governments. Nonetheless, a range of policies have been utilized in emerging economies (here, low- and middle-income countries), in some cases in a similar fashion to more developed nations. As displayed in Figure 3.5, the most utilized policy response in the middle-income group was training (twenty-five countries) followed by job-search assistance, entrepreneurship incentives and public works programmes. For example, China announced in November 2008 a four trillion yuan (US$586 billion) economic stimulus package for two years, which amounted to 14 per cent of estimated GDP (2008 level). As part of this package, there was an announced nation-wide vocational training scheme, which would especially assist laid-off and migrant workers with the view of easing pressure on the Chinese job market (Lee 2009). Recognizing the potential benefits of the latter type of schemes, South Africa established in 2004 the Extended Public Works Programme (EPWP) with the aim of 'creating at least 1 million work opportunities, of which at least 40 per cent of beneficiaries will be women, 30 per cent youth and 2 per cent people with disabilities'.[26] A second phase launched in 2009 aimed to increase the number of beneficiaries to two million full-time equivalent jobs. EPWP beneficiaries participate in a range of infrastructure, economic, environmental and social projects (see Chapter 6 for more details).

In India, the Mahatma Gandhi National Rural Employment Guarantee (MGNREG) scheme also received considerable attention, particularly because it enshrines a right to employment and provides a wage floor for the rural poor.[27] Taking a rights-based approach, the MGNREG scheme confers the right of employment of up to 100 days per year in public works programmes per rural household. The government is, hence, acting as the employer of last resort, providing work to those who are unable to gain employment elsewhere. The MGNREG scheme should have helped India in mitigating the impact of the crisis on the rural poor, which underscores the importance of having safety nets in place, supported by existing institutions and policies, to be able to respond to an economic shock. Recognizing the role of these programmes during the current crisis, the Government of India announced as part of its stimulus package additional resources for such schemes as the MGNREG (ILO 2009; Kannan 2009).[28]

The most widely discussed measure taken during the global financial crisis has been short-time working arrangements, which involves the reduction of working hours together with a reduction in wages that may be subsidized by governments to ease the burden on workers (see, for example, Cazes et al. 2010). The German 'Kurzarbeit' and other similar schemes clearly helped employers respond to the downturn by relying on internal numerical adjustment (reduction in working hours) rather than external adjustment (shedding employment). This was crucial for export-oriented firms in Germany and other European countries, which had been experiencing skills shortages in the period leading up to the global financial crisis. Their strategy paid off with a return to strong export growth, which had been largely driven by demand in China and other emerging economies.

In developing countries, measures such as reducing working hours received little attention, partly because they are difficult to implement or because of their costs, although depending on whether a social security system is in place, a subsidized reduction of working hours can be less expensive than the payment of unemployment benefits and the further consequences of increased unemployment. Alternatively, unsubsidized measures would result in reduced wages for workers, who are often living near or below the poverty line, and thus the measure would subsequently have had long-lasting negative consequences for the welfare of these workers and their families.

Overall, these policy options lose some relevance in countries where the formal economy may represent only ten per cent of workers and where labour costs are not a major constraint for employers. In addition, such interventions require constructive social dialogue, which is often absent. Despite the many challenges middle-income countries are facing to implement such labour market programmes,[29] countries such as Mauritius have looked for ways to keep people in jobs. In May 2009, the Government of Mauritius announced that its National Employment Foundation would run a 'Work cum Training' scheme to enable companies in the manufacturing and tourism sectors, facing a reduction in their turnover, to send their employees on training programmes instead of laying them off.[30] There are far fewer low-income countries implementing such policies in response to the crisis. In general, low- and middle-income countries tend to rely on labour market policy measures that do not require complex institutional structures and social dialogue.

In addition to these interventions, a common form of support for the unemployed/underemployed, particularly in developing countries, is entrepreneurship incentives, which usually consist of training, credit or a combination of both. Entrepreneurship training focuses on developing skills in business planning, marketing and product development, often coupled with mentoring. Entrepreneurship credit schemes, usually micro-credit, seek to overcome barriers the under-/unemployed face in accessing funds from formal lending institutions, which are especially severe because these individuals lack a credit history and collateral. A major constraint is that these schemes can assist only a small proportion of the unemployed since not all individuals are suited to becoming entrepreneurs (though it can be argued that entrepreneurship skills can be beneficial for a broader range of roles). Prior to the crisis, a number of developing countries had already established entrepreneurship funds that provide both training and access to credit, mostly targeting youth. In Africa alone, Algeria, Botswana, Kenya, Malawi, Mali, Nigeria, Senegal, South Africa, United Republic of Tanzania, Uganda and Zambia have set up youth entrepreneurship funds in recent years. These programmes could be used as vehicles to accelerate any labour market response to the impact of the current global economic downturn, which would nonetheless require increased resources.

The downturn of the last couple of years has underscored the point that governments can respond most effectively to such crises when they rely on existing labour market institutions and programmes, which all rest on permanent structures. For example, a well-staffed and equipped public employment service is needed to manage programmes that target the unemployed. Subsidies require legislation that stipulates how these financing measures are provided to employers. The lesson learnt from the East Asian crisis in the late 1990s was that the lack of institutions and programmes, especially in terms of established social security schemes, hindered the ways these countries could respond to the adverse impact on labour markets and household welfare across the region. This situation, however, was repeated in many countries during the global financial crisis of 2008–2010.[31]

As emphasized before, unemployment benefit schemes are crucial in maintaining income levels and consumption during a downturn. In such situations, unemployment benefits act as automatic stabilizers because the overall coverage of assistance to the unemployed increases by design during a recession as more jobless submit claims for benefits, without any specific government intervention.[32] However, during the current crisis, large numbers of laid-off workers have not been eligible for unemployment benefits. In response to this, many governments have made changes during the current crisis to unemployment benefits schemes, including extending coverage and increasing generosity of payments. For example, some countries have extended unemployment benefits to those who have not previously been eligible (for example, through a reduction of minimum of months worked to be eligible). Others, such as Brazil and the Republic of Korea, have extended the duration of unemployment benefits.

The main challenge to expanding coverage and increasing unemployment benefits is the cost for governments, though these measures are mostly meant to be temporary. As shown in section 3.2.4 above, most developing and emerging countries do not have unemployment benefit schemes due to their cost, and lack capacity and institutional requirements such as a functioning public employment service. In Africa, only Algeria, Egypt, South Africa and Tunisia provide any form of unemployment insurance programme. Viet Nam is the only low-income country to establish an unemployment insurance scheme, which commenced in January 2009, though Vietnamese employees can only benefit from this scheme from the beginning of 2010 (Pham 2009). In other countries, new social security systems can only be envisaged over a longer-term horizon, which limits the applicability of this policy option as an immediate response to the current crisis in developing economies. Nonetheless, it remains an important goal as a means of protecting the welfare of the poor (Townsend 2009). Since most of the poor in developing countries are beyond the reach of formal income protection schemes, countries in Latin America, such as Brazil, support those in poverty through targeted cash transfers (usually conditional on the participation of children in schools or health-related requirements), but those schemes should not be substitutes for unemployment compensation schemes.[33]

3.5 Conclusion

Relevant to a wider discourse on labour market policies and institutions, this chapter addresses much-debated themes such as the role of EPL and minimum wages in emerging economies. It goes beyond a narrow approach based on the negative effects of labour market regulations on labour market outcomes and argues that empirical evidence on the role of minimum wages and EPL, in particular, faces serious measurement and econometric challenges. This may partly explain why the debate on the effects of labour market regulations on labour markets is still not settled and empirical findings, in particular cross-country ones, are far from robust. However, beyond measurement issues, there are also conceptual problems as well. Most of the empirical research carried out in this field has systematically assumed causality to go from institutions to economic performance without considering the possibility of reverse causality.

The cross-country overview of existing policies and institutions in the main emerging economies showed considerable variation within countries in terms of the policy and institutional mix that is not only explained by differences in income level and labour market characteristics, but also by the different priorities governments have set to achieve some security and flexibility. But, interestingly, it also reveals that, despite the various constraints mentioned above, some building blocks are already in place even if not sufficiently developed. However, the predominance of the informal economy, the low levels of enforcement (even for formal sector workers), weak institutional capacity and the lack of fiscal space mean that workers are afforded little protection in practice. This deficit in worker protection remains one of the key challenges to policymakers in emerging economies.

Labour market policies, as a tool to improve the match between demand and supply, have also a role to play in emerging economies. In contrast to earlier decades, these economies are increasingly developing and implementing labour market policies to address both structural and demand-related unemployment and underemployment, such as public employment programmes, entrepreneurship incentives and training which often targets women and youth.

In designing and implementing labour market policies, policymakers should keep in mind the following principles: the policy response should build on existing measures; the interventions should match the objectives, for example, react to the drop in labour demand or set longer-term goals; and weigh up the relative costs and benefits of different policies. The response is also development-dependent: due to financial and technical constraints, the set of options available to OECD countries is far larger than that suitable for emerging and developing economies, particularly low-income countries.

Moreover, over the medium and long term, governments should aim to develop a comprehensive and integrated policy and institutional framework that will enable them to better respond to labour market challenges, which emanate from not only global shocks but also from local and regional phenomena. This involves the development of labour market institutions and a broad-based social security system that acts as an automatic stabilizer during a crisis.

Overall, labour market regulations (institutions and policies) can play a positive role but effectiveness remains a challenge: while there has been a strong tendency around the world towards deregulating labour markets, emerging economies are showing that regulations such as minimum wages can be used effectively to address poverty and inequality, without hampering formal sector job creation. Institutions also have an important role to play during crises because they provide protection to workers. At the same time, many regulations in these countries are not adequately enforced, an issue that needs to be addressed if effectiveness is to improve.

Appendix

Table 3.A1   Strictness of employment protection, OECD indicators, 2008

	Permanent contracts	Temporary contracts	Collective dismissal	Overall EPL index
Argentina	2.10	3.00	4.00	2.80
Brazil	1.49	3.96	0.00	2.27
Chile	2.59	2.04	0.00	1.93
China	3.31	2.21	3.00	2.80
Czech Republic	3.00	1.71	2.13	2.32
Estonia	2.27	2.17	3.25	2.39
France	2.60	3.75	2.13	3.00
Germany	2.85	1.96	3.75	2.63
Georgia	0.60	0.20	0.00	0.30
Hungary	1.82	2.08	2.88	2.11
India	3.65	2.67	0.00	2.63
Indonesia	4.29	2.96	0.00	3.02
Israel	2.19	1.58	1.88	1.88
Japan	2.05	1.50	1.50	1.73
Republic of Korea	2.29	2.08	1.88	2.13
Kazakhstan	2.10	1.50	0.00	1.50
Kyrgyzstan	1.90	0.80	3.60	1.70
Lithuania	2.60	2.30	3.60	2.70
Malaysia	2.20	0.30	0.00	1.10
Mexico	2.25	4.00	3.75	3.23
Morocco	4.00	3.60	0.00	3.20
Nepal	4.30	5.00	0.00	3.90

Table 3.A1   (Continued)

	Permanent contracts	Temporary contracts	Collective dismissal	Overall EPL index
Poland	2.01	2.33	3.63	2.41
Russian Federation	2.79	0.79	1.88	1.80
Slovakia	2.45	1.17	3.75	2.13
South Africa	1.91	0.58	1.88	1.35
Spain	2.38	3.83	3.13	3.11
Turkey	2.48	4.88	2.38	3.50
United Kingdom	1.17	0.29	2.88	1.09
United States	0.56	0.33	2.88	0.85
Viet Nam	3.30	0.80	3.80	2.30

Sources: OECD and authors' calculations.

Notes

1. Labour institutions can be formal and informal, written or unwritten, to the extent they affect the labour market (see for example Berg and Kucera 2008). This chapter concentrates on formal ones.
2. EPL relates to hiring and firing rules governing unfair dismissals, lay-offs for economic reasons, severance payments, minimum notice periods, administrative authorization for dismissals and prior discussion with labour representatives.
3. Labour market policies encompass all kinds of regulative policies that influence the interaction between labour supply and demand. They consist of policies that provide income replacement without an obligation to join work or training schemes (such as unemployment compensation, often called passive labour market policies for OECD countries) as well as labour market integration measures available to the unemployed or those threatened by unemployment (active labour market policies in the OECD terminology). Particularly in advanced countries, there has been increasing effort to 'activate' passive measures in order to enhance the integration of the unemployed and underemployed.
4. The ILO adopted the Accommodation of Crews (Fishermen) Convention, 1966 (No. 126) and the minimun Wage Fixing Convention, 1970 (No. 131), both minimum wage-fixing conventions. Convention No. 131, which provides more general protection to wage earners against 'unduly low wages' and calls for 'a system of minimum wages which covers all groups of wage earners whose terms of employment are such that coverage would be appropriate'.
5. See, for example, an overview of theoretical consideration in Boeri et al. (2008).
6. Informal employment being defined as the self-employed and unpaid family workers.

7. In Brazil, informal salaried workers are those who report working without a signed work contract.
8. For a summary of these effects in OECD and transition economies see, for example, Holmlund (1998) and Van Ours and Vodopivec (2005).
9. Job-to-job flows are very important workers' flows that may actually explain cross-country differences in the way labour markets adjust: typically the coexistence of low unemployment turnover and large job turnover rates can, for example, be explained by the occurrence of many direct shifts of workers from one job to another.
10. In order to carry out international comparisons of employment protection regimes, various summary indicators have been computed by academics and international organizations (for example, OECD 1994, 1999; Holzmann et al. 2011).
11. While those indicators were originally produced for advanced economies, they are now available for an increasing number of emerging economies (see Table 3A.1).
12. Average tenure is 6.2 years in Latin America and about half of the labour force had one or fewer years on the job (Berg and Cazes 2008).
13. As was the case, for example, in previous Doing Business reports, until 2011 for the EWI Index.
14. At the same time, the assumption that employers in the informal sector of developing countries have maximum flexibility is not entirely accurate, particularly when firms want to expand, but are constrained by poor access to credit or infrastructure issues.
15. Ninety per cent of ILO member states have a minimum wage system (major exceptions include Gulf countries).
16. This is particularly in the case of developing countries where income distributions are highly skewed.
17. For example, 1171 minimum wage rates exist in India (Belser and Rani 2011)
18. As in most Asian countries, the rate of unionization as well as the coverage rate is very low.
19. A threshold usually used for computing the CB coverage index which takes a value of 1 when CB covers less than 25 per cent of all salaried workers unionized or not; 2 if this number is between 26 and 69 per cent, and 3 when coverage is above 70 per cent;
20. Unemployment insurance systems exist, however, in the Russian Federation, Brazil, China, South Africa and Turkey.
21. See, for example, Acevedo, Eskenazi and Pagès, 2006
22. In the Philippines, for example, employers are obliged to pay one month's salary for every year of previous employment.
23. Beneficiaries are entitled in the Russian Federation to unemployment assistance after unemployment insurance stops.
24. But, of course, involuntary unemployment may also be due to insufficient aggregate demand.
25. See Council of the EU (2009), ECLAC (2009), ILO (2009a, 2009b), Kannan (2009), Lee (2009), OECD (2009), and Titiheruw et al. (2009).
26. See www.epwp.gov.za/index.asp?c=Home.
27. See http://nrega.nic.in/ and Sjoblom and Farrington (2008).

28. The NREG Act was enacted in 2005, building on a previous initiative in the state of Maharashtra (the Maharashtra Rural Employment Guarantee Programme). The MGNREG scheme was extended in 2008 to cover 615 districts previously 330) and provide work for 32 million people (at a cost of US$4 billion in the 2008/2009 budget). At least one-third of the beneficiaries shall be women (they made up half of the beneficiaries in 2008) (ILO 2009a).

29. Labour markets in developing countries have different characteristics (unemployment is less of an issue, but informality is); institutional and technical capacity are limited, regulations are not enforced, training facilities are inadequate, and so on (Cazes and Verick 2010).

30. See Budget Speech from 22 May 2009, www.gov.mu/portal/goc/mof/files/budspeech09.pdf.

31. See the discussion in ILO (2009).

32. In contrast, most active labour market policies have to be increased through actions of policymakers, except for such countries as Denmark and Switzerland where funding for such policies rises automatically with the unemployment rate (OECD 2009a).

33. The Brazilian Minister of Social Development and Fight against Hunger, Patrus Ananias, announced during his presentation of the programme at the ILO's Governing Body meeting in March 2009, that the Bolsa Família scheme will be expanded; see: www.ilo.org/global/About_the_ILO/Media_and_public_information/Feature_stories/lang–en/WCMS_103947/index.htm. Paraguay also plans to expand its conditional cash transfer programme to benefit 120,000 extremely poor families (ECLAC 2009).

References

Angrist, J. D. and J. S. Pischke (2008) *Mostly Harmless Econometrics: An Empiricist's Companion* (Princeton: Princeton University Press).

Acevedo G., P. Eskenazi and C. Pagès (2006) 'Unemployment Insurance in Chile: A New Model of Income Support for Unemployed Workers', World Bank Social Protection Discussion Paper No. 0612 (Washington, DC: World Bank).

Addison, J. T. and P. Teixeira (2003) 'The Economics of Employment Protection', *Journal of Labor Research*, Vol. 24, No. 1, pp. 85–129.

Addison, J. T. and P. Teixeira (2005) 'What Have We Learned about the Employment Effects of Severance Pay? Further Iterations of Lazear et al.', *Empirica*, Vol. 32, No. 3–4, pp. 345–368.

Ahn, P. S. (2010) The Growth and Decline of Political Unionism in India: The Need for a Paradigm Shift (Bangkok: ILO Decent Work Team for East and South East Asia and the Pacific).

Aleksynska, M. and M. Schindler (2011) 'Labor Market Regulations in Low-, Middle- and High-Income Countries: A New Panel Database', IMF Working Paper 11/154 (Washington, DC: IMF).

Alerkof, G. A. (1984) *An Economic Theorist's Book of Tales* (Cambridge: Cambridge University Press).

Almeida, R. K. and P. Carneiro (2008) 'Enforcement of Labor Regulation and Firm Size', World Bank Discussion Paper No. 0814 (Washington, DC: World Bank).

Andalon, M. and C. Pagès (2008) 'Minimum Wage in Kenya', IZA Discussion Paper No. 3390 (Bonn: IZA).

Auer, P., U. Efendioglu and J. Leschke (2008) *Active Labour Market Policies around the World: Coping with the Consequences of Globalization* (Geneva: ILO).

Autor, D., J. Donohue and S. Schwab (2006) 'The Costs of Wrongful Discharge Laws', *Review of Economics and Statistics*, Vol. 88, No. 2, pp. 211–231.

Banerjee, A. and E. Duflo (2009) 'The Experimental Approach to Development Economics', *Annual Review of Economics*, Vol. 1, No. 1, pp. 151–178.

Becker, G. (1964) *Human Capital* (Chicago: University of Chicago Press).

Belot, M. and J. van Ours (2001) 'Unemployment and Labor Market Institutions: An Empirical Analysis', *Journal of the Japanese and International Economies*, Vol. 15, No. 4, pp. 403–418.

Bell, L. A. (1997) 'The Impact of Minimum Wages in Mexico and Colombia', *Journal of Labor Economics*, Vol. 15, No. S3, pp. S102–S135.

Belser, P. and U. Rani (2011) 'Extending the Coverage of Minimum Wages in India: Simulations from Household Data', *Economic and Political Weekly*, Vol. 46, No. 22, pp. 47–55.

Bentolila, S. and G. Bertola (1990) 'Firing Costs and Labour demand: How Bad Is Eurosclerosis?', *Review of Economic Studies*, Vol. 57, No. 3, pp. 381–402.

Berg J. and D. Kucera (eds) (2008) *In Defence of Labour Market Institutions: Cultivating Justice in the Developing World* (Basingstoke and Geneva: Palgrave Macmillan and ILO).

Berg J. and S. Cazes (2008) 'Policymaking Gone Awry: The Labour Market Regulations of the Doing Business Indicators', *Comparative Labour Law and Policy Journal*, Vol. 29, No. 4. pp. 349–381.

Bertola G. (1990) 'Job Security Employment and Wages', *European Economic Review*, Vol. 34, No. 4, pp. 851–866.

Besley T. and R. Burgess (2004) 'Can Labor Regulation Hinder Economic Performance? Evidence from India', *Quarterly Journal of Economics*, Vol. 119, No. 1, pp. 91–134.

Betcherman, G., K. Olivas and A. Dar (2004) 'Impact of Active Labour Market Programs: New Evidence from Evaluations with Particular Attention to Developing and Transition Countries', World Bank Social Protection Discussion Paper No. 0402 (Washington, DC: World Bank).

Betcherman, G., M. Godfrey, S. Puerto, F. Rother and A. Stavreska (2007) 'A Review of Interventions to Support Young Workers: Findings of the Youth Employment Inventory', World Bank Social Protection Discussion Paper No. 0715 (Washington, DC: World Bank).

Blanchard, O. and J. Wolfers (2000) 'The Role of Shocks and Institutions in the Rise of European Unemployment: The Aggregate Evidence', *Economic Journal*, Vol. 110, pp. 1–33.

Boeri T. (1999) 'Enforcement of Employment Security Regulations, On-the-Job Search and Unemployment Duration', *European Economic Review*, Vol. 43, No. 1, pp. 65–89.

Boeri T., B. Helppie and M. Macis (2008) 'Labour Regulations in Developing Countries: A Review of the Evidence and Directions for Future Research', Social Protection Discussion Paper No 46306 (Washington, DC: World Bank).

Boeri T. and J. Van Ours (2008) *The Economics of Imperfect Labour Markets* (Princeton: Princeton University Press).

Boeri T. and J. Jimeno (2005) 'The Effects of Employment Protection: Learning from Variable Enforcement', *European Economic Review*, Vol. 49, No. 8, pp. 2057–2077.

Botero, J. C., S. Djankov, R. La Porta, F. Lopez-de-Sinales and A. Shleifer (2004) 'The Regulation of Labor', *Quarterly Journal of Economics*, Vol. 119, No. 4, pp. 1339–1382.

Cahuc, P. and A. Zylberbeg (2004) *Labour Economics* (Cambridge, MA: MIT Press).

Card, D., J. Kluve and A. Weber (2009) 'Active Labour Market Policy Evaluations: A Meta-analysis', IZA Discussion Paper, No. 4002 (Bonn: IZA).

Calmfors, L., J. Driffill, S. Honkapohja and F. Giavazzi (1988) 'Bargaining Structure, Corporatism and Macroeconomic Performance', *Economic Policy*, Vol. 3, No. 6, pp. 13–61.

Card, D. and A. Kruger (1995) *Myth and Measurement: The New Economics of the Minimum Wage* (Princeton: Princeton University Press).

Cazes, S., T. Boeri and G. Bertola (1999) 'Employment Protection and Labour Market Adjustment in OECD Countries: Evolving Institutions and Variable Enforcement', ILO Employment Working Paper No. 48 (Geneva: ILO).

Cazes, S. and S. Scarpetta (1998) 'Labour Market Transitions and Unemployment Duration: Evidence from Bulgarian and Polish Micro-data', *Economics of Transition*, Vol. 6, pp. 113–144.

Cazes, S. and S. Verick (2010) 'What Role for Labour Market Policies and Institutions in Development? Enhancing Security in Developing Countries and Emerging Economies', ILO Employment Working Paper No. 67 (Geneva: ILO).

Cazes, S. and S. Verick (2012) *Perspectives on Labour Economics for Development* (Geneva: ILO).

Cazes, S., S. Verick and C. Heuer (2011) 'Labour Market Policies in Times of Crisis', in I. Islam and S. Verick (eds) *From the Great Recession to Labour Market Recovery: Issues, Evidence and Policy Options* (Basingstoke and Geneva: Palgrave Macmillan and ILO), Chapter 8.

Dolado, J., F. Kramarz, S. Machin, A. Manning, D. Margolis and C. Teuling (1996) 'The Economic Impact of Minimum Wages in Europe', *Economic Policy*, Vol. 11, No. 23, pp. 317–372.

Donohue, J. and P. Siegelman (1995) 'The Selection of Employment Discrimination Disputes for Litigation: Using Business Cycle Effects to Test the Priest-Klein hypothesis', *The Journal of Legal Studies*, Vol. 24, No. 2, pp. 427–462.

Doucouliagos, H. and T. D. Stanley (2009) 'Publication Selection Bias in Minimum Wage? A Meta-regression Analysis', *British Journal of Industrial Relations*, Vol. 60, No. 2, pp. 406–428.

Emerson, M. (1988) 'Regulation or Deregulation of the Labour Market. Policy Regimes for the Recruitment and Dismissal of Employees in Industrialized Countries', *European Economic Review*, Vol. 32, No. 4, pp. 775–817.

Duflo, E., (2006) 'Field Experiments in Development Economics', in R. Blundell, W. Newey and T. Persson (eds), *Advances in Economics and Econometrics: Theory and Applications, Ninth World Congress* (Cambridge: Cambridge University Press), Vol. 2, pp. 322–348.

Duflo, E. and M. Kremer (2005) 'Use of Randomization in the Evaluation of Development Effectiveness', in G. Pitman, O. Feinstein and G. Ingram (eds), *Evaluating Development Effectiveness* (New Brunswick: Transaction Publishers), pp. 205–232.

Duflo, E., R. Glennerster and M. Kremer (2007) 'Using Randomization in Development Economics Research: A Toolkit', in T. Paul Schults and J. Strauss (eds), *Handbook of Development Economics* (North Holland: Elsevier Science), Vol. 4, pp. 3895–3862.

Fajnzylber, P. (2001) 'Minimum Wage Effects throughout the Wage Distribution: Evidence from Brazil's Formal and Informal Sectors', *Anais do XXIX Encontro Nacional de Economia*, Brazil.

Fajnzylber, P. (ed.) (2004) *Law and Employment: Lessons from Latin America and the Caribbean* (Chicago: University of Chicago Press).

Feldstein (2005).

Feliciano, Z. M. (1998) 'Does the Minimum Wage Affect Employment in Mexico?', *Eastern Economic Journal*, Vol. 24, No.2, pp. 165–180.

Freeman, R. B. (2005) 'Labour Market Institutions without Blinders: The Debate about Flexibility and Labour Market Performances', NBER Working Paper No. 11286 (Cambridge, MA: NBER).

Gindling, T. H. and K. Terrel (2007a) 'The Effects of Multiple Minimum Wages throughout the Labor Market: The Case of Costa Rica', *Labour Economics*, Vol. 14, No. 83, pp. 485–511.

Ghose, A. K., N. Majid and C. Ernst (2008) *The Global Employment Challenge* (Geneva: ILO).

Grubb, D. and W. Wells (1993) 'Employment Regulation and Patterns of Work in EC Countries', OECD Economic Studies No. 21 (Paris: OECD).

Heckman, J. J. (1992) 'Randomization and Social Policy Evaluation', in C. Manski and I. Garfinkel (eds), *Evaluating Welfare and Training Programs* (Cambridge, MA: Harvard University Press).

Heckman, J. J. and C. Pagés-Serra (2000) 'The Cost of Job Security Regulation: Evidence from Latin American Labor Markets', *Economía*, Vol. 1, No. 1, pp. 109–144.

Heckman, J. J and C. Pages (eds) (2004) *Law and Employment: Lessons from Latin America and the Caribbean* (Chicago: University of Chicago Press).

Heckman, J., R. Lalonde and J. Smith (1999) 'The Economics and Econometrics of ALMPs', *Handbook of Labour Economics*, Vol. 3 (Amsterdam: North-Holland).

Herr, H., M. Kazandziska and S. Mahnkopf-Praprotnik (2009) 'The Theoretical Debate about Minimum Wages', Global Labour University Working Paper No. 6 (Berlin: GLB).

Holmlund, B. (1998) 'Unemployment Insurance in Theory and Practice', *Scandinavian Journal of Economics,*Vol. 100, No. 1, pp. 113–141.

Holzmann, R., Y. Pouget, M. Vodopivec and M. Weber (2011) 'Severance Pay Programs around the World: History, Rationale, Status and Reforms', IZA Discussion Paper No. 5731 (Bonn: IZA).

International Labour Office (ILO) (2012) *Global Wage Report 2012/13* (Geneva: ILO).

International Labour Office (ILO) (2013) *World Social Security Report 2012/13* (Geneva: ILO) (forthcoming).

Islam, I. and S. Verick (eds) (2011) *From the Great Recession to Labour Market Recovery: Issues, Evidence and Policy Options* (Basingstoke and Geneva: Palgrave Macmillan and ILO).

Kluve, J. (2006) 'The Effectiveness of European Active Labour Market Policy', IZA Discussion Paper No. 2018 (Bonn: IZA).

Kluve, J. (2007) 'The Effectiveness of European ALMPs', in J. Kluve et al. (eds), *Active Labour Market Policies in Europe: Performance and Perspectives* (Berlin and Heidelberg: Springer), pp. 153–203.

Kugler, A. (1999) 'The Impact of Firing Costs on Turnover and Unemployment: Evidence from the Colombian Labour Market Reforms', *International Tax and Public Finance*, Vol. 6, No. 3, pp. 389–410.

Lafontaine, F. and J. Sivadasan (2009) 'Do Labor Market Rigidities Have Microeconomic Effects? Evidence from within the Firm', *American Economic Journal: Applied Economics*, Vol. 1, No. 2, pp. 88–107.

Lazear, E. P. (1990) 'Job Security Provisions and Unemployment', *Quarterly Journal of Economics*, Vol. 105, No. 3, pp. 699–726.

Lechner, M. and C. Wunsch (2009) 'Are Training Programs More Effective When Unemployment Is High?', *Journal of Labour Economics*, Vol. 27, No. 4, pp. 653–692.

Maloney, W. and J. Nunez Mendez (2004) 'Measuring the Impact of Minimum Wages: Evidence from Latin America', NBER Working Paper 9800 (Cambridge, MA: NBER).

Martin, J. P. (2000) 'What Works among Active Labour Market Policies: Evidence from OECD Countries' Experiences', OECD Economic Studies No. 30, 2000/I (Paris: OECD).

Ministry of Rural Development, Government of India (2012) *MGNREGA Sameeksha: An Anthology of Research Studies on the Mahatma Gandhi National Rural Employment Guarantee Act, 2005, 2006–2012* (New Delhi: Orient Blackswan).

Micco, A. and C. Pagès (2006) 'The Economic Effects of Employment Protection: Evidence from International Industry-level Data', IZA Discussion Paper No. 2433 (Bonn: IZA).

Montenegro, C. E. and C. Pagès (2004) 'Who Benefits from Labor Market Regulations? Chile, 1960–1998', in J. J. Heckman and C. Pagès (eds), *Law and Employment: Lessons from Latin America and the Caribbean* (Chicago: University of Chicago Press).

Neumark, D., W. Cunningham and S. Siga (2007) 'The Effects of the Minimum Wage in Brazil on the Distribution of Family Incomes: 1996–2001', *Journal of Development Economics*, Vol. 80, No. 1, pp. 136–159.

Nickell, S. (1997) 'Unemployment and Labor Market Rigidities: Europe versus North America', *Journal of Economic Perspectives*, Vol. 11, No. 3, pp. 55–74.

Nickell, S. and R. Layard (2005) 'Labor Market Institutions and Economic Performance', in O. Ashenfelter and D. Card (eds), *Handbook of Labor Economics*, Vol. 3B, pp. 3029–3084 (Amsterdam: Elsevier).

Nickell S., L. Nunziata and W. Ochel (2005) 'Unemployment in the OECD since the 1960s: What Do We Know?', *Economic Journal*, Vol. 115, No. 500, pp. 1–27.

Organisation for Economic Co-operation and Development (OECD) (1994) *Jobs Study* (Paris: OECD).

Organisation for Economic Co-operation and Development (OECD) (1998) 'Making the Most of the Minimum: Statutory Minimum Wages, Employment, and Poverty', in *Employment Outlook*, pp. 31–77 (Paris: OECD).

Organisation for Economic Co-operation and Development (OECD) (1999) *Employment Outlook* (Paris: OECD).

Organisation for Economic Co-operation and Development (OECD) (2004) *Employment Outlook* (Paris: OECD).

Organisation for Economic Co-operation and Development (OECD) (2006) *Employment Outlook* (Paris: OECD).

Organisation for Economic Co-operation and Development (OECD) (2009) *Employment Outlook* (Paris: OECD).

Organisation for Economic Co-operation and Development (OECD) (2010) *Employment Outlook* (Paris: OECD).

O'Higgins, N. (2001) *Youth Unemployment and Employment Policy* (Geneva: ILO).

Piore M. (1986) *Labor Market Flexibility* (Berkeley: University of California Press).

Pissarides C. (1979) 'Job Matchings with State Employment Agencies and Random Search', *Economic Journal*, Vol. 89, No. 356, pp. 818–833.

Reinecke G. and S. White (2004) *Policies for Small Enterprises. Creating the Right Environment for Good Jobs* (Geneva: ILO).

Robalino D., M. Vodopivec and A. Bodor (2009) 'Savings for Unemployment in Good or Bad Times: Options for Developing Countries', IZA Discussion Paper No. 4516 (Bonn: IZA).

Scarpetta S. (1996) 'Assessing the Role of Labor Market Policies and Institutional Factors on Unemployment. A Cross-Country Study', *OECD Economic Studies*, Vol. 26, pp. 43–98.

Social Security Administration and the International Social Security Association (SSA/ISSA) (2009) *Social Security Programs Throughout the World: Africa, 2009* (Washington, DC: SSA Publications).

Townsend, P. (ed.) (2009) *Building Decent Societies: Rethinking the Role of Social Security in Development* (Basingstoke and Geneva: Palgrave Macmillan and ILO).

Tzannatos, Z. (2008) 'The Impact of Trade Unions: What Do Economists Say?', in J. Berg and D. Kucera (eds), *In Defence of Labour Market Institutions: Cultivating Justice in the Developing World* (Basingstoke and Geneva: Palgrave Macmillan and ILO), pp. 150–191.

Verick, S. (2004). 'Threshold Effects of Dismissal Protection Legislation in Germany', IZA Discussion Paper No. 991 (Bonn: IZA)

Van Ours, J. C. and M. Vodopivec (2005) 'How Changes in Benefits and Entitlements Affect the Duration of Unemployment', CEPR Discussion Paper No. 4962 (London: Centre for Economic Policy Research).

Van Ours, J. C. and M. Vodopivec (2008) 'Does Reducing Unemployment Insurance Generosity Reduce Job Match Quality?', *Journal of Public Economics*, Vol. 92, No. 3–4, pp. 684–695.

Part II

4
Transitions out of Informality and Falling Unemployment: The Transformation of the Brazilian Labour Market since the 2000s

4.1 Introduction

During the 1960s and 1970s, Brazil grew rapidly, thanks largely to strong commodity prices, but this was accompanied by rising inequality. The military junta, which ruled from 1965 to 1985, followed a policy of import substitution. Despite the large accumulation of foreign debt, which financed industrialization, this approach proved unsuccessful and growth slowed considerably in the late 1970s and early 1980s. This downturn and economic mismanagement culminated in the default in 1983 of external debt, which had risen dramatically as a consequence of large inflows of capital. Despite the move to democracy in 1985 and liberalization of the economy over the following decade or so, Ferreira et al. (2009) conclude that the very low GDP growth in Brazil between 1985 and 2004 left the problem of poverty largely unchanged.

Following decades of high inequality and poverty along with bouts of high inflation and crises, the performance of the Brazilian economy and labour market over the last decade is, therefore, remarkable. This achievement is the outcome of not only strong economic growth and macroeconomic stability, but also effective government interventions in the area of taxation and social policies. Notably, the government under President Luiz Inacio 'Lula' da Silva increased spending on the famous Bolsa Família scheme that provides conditional cash transfers to poor households. With, as well, important implications for pensions, the government raised minimum wages, which had been stagnant or falling during the 1990s and early 2000s. During the period of Lula's government, the real minimum wage almost doubled from R$281 in 2002 to

R$510 in 2010. Another important contribution to falling inequality is the improvement in educational attainment, which has helped get the poor into better jobs.

Though starting from a poor initial situation, the resulting fall in poverty and inequality is impressive. The poverty headcount ratio (based on the national poverty line) fell from 48 per cent in 1990 to 24.9 per cent in 2009; the ratio decreased by 11.5 percentage points from 2005 to 2009 alone (from 36.4 to 24.9 per cent). At the same time, the Gini coefficient, a measure of income distribution that is slow-moving, decreased from 0.627 in 1990 to 0.576 in 2009.[1]

This turnaround is also evident when looking at Brazil in terms of how economic shocks have affected the country. Indeed, crises are nothing new for Brazil: the country has defaulted on external debt seven times over 175 years (Reinhart and Rogoff 2009). Most recently, Brazil was hit following the Russian debt default in 1998, which exposed the fragility of an economy that was characterized by large current account deficits (financed by capital inflows). Once investors lost their appetite for Brazilian debt and speculators turned on the currency, the government was forced to turn to the IMF for a bailout and abandon the fixed exchange rate regime and, hence, devalue the Brazilian real.

Thus, the performance of Brazil during the global financial crisis is a stark departure from the experience of previous episodes that resulted in recessions and rising poverty and inequality. The Brazilian economy contracted by 0.9 per cent in 2009, which was mainly due to a fall in exports and investments rather than consumption (ILO/IILS 2011). Due to the resilience of the economy, the recovery was, however, swift: in 2010, GDP grew by a robust 7.5 per cent, thanks to both strong domestic demand arising from the new middle class and rapid growth in exports of raw commodities (particularly to China). In terms of the latter trend, the share of Brazilian exports destined for China rose from 8 per cent in 2008 to 14 per cent in 2009, more than making up for the fall in exports to the United States. Bilateral trade between Brazil and China increased from just $2 billion in 2000 to $56.2 billion in 2010, while China became Brazil's largest source of FDI (which reached $17 billion in 2010).[2] Inflation in consumer prices has nonetheless remained subdued, falling to just 4.9 per cent in 2009.[3]

A key difference between the impact of previous shocks and the resilience of the Brazilian economy to the global financial crisis is the improved policy space. In this respect, the primary budget had been in surplus since 1999 (in 1998, for example, the government had a large external debt) (ILO/ILLS 2011). In turn, this fiscal space allowed the

Brazilian government to respond to the downturn in 2009 through fiscal stimulus and expansion of safety nets (such as Bolsa Família). With a floating exchange rate mechanism, there was no need to defend any speculative attacks, while the financial sector has been reformed and strengthened during the 2000s. Of course, exports to China and the inflows of FDI in 2009 and onwards have bolstered growth on top of the strong domestic demand that is being generated by the emerging middle class in Brazil.

These factors provide an explanation for the benign impact of the crisis on the labour market. Prior to the onset of the global financial crisis, the unemployment rate in the six metropolitan areas fell from 11.5 per cent in 2004 to 7.9 per cent in 2008. The rate increased only by 0.2 percentage points during the year of the recession (up to 8.1 per cent) and then continued on its downward trend in 2010. In November 2011, the unemployment rate stood at just 5.2 per cent. More importantly, formal employment has grown strongly: the Brazilian economy created 15.3 million formal jobs from 2003 to 2010, which continued during the recession of 2009.[4]

As a consequence of the successes over the last decade, Brazil has become a beacon of an alternative path to development that does not rely on complete laissez-faire policies; in fact the Brazilian government has taken a strong interventionist approach to both promoting growth and tackling inequality and poverty. Nonetheless, Brazil continues to face many challenges, especially the high level of inequalities across regions and segments of the population that still persist, which is due to such factors as the low quality of education and inadequate infrastructure. Moreover, the economy has begun to slow down (growth reached only 2.7 per cent in 2011), while inflation has remained a concern.

Against this background, this chapter seeks to address both the transformation of the labour market, especially in terms of the movements out of informal employment, and the nature of policies and institutions in Brazil. In terms of the latter, this chapter stresses that, although the government does not rely extensively on labour market policies, social protection schemes and minimum wage policies have played an important role in impacting poverty and inequality.

In terms of the framework outlined in the opening chapter, this contribution focuses firstly on the longer-term labour market trends and situation, especially on the phenomenon of transiting out of informality, which is notable considering the absence of this feature in most emerging economies. Secondly, this chapter addresses important labour market institutions, such as the minimum wage, along with social policies including Bolsa Família, and their relationship to labour market outcomes and the overall improvement in poverty and inequality. In comparison to other emerging economies such as South Africa, specific labour market policies receive less priority in Brazil (for example, utilization of training or public employment programmes).

The remainder of this chapter is structured as follows. Section 4.2 summarizes the main labour market trends over the last decade, while section 4.3 presents findings on the individual and household characteristics that drive labour market status in Brazil. Section 4.4 focuses on factors that are associated with transitions in the labour market, especially into formal employment. Section 4.5 switches to labour market policy and the institutional environment, with reference also to the broader range of social policies in place in Brazil. Finally, section 4.6 concludes.

4.2   Labour market trends from 2001: falling unemployment and rising formal employment

This section presents aggregate trends on key indicators of the labour market (unemployment rate, informal employment, participation rate, employment-population rate, wages, earnings, hours worked and NEET rate) to illustrate improvements for the population as a whole and by specific characteristics, namely age and gender. The data in this section and the next come from either the National Household Survey (Pesquisa Nacional por Amostra de Domicílios, or PNAD), a nationally representative household survey that samples more than 100,000 households in Brazil every year in September, or the Monthly Employment Survey (Pesquisa Mensal de Emprego, or PME), which covers only six metropolitan areas. The focus is on the working-age population between 15 and 65 years old.

Firstly, trends over the last decade reveal that the increase in the labour force participation rate has increased, driven mostly by more Brazilian women joining the labour force. From 2001 to 2009, the rate for women (aged 15+) went up by 3.8 percentage points (from 54.1 to 57.9 per cent) compared to a decrease of 0.8 points for men (from 81.0 to 80.2 per cent) (Figure 4.1). The downward trend in male participation is being driven by increased enrolment in education (this has happened for young Brazilian women as well, but this is outweighed by an increase among prime-age women). During the 2000s, there has been a greater rise in participation in rural areas (ILO 2009).

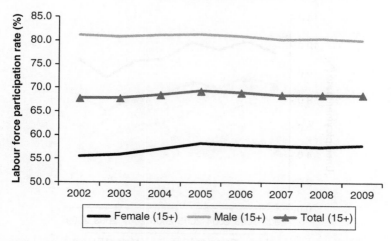

Figure 4.1 Gender gap in labour force participation falling from 2001 to 2009
Source: PNAD reported in ILO Key Indicators of the Labour Market, 7th Edition; accessed online 3 September 2012.

These trends in the labour force participation rate reflect two under-lying changes in the Brazilian labour market: a rise in employment–population ratio among both men and women accompanied by a fall in the unemployment rate. Over the period 2002–2008, the employment–population ratio rose by 1.1 percentage points for men (from 75.2 to 76.3 per cent), while it increased by 2.9 points for women (from a low of 49.2 to 52.1 per cent).

In terms of the unemployment rate, there has been a consistent fall since the mid-2000s for both Brazilian men and women, particularly in the metropolitan areas. Starting with national figures from PNAD, the unemployment rate dropped from 9.3 per cent in 2001 to 8.3 per cent in 2009, despite the increase during the recession from the rate in 2008 (Figure 4.2). This downward trend is evident for both men and women. Long-term unemployment has also fallen, notably from 2007 to 2008 (ILO 2010). As found in the cases of most developing countries and emerging economies (see the cases of Indonesia, South Africa and Turkey presented elsewhere in this volume), there is an inverse U-shaped rela-tionship between education and unemployment. In the case of Brazil, the unemployment rate is the highest for individuals with incomplete secondary school (but more than primary) (Ernst 2008).

An even more optimistic picture on the unemployment situation in Brazil is provided by the PME data for the metropolitan areas: the

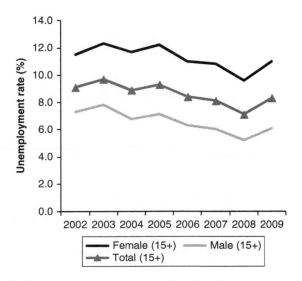

Figure 4.2 Falling unemployment rates for Brazilian men and women, 2001–2009 (national)

Source: PNAD reported in ILO Key Indicators of the Labour Market, 7th Edition; accessed online 3 September 2012.

unemployment rate in the six metropolitan areas fell from 11.5 per cent in 2004 to 7.9 per cent in 2008. The rate increased only by 0.2 percentage points during the year of the recession (up to 8.1 per cent) and then continued on its downward trend in 2010. In November 2011, the unemployment rate stood at just 5.2 per cent in these urban areas.

A less positive characteristic of the labour market is the share of youth not in employment, education or training (NEET). According to the national PNAD data, the NEET rate has remained relatively stable during the 2000s. Moreover, it is of great concern that around 16 per cent of 19-year-old men and 30 per cent of young women of the same age were not participating in school or the labour market in 2008. Though young women have a higher NEET rate than men, there was a reduction in the gender gap between 2001 and 2008: the rate for young men increased by 1 percentage point, while it fell for young women by 2.3 points.

With respect to sectoral shares in employment, the Brazilian labour market is more similar to advanced economies in the sense that the service sector accounts for the largest proportion. In 2008, the share of employment in services reached 64 per cent, while the respective shares in industry and agriculture were just 22 and 12 per cent. These figures were rather stable during the first half of the 2000s before an increase in the service sector share and accompanying decline in the proportion of workers in agriculture.

Related to the sectoral distribution of employment is the nature of informality in the Brazilian labour market, which, as evident in most developing countries and emerging economies, has been a major challenge. As highlighted in this chapter, the downward trend in the share of informal employment has been a major achievement for the country: 15.3 million formal jobs have been created in Brazil since 2003. Moreover, during the 2000s, three formal jobs were created for every informal one (ILO/OECD 2011).

While there is no consensus in defining informality, this chapter uses the approach of Mello et al. (2006) and Scorzafave and Lima (2010): informal workers are defined as those who fit one of the following descriptions: employees without signed labour booklets, including domestic maids; self-employed people; those producing for their own consumption; those constructing their own homes; and unpaid workers.[5] In terms of the Labour and Social Security Booklet, or CTPS, this document must be signed by the employer in the formal sector. It guarantees access to some of the main labour rights, such as unemployment insurance, social security benefits and FGTS. In its 74 years of existence, it has undergone many changes. When it was created in 1932, it was a simple card. Today, the CTPS contains information about worker's qualifications, professional life and social security contributions.

As shown in Figure 4.3, informality in Brazil based on this definition dropped consistently in the 2000s, from 52.4 per cent in 2001 to 46.3 per cent in 2008. This drop is highly correlated with the economic recovery process in Brazil over the last two years, along with measures to promote formalization, including access to social security. The most significant fall over this period happened for men aged 51 to 61 years old (7.7 percentage points), followed by men from 15 to 24 years old (7 points). Though smaller, the decrease for women was also very considerable; 6.8 points for those between 51 and 65 years old. The trend in informality for Brazilian women shows a flatter pattern for all age groups. In 2008, female informality was higher than the male rate, except for the youngest group. The downward trend in informality in Brazil presented in Figure 4.3 continued during and following the recession of 2009. As a result of this registration of workers, there has been a commensurate rise in the share of workers with social security, from 45.7 per cent in 2001 to 54.1 per cent in 2009. As reported in ILO/OECD

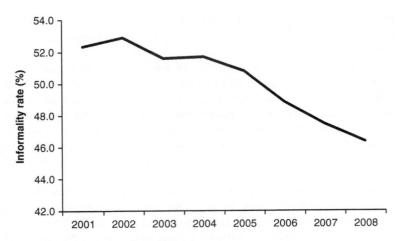

Figure 4.3   Falling informality in the 2000s
Source: PNAD as reported in ILO (2010).

(2011), data from the metropolitan areas show that the share of workers without a registered labour booklet decreased from 19.7 per cent in October 2008 to 18 per cent in October 2010.

One interesting aspect in the Brazilian case is that prime-age workers have lower informality rates than younger or older ones. For young workers, the high informality can be explained by the difficulty in entering the labour market, because most formal jobs require previous experience and high school diplomas. Younger workers can see the informal sector as a way into the labour market, sometimes an activity along with school. After gathering some experience, these workers try to migrate to the formal sector. This explains why there is a fall in informality after the age of 25. On the other hand, there is a considerable contingent of old workers engaged in informal activities. Many of them are retirees who keep working to supplement their pensions. For example, Mello et al. (2006) found that, in 2004, a third of Brazil's retirees were still working.

Finally, in terms of earnings and wages, there has been, in general, an improvement during the latter half of the 2000s. Using figures on real monthly labour income, in constant R$ terms, average earnings dropped almost 10 per cent from 2001 to 2004, which was followed by an increase of R$153.10 (US$ 75.00) (Figure 4.4). In this period, the gender earnings gap remained constant, with men earning 40 per cent more than women.

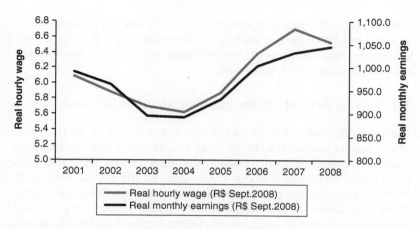

Figure 4.4 Monthly earnings and hourly wages ($R)
Source: PNAD, authors' calculations.

As shown in Figure 4.4, the pattern for wages (measured in reals per hour) is similar to that for earnings, with a decrease from 2001 to 2004 and an increase thereafter. The only difference in these figures is that wages declined from 2007 to 2008. In the whole period, wages increased by 7.3 per cent. For men and women, the prime-age group experienced the lowest wage increases (2.2 and 3.3 per cent, respectively). On the other hand, younger and older workers experienced increases of more than 10 per cent, reflecting improvements in the wage distribution. In this respect, it is important to understand the effect of these trends in wages and earnings on inequality levels. Scorzafave and Lima (2010) decompose several inequality indexes in order to assess the impact of different income sources on per capita household income inequality. They conclude that the 13 per cent reduction in the concentration rate of wages was the most important factor explaining the recent drop in Brazilian inequality, as labour income accounts for more than 60 per cent of total household income.

In summary, the aggregate trends from both the nationally representative data (PNAD) and the survey of metropolitan areas (PME) reveal that the Brazilian labour market has been improving over the 2000s as reflected by falling unemployment rates, increasing formalization of employment and growing wages. Moreover, the impact of the global financial crisis on labour market outcomes was short-lived and the improving situation continued in 2010 and 2011. Nonetheless, as addressed below in the analysis of the results from the micro-data, challenges remain such as the barriers faced by those with low levels of educational attainment, and youth.

4.3   Factors behind labour market outcomes in Brazil

The preceding subsection depicted the recent evolution of the main labour market indicators in Brazil. Here, results from a multinomial logit model are presented to disentangle the main factors associated with the 'choice' of different labour force status in the period from 2001 to 2008. The data used in the estimation also come from the PNAD. These data allow for the identification of four labour states: formal employment, informal employment, unemployment and out-of-labour force. Unfortunately, it is not possible to identify discouragement in the PNAD data.

Separate models for each year and gender are estimated. Table 4.1 reports the results for 2001 and 2008 for men and Table 4.2 reports female figures. The results indicate that urban men are more likely to be in the formal sector and to be unemployed compared to rural men; however, they are less likely to be in the informal sector. This is also true for women, although the marginal effects are smaller. This result is consistent with anecdotal evidence that informality is very high in rural areas of Brazil. The older a man is, the higher is the probability of being out of the labour force. The same is true for women.

There are also differences across Brazilian regions in the multinomial logit marginal effects, with men living in the South and Southeast regions having more chance of being in the formal sector and the opposite happening in the North and Northeast regions compared to the Midwest (reference group).[6] So, there is a relationship between the development level and institutions of a region and the probability of being in a formal job. Exactly the opposite happens regarding informal employment. There is also a higher probability of unemployment in less developed regions of the country. For women, the pattern is similar, although in the North women are less likely to be unemployed, but with a very small marginal effect.

Another interesting result is that number of children affects the labour market sector occupied by men. One additional very young child decreases the probability of being in the formal (or in the informal) sector by 6 percentage points compared to being out of the labour force. This result is weaker for children between five and nine years old and

Table 4.1 Multinomial logit marginal effects – men

Base category	Out of labour force			Out of labour force		
	2001			2008		
	Formal	Informal	Unemployed	Formal	Informal	Unemployed
Age	-0.003***	-0.001***	-0.001***	-0.004***	-0.001	-0.001***
	(0.000)	(0.000)	(0.000)	(0.000)	(0.000)	(0.000)
Urban	0.067***	-0.291***	0.041***	0.072***	-0.203***	0.024***
	(0.003)	(0.004)	(0.001)	(0.003)	(0.004)	(0.001)
Southeast	0.033***	-0.095***	0.009***	0.039***	-0.071***	-0.001
	(0.004)	(0.004)	(0.002)	(0.004)	(0.004)	(0.002)
Northeast	-0.051***	0.001	0.006***	-0.080***	0.039***	0.008***
	(0.003)	(0.004)	(0.002)	(0.004)	(0.004)	(0.002)
South	0.046***	-0.067***	-0.002	0.041***	-0.060***	-0.005**
	(0.004)	(0.005)	(0.002)	(0.005)	(0.004)	(0.002)
North	-0.060***	0.002	-0.008***	-0.067***	0.044***	-0.006***
	(0.004)	(0.006)	(0.002)	(0.004)	(0.006)	(0.002)
No. of children 0–4	-0.054***	-0.066***	-0.010***	-0.062***	-0.056***	-0.010***
	(0.002)	(0.002)	(0.001)	(0.003)	(0.003)	(0.001)
No. of children 5–9	-0.039***	-0.065***	-0.012***	-0.048***	-0.052***	-0.009***
	(0.002)	(0.002)	(0.001)	(0.002)	(0.002)	(0.001)
No. of children 10–15	-0.054***	-0.048***	-0.014***	-0.072***	-0.049***	-0.011***
	(0.002)	(0.002)	(0.001)	(0.002)	(0.002)	(0.001)
4–7 yrs of schooling	0.150***	0.093***	0.045***	0.160***	0.076***	0.030***
	(0.003)	(0.003)	(0.002)	(0.004)	(0.004)	(0.002)

Table 4.1 (Continued)

Base category	Out of labour force 2001			Out of labour force 2008		
	Formal	Informal	Unemployed	Formal	Informal	Unemployed
8–11 yrs of schooling	0.346***	0.036***	0.049***	0.376***	0.049***	0.042***
	(0.004)	(0.004)	(0.002)	(0.004)	(0.003)	(0.002)
12+ yrs of schooling	0.491***	−0.103***	−0.001	0.483***	−0.093***	0.016***
	(0.006)	(0.005)	(0.003)	(0.005)	(0.004)	(0.003)
Household head	0.358***	0.272***	−0.003*	0.394***	0.191***	−0.008***
	(0.003)	(0.004)	(0.001)	(0.004)	(0.004)	(0.001)
Spouse	0.346***	0.058***	−0.015***	0.397***	0.027***	−0.018***
	(0.011)	(0.011)	(0.003)	(0.006)	(0.006)	(0.001)
White	−0.018***	−0.047***	−0.019***	−0.026***	−0.036***	−0.013***
	(0.002)	(0.003)	(0.001)	(0.003)	(0.003)	(0.001)
No. of adults	0.031***	0.048***	0.006***	0.035***	0.033***	0.004***
	(0.001)	(0.001)	(0.000)	(0.001)	(0.001)	(0.000)
Observations	183,697	183,697	183,697	185,082	185,082	185,082

Note: *** significant at 1%; ** significant at 5%; * significant at 10%; standard errors in parentheses.
Source: PNAD; authors' calculations.

Table 4.2 Multinomial logit marginal effects – women

Base category	Out of labour force					
	2001			2008		
	Formal	Informal	Unemployed	Formal	Informal	Unemployed
Age	-0.001***	-0.001***	-0.001***	-0.002***	-0.001***	-0.001***
	(0.000)	(0.000)	(0.000)	(0.000)	(0.000)	(0.000)
Urban	0.042***	-0.104***	0.028***	0.057***	-0.041***	0.020***
	(0.002)	(0.003)	(0.001)	(0.002)	(0.003)	(0.001)
Southeast	0.010***	-0.025***	0.008***	0.019***	-0.020***	0.001
	(0.002)	(0.003)	(0.002)	(0.002)	(0.003)	(0.001)
Northeast	-0.018***	0.002	0.003*	-0.035***	0.013***	0.002
	(0.002)	(0.003)	(0.002)	(0.002)	(0.003)	(0.001)
South	0.034***	0.009*	0.003	0.043***	-0.004	-0.005**
	(0.003)	(0.004)	(0.002)	(0.003)	(0.004)	(0.002)
North	-0.028***	-0.012**	-0.008***	-0.034***	0.001	-0.008***
	(0.002)	(0.004)	(0.002)	(0.003)	(0.004)	(0.001)
No. of children 0–4	-0.048***	-0.066***	-0.010***	-0.060***	-0.066***	-0.007***
	(0.001)	(0.002)	(0.001)	(0.002)	(0.002)	(0.001)
No. of children 5–9	-0.020***	-0.024***	-0.009***	-0.027***	-0.029***	-0.005***
	(0.001)	(0.002)	(0.001)	(0.002)	(0.002)	(0.001)
No. of children 10–15	-0.016***	-0.010***	-0.013***	-0.022***	-0.020***	-0.009***
	(0.001)	(0.002)	(0.001)	(0.001)	(0.002)	(0.001)
4–7 yrs of schooling	0.085***	0.073***	0.054***	0.121***	0.073***	0.052***
	(0.003)	(0.003)	(0.002)	(0.004)	(0.003)	(0.003)

Table 4.2 (Continued)

Base category	Out of labour force 2001			Out of labour force 2008		
	Formal	Informal	Unemployed	Formal	Informal	Unemployed
8–11 yrs of schooling	0.255***	0.089***	0.087***	0.289***	0.097***	0.087***
	(0.004)	(0.003)	(0.002)	(0.004)	(0.003)	(0.002)
12+ yrs of schooling	0.552***	0.015***	0.040***	0.567***	−0.009*	0.053***
	(0.006)	(0.004)	(0.004)	(0.006)	(0.004)	(0.003)
Household head	0.159***	0.294***	0.048***	0.155***	0.262***	0.025***
	(0.004)	(0.006)	(0.003)	(0.004)	(0.005)	(0.002)
Spouse	0.097***	0.221***	0.026***	0.123***	0.214***	0.014***
	(0.002)	(0.003)	(0.002)	(0.003)	(0.004)	(0.001)
White	−0.010***	−0.033***	−0.018***	−0.012***	−0.037***	−0.013***
	(0.001)	(0.002)	(0.001)	(0.002)	(0.002)	(0.001)
No. of adults	0.010***	0.024***	0.006***	0.011***	0.024***	0.003***
	(0.001)	(0.001)	(0.000)	(0.001)	(0.001)	(0.000)
Observations	193,391	193,391	193,391	196,021	196,021	196,021

Note: ***significant at 1%; **significant at 5%; *significant at 10%; standard errors in parentheses.
Source: PNAD; authors' calculations.

is also stronger for older children. For women, however, the effect is similar but becomes smaller as children get older. These results are very interesting, since it is counterintuitive for the number of children to affect men's employment status. Although significant, the effect of family size regarding unemployment is lower than the other categories for both women and men.

So, families with many children exhibit lower ability to participate in the labour market. As Brazil is at the tail end of its demographic transition, the number of children in families is decreasing over time, although this drop is less pronounced in poorer households. So, in the coming years this variable should become less important in explaining allocation in the labour market.

The results concerning schooling are very interesting. The omitted reference group is 0–3 years of schooling. So, the more educated people are, the higher is the probability that they are formal workers, compared to being out of the labour force. The opposite result is found for informal work, mainly for men. So, with the continuing growth of the Brazilian labour force's educational attainment, there should be some effect on formality rates. In the case of unemployment, the results reflect the stylized fact that education and probability of unemployment have an inverted-U relationship for both males and females. This result is associated with the growth in the relative supply of workers with eight to 11 years of schooling in recent years who cannot find jobs.

For men and women, household heads and spouses have both higher probabilities of being in formal jobs than people in other household positions (reference group: sons, other parent, and so on). For informality, again there is considerably more chance for household heads to be out of the labour force. The opposite happens regarding male unemployment, but not for female household heads and spouses, who face a higher probability of being unemployed compared to other women.

Non-white men and women both have a higher probability of being out of the labour force than white men (and white women) respectively, for every occupational situation, but the magnitude of these marginal effects is not so high, especially for formal jobs and unemployment. Also, the presence of more adults inside the household increases the probability of insertion in the labour market, as formal workers, informal workers and, to a lesser extent, as unemployed for both men and women, although the marginal effects are higher for the former group. Finally, the marginal effects for both men and women in general did not change appreciably between 2001 and 2008, with very few exceptions.

4.4   Drivers of transitions in the labour market

This section investigates the labour market transitions in Brazil by firstly describing the raw labour market transition probabilities and then estimating another multinomial logit model in an attempt to disentangle the effect of individual and household characteristics on the probability of moving from one labour market state to another. The main differential of this analysis is that here individuals are tracked over time in a panel data set, using the Monthly Employment Survey (Pesquisa Mensal de Emprego, or PME).[7]

Using a more narrow specification than above, informal workers are defined as those who do not have a formal labour contract (meaning a labour booklet signed by the employer). The unemployed category refers to those who were not working and were looking for a job in the last 30 days, whether or not they had worked before. People out of the labour force are those neither working nor looking for a job in the last 30 days.

In all the results of this section, the transitions reflect movements over two periods from time t and 3 months later (t+3). This analysis permits understanding the persistence of each labour market state and also if there are considerable transitions between categories. This is interesting, since higher persistence and low transitions can be related to a more segmented labour market.

4.4.1   Raw labour market transitions

As a starting point, the raw labour market transitions are presented for two periods; pre-crisis (2003–2007) and for the beginning of the crisis period (2008).[8] The transition rates are calculated separately for men and women and for three age groups: 15–24, 25–50 and 51–65 years old. The relative transition tables reveal the proportions of people who transited from one situation (in the first interview) to another situation three months later (in the fourth PME interview). The diagonal of each table reveals the percentage of people who stayed in the same situation in the period.

As can be seen from Table 4.3, the percentages of male transitions for the period 2003 to 2007 does not differ greatly from those in 2008. In the first period, 90.1 per cent of men stayed in the formal sector, which is the most absorbent sector, as found in Chapter 5 on South Africa. The most significant transitions were from formal to informal (3.8 per cent) and for inactivity (2.7 per cent). For 2008, there was a slight change in these figures, but the portrait is almost the same.

Table 4.3 Raw labour market transitions – men

Men (2001–2007)

		To					
		Formal	Informal	Unemployed	Self-employed	Out of labour force	Discouraged
From	Formal	90.1	3.8	1.7	1.6	2.7	0.0
	Informal	16.0	61.8	5.0	10.4	6.9	0.0
	Unemployed	10.4	12.9	45.3	8.2	22.9	0.3
	Self-employed	4.4	9.4	2.7	77.9	5.6	0.0
	Out of labour force	3.6	5.7	8.8	4.7	77.1	0.1
	Discouraged	3.3	9.2	20.8	15.0	45.0	6.7

Men (2008)

		To					
		Formal	Informal	Unemployed	Self-employed	Out of labour force	Discouraged
From	Formal	89.8	3.3	1.7	2.0	3.1	0.0
	Informal	17.4	60.0	3.9	11.0	7.6	0.0
	Unemployed	16.1	12.6	37.2	8.1	26.0	0.0
	Self-employed	5.4	8.7	2.1	78.4	5.4	0.0
	Out of labour force	4.2	5.8	6.4	4.4	79.1	0.0
	Discouraged	8.3	0.0	8.3	8.3	66.7	8.3

Source: Monthly Employment Survey (Pesquisa Mensal de Emprego–PME); authors' calculations.

Despite these similarities, there is an important change in transitions out of unemployment: the number of people who persisted in unemployment decreased from 45.3 per cent for 2003–2007 to 37.2 per cent in 2008.

Table 4.3 also shows that, from 2001 to 2008, fewer people remained unemployed or in the informal sector for more than three months and transitions increased from these categories to formal and self-employed activities. For example, the transition from unemployment to formal employment rose from 10.4 to 16.1 per cent in the period. These figures indicate an improvement in working opportunities and probably a reduction in unemployment duration for men.

Another encouraging signal is that the percentage of people who were discouraged in the first interview and went to the formal sector later also rose significantly: from 3.3 per cent in the first period to 8.3 per cent in 2008. The number of people identified as discouraged was very low in both periods (0.1 per cent of the sample), which is in great contrast to the situation in South Africa as outlined in Chapter 5.

As illustrated in Table 4.4, the situation for Brazilian women is similar to men: 88.2 per cent of them stayed in the formal sector in the first period (2003–2007) against 87.7 per cent in 2008. Most of the women who did not stay in this situation passed to the informal sector or to inactivity, just like men. However, the number of women who went from the formal sector to inactivity increased in 2008 to 4.7 per cent (against 4.2 per cent in the period from 2003 to 2007). Also, the number of women who were discouraged and then transited to the formal sector dropped from 2.1 per cent in the period 2003–2007 to 0 per cent in 2008. The most stable situations were formal and out of the labour force, with over 80 per cent persistence in each. Unlike men, the pattern of transitions from unemployment did not improve in 2008 vis-à-vis 2003–2007; the only change was a reduction in the proportion of women who remained unemployed and an increase in the fraction that transited to inactivity.

The raw transitions rates for youth also show a fall in the percentage of people who stayed unemployed (Table 4.5). From 2003 to 2007, 48.0 per cent of these people remained unemployed, while in 2008 this percentage was only 39.2 per cent. It can also be seen that, in 2008, there were fewer self-employed people (57.0 versus 60.6 per cent in the first period). In 2008, most of these young people went to the informal sector (17.4 per cent) or to the out-of-the labour force group (13.5 per cent). The percentage of people staying out of the labour force rose to 79.5 per cent. The number of people staying in the informal sector diminished

Table 4.4 Raw labour market transitions – women

Women (2003–2007)

		To					
		Formal	Informal	Unemployed	Self-employed	Out of labour force	Discouraged
From	Formal	88.2	5.2	1.7	0.8	4.2	0.0
	Informal	12.3	68.0	4.4	4.8	10.4	0.0
	Unemployed	6.5	11.2	46.1	3.2	32.4	0.6
	Self-employed	2.4	8.8	2.2	73.2	13.4	0.0
	Out of labour force	1.7	3.9	6.4	3.2	84.7	0.2
	Discouraged	1.5	9.2	20.2	6.5	54.6	8.0

Women (2008)

		To					
		Formal	Informal	Unemployed	Self-employed	Out of labour force	Discouraged
From	Formal	87.7	5.1	1.8	0.8	4.7	0.0
	Informal	14.1	66.4	3.6	4.6	11.4	0.0
	Unemployed	9.9	11.6	39.6	3.2	35.3	0.4
	Self-employed	2.9	8.9	1.5	71.4	15.3	0.0
	Out of labour force	1.9	4.3	5.2	2.9	85.5	0.1
	Discouraged	0.0	7.6	19.2	7.6	57.7	7.7

Source: Monthly Employment Survey (Pesquisa Mensal de Emprego – PME); authors' calculations.

Table 4.5 Raw labour market transitions – youth (15–24)

(2003–2007)

			To				
		Formal	Informal	Unemployed	Self-employed	Out of labour force	Discouraged
From	Formal	86.1	5.9	3.0	0.6	4.5	0.0
	Informal	13.9	64.0	7.5	3.6	11.0	0.0
	Unemployed	7.7	11.8	48.0	2.5	29.6	0.4
	Self-employed	4.8	16.7	6.3	60.6	11.7	0.0
	Out of labour force	2.7	6.2	11.8	1.5	77.7	0.2
	Discouraged	2.2	11.1	31.1	5.6	42.2	7.8

(2008)

			To				
		Formal	Informal	Unemployed	Self-employed	Out of labour force	Discouraged
From	Formal	86.5	4.6	3.0	0.6	5.3	0.0
	Informal	17.0	60.5	5.9	3.7	12.9	0.0
	Unemployed	11.7	12.2	39.2	2.8	33.8	0.3
	Self-employed	6.4	17.5	5.6	57.0	13.5	0.0
	Out of labour force	3.4	6.7	9.0	1.4	79.5	0.1
	Discouraged	0.0	0.0	33.3	0.0	66.7	0.0

Source: Monthly Employment Survey (Pesquisa Mensal de Emprego – PME); authors' calculations.

3.5 percentage points. Many of them went to the formal sector or to the out-of-labour force. For this age group, higher migration to inactivity is not necessarily bad news, as this can reflect a movement to returning to school. This can be related to a strategy of increasing human capital to increase the chances of finding more qualified jobs in the future.

In comparison, for adults between 25 and 50 years of age (transition rates are not displayed here) there was also a decline in the percentage of people remaining unemployed: from 44.8 per cent over 2003–2007 to 38.8 per cent in 2008. There were no significant changes in the persistence of other states. In 2008, there is evidence of a higher rate of transitions to the formal sector compared to the first period. While between 2003 and 2007, 9.0 per cent of unemployed prime-age adults moved to the formal sector, the rate was 13.7 per cent in 2008.

The analysis of the above tables indicates that labour market segmentation is not as strong in Brazil, since at least one third of informal workers transit out of this kind of occupation a few months later. The same is true for unemployed people: there are considerable transitions from unemployment for most groups. The good news is the high persistence in formal jobs (over 80 per cent for all groups) and the decline in unemployment persistence between 2003–2007 and 2008.

4.4.2 Determinants of labour market transition probabilities

This section disentangles the factors associated with labour market transition probabilities, using PME data from 2001 to 2008. Instead of reporting all results, the focus here is on factors that drive transitions out of informal employment and unemployment.[9]

The results of the multinomial logit for the transition from the informal sector are in Table 4.A1 (all) and 4.A3 (women) in the Appendix. Here, there are dissimilar patterns of transition probabilities in different regions of the country. For example, informal male and female workers in Rio de Janeiro have less chances to transit to other categories than do workers in other regions. Also, for both men and women the more educated an informal worker is, the higher is the probability of passing to a formal job. On the other hand, for men there is not a significant relationship between schooling and transition probabilities from informality, except that male high school graduates have less chance to transit to the out-of-labour market category. For women, the result is similar: the more schooling, the lower the probability of transition from informality to being out of the labour force, after controlling for other explanatory variables.

Household male heads have a higher probability of escaping from informal to formal jobs (and to self-employment) than other family members. On the other hand, they have less chance to transit to unemployment and to out-of-labour force, an expected result. Female heads and spouses have higher chances than others to transit from informal to self-employment. For men, race does not affect transition probability from informality. However, black women have less chance to transit to formality than other groups. Finally, 2008 presents the highest probability of migration toward formal jobs for both men and women.

The marginal effects for the transitions out of unemployment are shown in Tables 4.A4 (women) and 4.A2 (all) in the Appendix. Again, the situation of women is worse than men, because they have less chance to escape unemployment and to find a job (formal, informal or self-employed). Again, the patterns of transition probabilities are very dissimilar across the country. Regarding education, the more educated an unemployed man is, the higher is the probability of him passing to a formal job (the most educated men have 11 percentage points more chance than other unemployed men to transit to formality!) and the lower the probability of passing to informal work (3.9 percentage points), self-employment (5.7 percentage points) or being out of the labour force (7.5 percentage points). For women, the relationship between schooling and transition probabilities is strongest in relation to formal jobs (3.9 percentage points) and to out of the labour force (8.8 percentage points).

Household heads have a higher probability of escaping from unemployment to any kind of job than other family members and less chance of transiting to inactivity than other family members. There is no difference in the probability of passing from unemployment among black, pardo and white unemployed men and women to formal, informal or self-employed occupations. Male and female black unemployed workers have less chance to transit from unemployment to out of labour force. Finally, 2008 presents the highest probability of movement from unemployment to any kind of job and the marginal effects are higher for men in this year. This reflects the good economic conditions in Brazil until the crisis hit in September 2008.

The analysis of this section shows very interesting patterns. First, education is undoubtedly very important for increasing the chances of finding a more qualified job in Brazil. Concerning raw labour market transitions, there is no important difference between men and women and the periods 2003–2007 and 2008. The figures indicate that more than 80 per cent of formal workers remain in this state three months later; on the other hand, in 2008 there was more mobility from the informal sector than in 2003–2007, indicating a low degree of labour market segmentation in Brazil. Finally, the determinants of transition reinforce the importance of education to increasing the chances of remaining in the formal sector and passing out of unemployment and informality.

4.5 Labour market policies and institutions: Brazil's emphasis on social policies

During the preceding decade, Brazil has increased social spending to OECD levels. In 2008 Brazil spent 26.1 per cent of GDP on social spending (though in per capita terms it is not as impressive). In other countries of the region, Argentina's public expenditure on social sectors reached 23.3 per cent in 2007, while it surpassed 19 per cent in Costa Rica. This outlay in Brazil can be broken down as follows: 5.6 per cent of GDP on education; 4.9 per cent on health; 13.4 per cent on social security; and 2.1 per cent on housing.[10] Human capital accumulation, which has been supported by the Bolsa Família scheme, has helped reduce informality (the young remain in school rather than finding an informal job) (Berg 2011), and contributed to a fall in inequality (OECD 2010). In terms of spending on social security, the average in OECD countries is around 14 per cent of GDP. In contrast to Brazil's approach, expenditure on this area is below 1 per cent of GDP in Asia (ILO/IILS 2011).

Therefore, Brazil has in recent years placed great emphasis on improving the access to social services and protection schemes, though it should be noted that spending on conditional cash transfers (CCTs; namely Bolsa Família) represents just 0.41 per cent of GDP. Altogether, social transfers (CCTs, pensions and other forms of assistance) have impacted inequality: the Gini coefficient for the distribution of individual's income falls from 0.626 to 0.595 thanks to these payments.[11]

The remainder of this section focuses on explanations for the rise in formality in Brazil along with a number of other key labour market institutions, particularly minimum wages and severance pay/individual savings accounts, along with a brief review of labour market policies, such as training schemes, which receive much less of a priority in Brazil. However, before doing so, it is important to reflect on Brazil's most famous scheme, though it is not directly linked to the labour market.

4.5.1   Explaining the rise in formality in Brazil in the 2000s

Due to the poor performance in the 1990s, most of the earlier literature had focused on the impediments to formal sector job creation. For example, Loyaza (1996, p. 148) concluded that 'the size of the informal sector is found to depend positively on tax burden and labour-market restrictions, and negatively on a proxy for the quality of government institutions'. Ulyssea (2006) also argued there is a consensus in the Brazilian literature that contractual rigidity and heavy payroll taxes are the main reasons for the high level of informality in Brazil (Barros 1993; Amadeo and Camargo 1996).

However, with the reversal of the rise of informality observed in the 1990s and the subsequent downward trend in informality in the 2000s, the focus of the discussion has shifted to understanding the factors behind the growing share of formal employment. As discussed in Berg (2011), and other references cited therein, a range of factors can be identified as drivers of formal job growth, from both a demand and supply perspective. Firstly, as noted above and in Chapter 2, the macroeconomic environment has improved, creating greater demand for labour, notably in export sectors but also in domestic-oriented businesses, which have benefited from the strong growth in domestic credit. In terms of the first factor, exports grew on average by 9.6 per cent per annum from 2000 to 2007, which was a time when Brazil (and other commodity-rich countries) have benefited from China's demand for minerals. With respect to the second factor, domestic credit in Brazil grew from 31.7 per cent of GDP in 2000 to 61.4 per cent in 2011.[12]

Another common factor highlighted is the introduction of a simplified and progressive tax system in 1996 (Simples Nacional), which reduced the burden for small and micro-enterprises (ILO/OECD 2011). More recently, the Individual Entrepreneur Law was enacted in 2009 to improve registration of micro-enterprises (no more than one employee). Under this law, micro-enterprises with annual revenues below R$36,000 per year can register their business and receive a taxation number, while remaining exempt from federal taxes. These enterprises need only to pay social security contributions of 5 per cent of the minimum wage. According to ILO/OECD (2011), over 1 million micro-enterprises had registered under this law, which has, in turn, increased the social security coverage of the self-employed. This outcome shows that, if policies are focused on incentives for formalization (such as access to social security), enterprises in the informal sector are more likely to register.

Such incentives for enterprises to register have been complemented by improved labour inspection in Brazil, which involved providing a better incentive structure (through bonuses and team rewards) (Berg 2011). As reported in Berg (2011), the number of registered workers as a result of labour inspection increased from 268,000 in 1996 to 669,000 in 2008. Despite the strong growth in jobs, studies such as Almeida and Carneiro (2009) argue, in contrast, that stricter enforcement through labour inspection is associated with a decline in employment in enterprises. Using firm-level data, this paper concludes that the more rigorous enforcement results in lower levels of informal employment.

In addition to these demand-side factors, Berg (2011) proposes the importance of demographics and increased education attainment reducing the supply of young workers to the labour market, who had traditionally taken up informal jobs. The evidence discussed above and presented in Table 4.A3 confirms the important role of education in driving the transition from informal to formal employment. Indeed, better-educated Brazilians, particularly women, are much more likely to be able to make such a move in the labour market than those with no or little education.

4.5.2 Bolsa Família

Bolsa Família is a conditional cash transfer that benefits poor families (with monthly per capita income from R$70.00 to R$140.00 in 2009) and extreme poverty (with monthly per capita income up to R$70.00). The average monthly transfer is R$70 or around US$35. The government under President Lula integrated a number of pre-existing programmes (such as Fome Zero (Zero Hunger)) and the Child Labour Eradication Programme (PETI) into the Bosla Família scheme, which has improved efficiency and delivery.

Bolsa Família is based on three steps for overcoming hunger and poverty. The first is the promotion of the immediate relief of poverty and hunger through direct transfer of income to needy families. The second is strengthening the exercise of social and basic rights in the areas of education and health, through the requirement to satisfy conditions, aiming to break the poverty cycle between generations. The third is coordination of complementary programmes that aim to develop families to overcome vulnerability and poverty. Some examples of these auxiliary are programmes for job and income-generation, adult literacy and registration to obtain documents.

Evidence in the literature suggests that Bolsa Família is a well-focused scheme and contributes to reducing both poverty and inequality in

Brazil. Soares et al. (2006) showed that 80 per cent of Bolsa Família beneficiaries belong to the targeted group and that Bolsa Família and BPC together account for 28 per cent of the fall in the Gini index between 1995 and 2004 (7 per cent from BPC and 21 per cent from Bolsa Família). Hoffman (2006) argued that a fifth of the overall reduction in inequality between 2001 and 2005 was due to conditional transfer programmes (Bolsa Família and BPC). In the poorest regions, like the Northeast, these CCTs are responsible for about 46 per cent of the reduction in the Gini index between 1998 and 2005 and 87 per cent in the period between 2002 and 2004. Scorzafave and Lima (2010) also show that Bolsa Família has been very important in reducing inequality. Furthermore, there is no evidence of collateral effects in terms of labour supply reduction among beneficiaries of the scheme (Ferro and Nicolella 2007; Mattos et al. 2008). Finally, the programme helps improve the consumption of basic staple foods by poor households (Resende and Hermeto 2006)

Barros et al. (2006) argued that the main factor behind the effect of these social programmes on inequality is the increase in their coverage between 2001 and 2005, especially in the case of Bolsa Família. In fact, there was a huge expansion of the scheme: in 2003, Bolsa Família served 3.6 million people, rising to 6.5 million in 2004, 8.7 million in 2005, 11 million in 2006 and 12.7 million in 2009 (IPEA 2010).

As highlighted above, another important social transfer in Brazil is the BPC (Benefício de Prestação Continuada de Assistência Social), which pays a welfare benefit of one times the minimum wage to people 65 years or older with disabilities that prevent them from leading independent lives and families whose per capita income does not reach a quarter of the minimum wage. In June 2006, over 1.3 million people received this benefit. There is robust evidence that BPC has helped fight poverty and inequality in recent years in Brazil. For example, Scorzafave and Lima (2010) found that a 1 per cent increase in BPC benefits is responsible for a 0.3 per cent reduction in the Gini index. Medeiros (2008) found that the BPC is important in reducing poverty in Brazil, while Soares et al. (2006) reported evidence that the BPC is responsible for 7 per cent of the decline in inequality in Brazil between 1995 and 2005.

4.5.3 Minimum wages

In recent years, Brazil has consistently increased minimum wages as a means to reduce poverty and inequality. The minimum wage in Brazil was first established in the 1930s. Under the Lula presidency, the minimum wage was rising in real terms, helping raise pay levels but also affecting the pension system, because these benefits are tied to the minimum wage (benefit levels are calculated in multiples of the minimum wage). Since 2004, the minimum wage has increased more than 130 per cent in real terms. In 2010, the national minimum wage in Brazil stood at R$510 (US$276) per month, which corresponds to roughly 45 per cent of mean monthly earnings. The states are free to set higher state-wide limits. For example, in 2010 São Paulo set its minimum wage at R$560 (US$303) and in Rio de Janeiro it is R$581 (US$316). The higher state wage floors do not apply to INSS pensioners, who are subject to federal legislation.

As highlighted in Chapter 3, the issue of minimum wages, like employment protection legislation, has generated polarized debates on the impact of such institutions on the labour market. According to standard economic theory, the introduction of a minimum wage in a dual labour market (with segmentation between formal and informal sectors) will lead to the loss of employment in the formal sector (because of the increase in wages above marginal productivity). It is assumed these workers would enter the informal sector (in the absence of unemployment benefits) which, in turn, would depress wages in that segment of the labour market. However, much of the recent empirical literature, especially that related to Latin America, shows that an increase in the minimum wage leads to a rise in the informal sector wage. Often referred to as the 'lighthouse effect', this outcome arises because the minimum wage helps the bargaining power of informal sector workers (assuming a monopsonistic labour market), which outweighs the impact of the increase in labour supply to the sector (Boeri et al. 2011).

Studies on Brazil such as those by Lemos (2007) and Fajnzylber (2001) find that the increases in the minimum wage in the country resulted in an increase in the informal sector wage. At the same time, there isn't any strong evidence that the minimum wage has increased unemployment in Brazil (Firpo and Reis 2006), or indeed informal employment given the positive trends noted above. Thus, labour market institutions, such as minimum wages, can be utilized to improve protection of workers without sacrificing jobs if the macroeconomic and policy environment is supportive of job creation (a 'win-win' situation can be achieved for employers and workers).

4.5.4 Unemployment benefits and severance pay

Brazilian workers in the formal sector are eligible to receive unemployment insurance benefits, which are managed by the Social Security

Administration (National Social Security Institute, or INSS). Besides financial support in the event of being laid off, the programme assists people to try to find new jobs. The resources are provided by the Fundo de Amparo ao Trabalhador (FAT), or Worker Support Fund, and the number of monthly payments varies from three to five, depending on how long the employee worked before being discharged. The amount of the benefit is based on an average of the last monthly salaries received by the worker, but cannot be less than the minimum wage. In 2009, 7.7 million workers received these payments (75 per cent of all unemployed), comprising R$19.7 billion (US$9.85 billion).

Another important characteristic of the Brazilian labour market is the FGTS, which stands for Time of Service Guarantee Fund (Fundo de Garantia por Tempo de Serviço). It was created in 1967 to assure a money reserve proportional to the tenure of work of every contributing worker in case of lay-off, death or at retirement. Each formal private worker has a compulsory saving account into which the employer deposits 8 per cent of the monthly salary. The worker can withdraw funds upon being laid off without cause (but not if fired), along with other particular moments, like the purchase of a home, in case of some serious diseases (cancer, AIDS) and at the time of retirement. In the case of lay-off, the employer must pay the worker an additional 40 per cent of the amount deposited during the work period, plus a 10 per cent fine to the government.

FGTS resources are legally earmarked to finance low-income housing programmes, environmental sanitation and urban infrastructure. In 2008, 44 per cent of Brazilian workers contributed R$54 billion (US$30 billion) to the fund. On the other hand, there was R$42 billion (US$23.3 billion) in withdrawals from 29 million accounts. So, in 2008, there was a net increase of US$6.7 billion (CAIXA 2010).

4.5.5   More mainstream active labour market policies?

Though the Brazilian government has prioritized Bolsa Família, the minimum wage (and the pension that is linked to it) and other schemes, a range of more traditional active labour market policies exists, such as training and wage subsidy schemes.

For example, the Programa Nacional de Estímulo ao Primeiro Emprego (PNPE), or First Job Incentive National Programme, which was set up in 2003, consists of several actions aimed at creating new jobs and preparing young people (16 to 24 years old) for better insertion in the labour market. Under the programme, the government gives financial incentives to firms to hire workers just entering the labour force. Companies can participate in the programme through two mechanisms: a) hiring youths registered but not yet receiving the benefit (in this case, they receive only a certification as partner of the First Job Programme); or b) for all firms that hire young people from this programme (the incentive is R$1,500.00 (US$700.00) annually for each job created).

To enter the programme, companies must prove tax regularity (no back taxes owed) and must respect all the labour obligations concerning the new hires (paying all payroll charges). The firm must also prove that the young worker is not crowding out an older one. Besides this, there is a limit on the percentage of such young workers from the programme; it cannot exceed 20 per cent of all the firm's workers. The aim of these rules is to avoid substitution between regular and subsidized employees. Young people interested in participating in the programme must have no prior formal employment, come from a family earning up to one-half minimum monthly wage[13] per capita and be regularly enrolled in school or any course for adults who did not complete their education.

Despite the good intentions, according to Ribeiro and Juliano (2005), the programme does not have any real impact on job creation. Excess bureaucracy and rules, and an incorrect diagnosis of the causes of juvenile unemployment are the reasons indicated by them for the programme's failure. They also argue that the programme itself does not necessarily raise the number of jobs for young people, which is crucial to overcome this problem. Rather, economic growth has a much larger impact on job creation than these policies.

In 2008, the federal government implemented another policy for young people. Projovem (Pro-youth) aims to prepare youths for the labour market and for alternative activities that can bring them and their families extra income. Any unemployed person between 18 and 29 years old and whose family earns up to half the minimum wage per person can participate in the programme. The participants receive a monthly benefit of R$100.00 (US$55.00) for six months if they prove their attendance at the training courses offered. Each course lasts 350 hours. The programme is developed in partnership with the states, civil society and the private sector. The objective is to stimulate the generation of job opportunities, business, social inclusion and entrepreneurship.

Projovem Adolescente is another part of the overall Projovem programme. It is a social and educative project serving people from 16 to 17 years old. The project integrates the actions of the Proteção Social Básica (Basic Social Protection) from the Sistema Único de Assistência Social (National Social Assistance System) and tries to improve the basic protection of families through the creation of mechanisms that guarantee harmony and collaboration among people in families and communities, to create a better setting for teen development. It also aims at the insertion, reinsertion and persistence of youths in the educational system. In 2009, Projovem Adolescente served more than 16,000 young people between 16 and 17 years old, at a cost of R$204 million according to the Social Development Ministry.

There is also the Projovem Urbano program, which has the objective of improving education in urban areas. The last modality of Projovem is the Projovem Campo, which tries to strengthen and amplify the access and continued participation of poor rural youths (from farmworker or smallholder families) in the educational system, by improving educational opportunities by the same means that the Projovem Urbano programme does. It is a reformulation of a previous programme called Saberes da Terra, taking into consideration the seasonal nature of the agricultural cycle. In 2007, R$2,743,228.00 (US$1,414,035) was spent on the whole Projovem program.

Among wage subsidies, there is the Wage Allowance (Abono Salarial), which is a benefit of one times the minimum wage paid once a year to low-wage workers. More specifically, every worker has the right to receive this benefit if his or her monthly wage is up to two times the minimum (currently US$530). The beneficiary also must have contributed to the Social Integration Programme (Programa de Integração Social, PIS) or to the Civil Servant Asset Formation Program (Programa de Formação do Patrimonio do Servidor Público, PASEP) for at least five years. So this programme benefits only formal sector workers. The last condition is to have held a formal job for at least 30 days in the previous year. In the period from July 2009 to June 2010 there were 12 million benefit payments made, at a cost of R$16.5billion (US$7.9 billion).

4.6   Conclusion

Following decades of high levels of inequality and poverty along with bouts of high inflation and financial and social crises, the performance of the Brazilian economy and labour market over the last decade is, therefore, remarkable. This achievement is the outcome of not only strong economic growth and macroeconomic stability, but also of effective government interventions in the areas of taxation and social policies. Notably, the government under President Luiz Inacio 'Lula' da Silva increased spending on the famous Bolsa Família scheme that provides conditional cash transfers to poor households. Also, with important implications for pensions, the government raised minimum wages, which had been stagnant or falling during the 1990s and early 2000s. In a stark departure from previous crises, Brazil responded effectively to the global financial crisis through a stimulus package and social protection measures. Thanks also to strong external demand, the economic recovery in 2010 was swift.

Turning to the labour market, the positive growth story and the effective implementation of various policies resulted in a fall in the unemployment rate from 11.5 per cent in 2004 to 5.2 per cent at the end of 2011. This was driven by the robust creation of jobs in the formal economy: the Brazilian economy created 15.3 million formal jobs from 2003 to 2010, a trend which continued during the recession of 2009. Formalization resulted from both a supportive macroeconomic environment, stronger incentives for formalization through the taxation and social security systems, improved labour inspection, reduced demographic pressures and increased educational attainment.

That said, the results from the micro-data show that inequalities in accessing formal sector jobs remain, particularly as a result of low levels of education. Indeed, there is an urgent need to improve education to diminish the NEET rate among youth and to enhance the skills of future Brazilian workers. It is particularly important to improve the job prospects of the poorest fraction of young Brazilians. For these reasons, Brazil needs to further expand education in terms of promoting transitions from high school to college education and vocational training.

Appendix

Table 4.A1   Transition probabilities from informal sector

To	Formal	Unemployed	Self-employed	Out of labour force
Female	−0.360***	−0.067	−1.049***	0.369***
	(0.030)	(0.049)	(0.042)	(0.039)
Age	0.049***	−0.030**	0.129***	−0.148***
	(0.008)	(0.014)	(0.011)	(0.009)
Age^2	−0.001***	−0.000	−0.001***	0.002***
	(0.000)	(0.000)	(0.000)	(0.000)
Recife	−0.103*	0.300***	0.216***	0.320***
	(0.061)	(0.095)	(0.077)	(0.066)
Salvador	−0.736***	−0.414***	−0.719***	−1.018***
	(0.063)	(0.100)	(0.086)	(0.079)
Bahia	0.180***	0.107	0.177***	0.104*
	(0.050)	(0.085)	(0.067)	(0.057)
Rio de Janeiro	−0.862***	−1.114***	−0.795***	−1.670***
	(0.055)	(0.105)	(0.073)	(0.080)
São Paulo	−0.261***	0.027	−0.277***	−0.565***
	(0.047)	(0.078)	(0.063)	(0.057)
Number of children	0.004	0.017***	0.002	0.004
	(0.004)	(0.006)	(0.005)	(0.004)
1–3 years of schooling	−0.121	0.326*	−0.186	−0.140
	(0.114)	(0.180)	(0.115)	(0.104)
4–7 years of schooling	0.154	0.282*	−0.023	−0.098
	(0.097)	(0.161)	(0.098)	(0.088)
8–10 years of schooling	0.497***	0.345**	0.089	−0.094
	(0.098)	(0.163)	(0.102)	(0.092)
11 or more years of schooling	0.792***	0.194	0.094	−0.493***
	(0.097)	(0.162)	(0.099)	(0.092)
Household head	0.134***	−0.217***	0.252***	−0.288***
	(0.042)	(0.069)	(0.058)	(0.055)
Spouse	0.004	−0.332***	0.377***	0.034
	(0.048)	(0.081)	(0.066)	(0.058)
Pardo	0.016	0.135**	0.052	0.024
	(0.035)	(0.056)	(0.046)	(0.043)
Black	−0.113**	0.176**	−0.000	0.012
	(0.053)	(0.080)	(0.067)	(0.062)
2003	−0.076	0.433***	0.015	−0.116*
	(0.049)	(0.081)	(0.066)	(0.060)
2004	−0.159***	0.226***	0.010	−0.251***
	(0.049)	(0.083)	(0.064)	(0.061)

2005	−0.109**	0.001	−0.174**	−0.253***
	(0.050)	(0.091)	(0.070)	(0.064)
2006	−0.188***	0.278***	−0.081	−0.106*
	(0.048)	(0.081)	(0.064)	(0.058)
2007	−0.236***	−0.055	−0.149**	−0.197***
	(0.048)	(0.086)	(0.065)	(0.058)
Constant	−2.291***	−1.985***	−4.404***	0.991***
	(0.174)	(0.281)	(0.227)	(0.181)
Observations	43,258	43,258	43,258	43,258

Note: *** significant at 1%; ** significant at 5%; * significant at 10%.
Source: Monthly Employment Survey (Pesquisa Mensal de Emprego – PME); authors' calculations.

Table 4.A2 Transition probabilities from unemployment

To	Formal	Unemployed	Self-employed	Out of labour force
Female	−0.572***	−0.118***	−0.947***	0.332***
	(0.051)	(0.043)	(0.065)	(0.033)
Age	0.104***	0.017	0.158***	−0.109***
	(0.016)	(0.013)	(0.017)	(0.009)
Age^2	−0.001***	−0.000	−0.002***	0.002***
	(0.000)	(0.000)	(0.000)	(0.000)
Recife	−1.054***	−0.214**	0.049	0.392***
	(0.101)	(0.087)	(0.112)	(0.065)
Salvador	−1.894***	−1.323***	−1.062***	−0.529***
	(0.103)	(0.091)	(0.122)	(0.064)
Bahia	0.034	0.272***	0.242**	0.274***
	(0.079)	(0.077)	(0.105)	(0.062)
Rio de Janeiro	−1.786***	−1.176***	−1.070***	−0.860***
	(0.095)	(0.084)	(0.115)	(0.063)
São Paulo	−1.115***	−0.286***	−0.728***	−0.337***
	(0.077)	(0.070)	(0.101)	(0.056)
Number of children	0.011*	0.020***	0.018***	0.012***
	(0.006)	(0.005)	(0.007)	(0.004)
1–3 years of schooling	0.165	0.194	−0.090	−0.118
	(0.259)	(0.162)	(0.180)	(0.126)
4–7 years of schooling	0.198	0.034	−0.182	−0.033
	(0.226)	(0.142)	(0.155)	(0.108)
8–10 years of schooling	0.451**	−0.253*	−0.490***	−0.075
	(0.226)	(0.144)	(0.161)	(0.108)
11 or more years of schooling	0.702***	−0.354**	−0.719***	−0.295***
	(0.224)	(0.142)	(0.159)	(0.107)
Household head	0.304***	0.254***	0.308***	−0.096**
	(0.068)	(0.059)	(0.080)	(0.046)

Table 4.A2   (Continued)

To	Formal	Unemployed	Self-employed	Out of labour force
Spouse	0.083	0.001	0.227**	0.301***
	(0.080)	(0.067)	(0.096)	(0.047)
Pardo	0.029	0.007	−0.059	−0.010
	(0.057)	(0.048)	(0.069)	(0.036)
Black	−0.157*	−0.108	−0.256**	−0.200***
	(0.084)	(0.070)	(0.100)	(0.052)
2003	−0.978***	−0.392***	−0.286***	−0.516***
	(0.083)	(0.073)	(0.101)	(0.054)
2004	−0.811***	−0.121*	−0.140	−0.267***
	(0.082)	(0.071)	(0.102)	(0.053)
2005	−0.694***	−0.371***	−0.456***	−0.358***
	(0.087)	(0.080)	(0.117)	(0.058)
2006	−0.609***	−0.257***	−0.192*	−0.345***
	(0.079)	(0.073)	(0.103)	(0.054)
2007	−0.554***	−0.279***	−0.277***	−0.377***
	(0.079)	(0.075)	(0.106)	(0.055)
Constant	−2.191***	−0.802***	−3.890***	1.513***
	(0.344)	(0.255)	(0.350)	(0.186)
Observations	26,638	26,638	26,638	26,638

Note: *** significant at 1%; ** significant at 5%; * significant at 10%.

Table 4.A3   Transition probabilities from informal sector – women

To	Formal	Unemployed	Self-employed	Out of labour force
Age	−0.000	−0.001***	0.001***	0.000
	(0.000)	(0.000)	(0.000)	(0.000)
Recife	−0.017*	0.005	0.006	0.016*
	(0.008)	(0.005)	(0.006)	(0.008)
Salvador	−0.054***	−0.011**	−0.020***	−0.070***
	(0.006)	(0.004)	(0.004)	(0.004)
Belo Horizonte	0.012	−0.002	0.000	0.004
	(0.007)	(0.004)	(0.005)	(0.006)
Rio de Janeiro	−0.068***	−0.026***	−0.011**	−0.092***
	(0.005)	(0.003)	(0.004)	(0.004)
São Paulo	−0.024***	−0.003	−0.007	−0.040***
	(0.006)	(0.004)	(0.004)	(0.005)
Number of children	0.000	0.001*	−0.000	0.000
	(0.001)	(0.000)	(0.000)	(0.000)

1–3 years of schooling	−0.001	0.019	−0.008	−0.019*
	(0.017)	(0.013)	(0.007)	(0.009)
4–7 years of schooling	0.040*	0.009	0.002	−0.024**
	(0.016)	(0.009)	(0.007)	(0.008)
8–10 years of schooling	0.067***	0.012	0.016	−0.020*
	(0.019)	(0.010)	(0.009)	(0.008)
11 or more years of schooling	0.120***	0.010	0.018*	−0.056***
	(0.018)	(0.009)	(0.008)	(0.008)
Household head	0.003	0.000	0.025***	−0.024***
	(0.006)	(0.003)	(0.005)	(0.005)
Spouse	−0.006	−0.007*	0.030***	−0.005
	(0.006)	(0.003)	(0.005)	(0.005)
Pardo	0.001	0.005	0.002	0.002
	(0.005)	(0.003)	(0.003)	(0.004)
Black	−0.023***	0.013**	−0.000	0.001
	(0.007)	(0.005)	(0.005)	(0.007)
2003	−0.007	0.021***	0.014*	−0.007
	(0.007)	(0.006)	(0.005)	(0.006)
2004	−0.009	0.010*	0.010*	−0.017**
	(0.007)	(0.005)	(0.005)	(0.006)
2005	−0.010	0.001	−0.001	−0.015*
	(0.007)	(0.005)	(0.005)	(0.006)
2006	−0.022***	0.010*	−0.001	−0.009
	(0.006)	(0.005)	(0.005)	(0.006)
2007	−0.027***	−0.001	−0.001	−0.016**
	(0.006)	(0.004)	(0.005)	(0.005)
Observations	23,445	23,445	23,445	23,445
Pseudo R2	0.045	0.045	0.045	0.045

Note: *** significant at 1%; ** significant at 5%; * significant at 10%.

Table 4.A4 Transition probabilities from unemployment – women

To	Formal	Informal	Self-employed	Out of labour force
Age	−0.000	−0.000	0.001***	0.002***
	(0.000)	(0.000)	(0.000)	(0.000)
Recife	−0.042***	−0.038***	0.020*	0.101***
	(0.004)	(0.008)	(0.008)	(0.018)
Salvador	−0.060***	−0.083***	−0.002	−0.076***
	(0.003)	(0.006)	(0.005)	(0.015)
Belo Horizonte	−0.007	0.011	0.012	0.033*
	(0.005)	(0.009)	(0.006)	(0.016)
Rio de Janeiro	−0.049***	−0.071***	−0.013**	−0.126***
	(0.003)	(0.006)	(0.004)	(0.014)

Table 4.A4   (Continued)

To	Formal	Informal	Self-employed	Out of labour force
São Paulo	−0.043***	−0.018*	−0.007	−0.045**
	(0.004)	(0.008)	(0.004)	(0.014)
Number of children	−0.000	0.001*	0.000	0.003**
	(0.000)	(0.001)	(0.000)	(0.001)
1–3 years of schooling	−0.014	0.054	0.008	−0.040
	(0.016)	(0.028)	(0.013)	(0.031)
4–7 years of schooling	0.002	0.009	0.006	−0.022
	(0.017)	(0.019)	(0.010)	(0.028)
8–10 years of schooling	0.009	−0.020	0.004	0.002
	(0.018)	(0.017)	(0.010)	(0.028)
11 or more years of schooling	0.039*	−0.015	0.007	−0.088**
	(0.017)	(0.018)	(0.009)	(0.028)
Household head	0.010	0.026**	0.012*	−0.045***
	(0.006)	(0.008)	(0.005)	(0.012)
Spouse	−0.005	−0.011	0.007	0.048***
	(0.005)	(0.007)	(0.004)	(0.011)
Pardo	−0.002	0.007	−0.004	0.007
	(0.004)	(0.006)	(0.003)	(0.009)
Black	−0.003	−0.007	−0.003	−0.033*
	(0.006)	(0.009)	(0.004)	(0.013)
2003	−0.033***	−0.019*	0.002	−0.081***
	(0.004)	(0.008)	(0.005)	(0.013)
2004	−0.032***	−0.002	0.003	−0.032*
	(0.004)	(0.009)	(0.005)	(0.013)
2005	−0.020***	−0.020*	−0.008	−0.037**
	(0.005)	(0.009)	(0.005)	(0.014)
2006	−0.019***	−0.011	−0.001	−0.050***
	(0.004)	(0.008)	(0.005)	(0.013)
2007	−0.018***	−0.010	−0.003	−0.056***
	(0.004)	(0.009)	(0.005)	(0.013)
Observations	15,036	15,036	15,036	15,036
Pseudo R2	0.049	0.049	0.049	0.049

Note: *** significant at 1%; ** significant at 5%; * significant at 10%.

Notes

1. Source: Economic Commission for Latin America and the Caribbean, Statistics and Economic Projections Division, Social Statistics Unit. See www.eclac.cl.
2. Source: International Monetary Fund, Direction of Trade Statistics.

3. Source: World Bank, World Development Indicators online database: http://data.worldbank.org/data-catalog/world-development-indicators
4. Source: ILO/OECD (2011) G20 Country Policy Brief: Brazil: www.oecd.org/els/48723896.pdf
5. Since the OECD used PME data, which only covers metropolitan regions, the informality rate calculated is lower than the rates reported here, as there is evidence of higher informality in non-metropolitan areas of Brazil.
6. Brazil is officially divided into five regions: North, Northeast, Midwest, Southeast and South.
7. As noted above, this database has some limitations because it is not nationally representative. Instead, it covers only six Brazilian metropolitan regions (São Paulo, Rio de Janeiro, Curitiba, Salvador, Recife and Porto Alegre). On the other hand, the PME provides the only panel data available in Brazil that permit tracking individuals in all aspects studied here (formal, informal, unemployed and inactive). Another advantage of the PME is that it allows identification of discouragement, which cannot be done with PNAD data.
8. As will be seen in more detail later, the effects of the international financial crisis on the Brazilian economy were relatively mild, causing recession in the fourth quarter of 2008 and first quarter of 2009, after which the economy rebounded strongly.
9. For a full set of estimates, see ILO (2010).
10. Source: Economic Commission for Latin America and the Caribbean, Social Expenditure Database, accessed 15 February 2012.
11. Source: Economic Commission for Latin America and the Caribbean, Social Expenditure Database, accessed 15 February 2012.
12. Source: World Bank World Development Indicators, online database; accessed 14 August 2012.
13. The federal government establishes a minimum monthly wage for those working what is considered a normal workweek. It is typically adjusted every year, and in recent years has been adjusted by more than inflation, to provide real gains.

References

Almeida, R. and P. Carneiro (2009) 'Enforcement of Labor Regulation and Firm Size', *Journal of Comparative Economics*, Vol. 37, No. 1, pp. 28–46.
Amadeo, E. and J. Camargo (1996) 'Instituições e o mercado de trabalho no Brasil', in J. Camargo (ed.), *Flexibilidade no Mercado de Trabalho no Brasil* (Rio de Janeiro: Fundação Getúlio Vargas).
Barros, R. (1993) 'The Informal Labour Market in Brazil', mimeo.
Barros, R., M. Carvalho and S. Franco (2006), 'O papel das transferências públicas na queda recente da desigualdade de renda brasileira', in R. Barros, M. Foguel and G. Ulyssea (eds), *Sobre a recente queda da desigualdade de renda no Brasil* (Brasília: IPEA).
Berg, J. (2011) 'Laws or luck? Understanding Rising Formality in Brazil in the 2000s', in S. Lee and D. McCann (eds), *Regulating for Decent Work: New Directions in Labour Market Regulation* (Basingstoke and Geneva: Palgrave Macmillan and ILO), Chapter 5.

Boeri, T., Garibaldi, P. and M. Ribeiro (2011) 'The Lighthouse Effect and Beyond', *Review of Income and Wealth*, Series 57, Special Issue, May 2011, pp. S54–S78.

CAIXA (2010) 'Demonstrações Contábeis do FGTS', available at: http://downloads.caixa.gov.br/_arquivos/fgts/demonstracao_financeira_fgts/DEMON STRACAO_FINANCEIRA_FGTS_2009.pdf

Ernst, C. (2008) 'Recent Dynamics in Brazil's Labour Market', Economic and Labour Market Paper 2007/10 (Geneva: ILO).

Fajnzylber, P. (2001) 'Minimum Wage Effects throughout the Wage Distribution: Evidence from Brazil's Formal and Informal Sectors', *Anais do XXIX Encontro Nacional de Economia*, No. 98.

Ferreira, F., P. Leite and M. Ravallion (2010) 'Poverty Reduction without Economic Growth?: Explaining Brazil's Poverty Dynamics, 1985–2004', *Journal of Development Economics*, Vol. 93, No. 1, pp. 20–36.

Ferro, A. and A. Nicolella (2007) 'The Impact of Conditional Cash Transfer Programs on Household Work Decisions in Brazil', FEA-RP Working Paper Series (Monte Alegre: FEA-RP).

Firpo, S. and M. Reis (2006) 'O Salário Mínimo e a Recente Queda da Desigualdade no Brasil', in R. Barros et al. (eds), *Desigualdade de Renda no Brasil: Uma Análise da Queda Recente* (Rio de Janeiro: IPEA).

Hoffmann, R. (2006) 'Transferências de renda e redução da desigualdade no Brasil e em cinco regiões entre 1997 e 2005', in R. Barros, M. Foguel and G. Ulyssea (eds), *Sobre a recente queda da desigualdade de renda no Brasil* (Brasilia: IPEA).

International Labour Office (ILO) (2009) *Decent Work Country Profile: Brazil* (Geneva: ILO).

International Labour Office (ILO) (2010) 'Developing More Effective Labour Market Policies and Institutions in Emerging Economies: The Brazilian Case', Background paper.

International Labour Office (ILO)/International Institute for Labour Studies (IILS) (2011) *Brazil: an Innovative Income-led Strategy, Studies on Growth with Equity* (Geneva: ILO/IILS).

International Labour Office (ILO) and Organisation for Economic Co-operation and Development (OECD) (2011) *G20 Country Policy Brief: Brazil* (Geneva: ILO).

IPEA (2010) 'Políticas sociais: acompanhamento e análise', DISOC/IPEA (Brasilia: Instituto de Pesquisa Econômica Aplicada).

Lemos, S. (2007) 'Minimum Wage Effects across the Private and Public Sectors in Brazil', *The Journal of Development Studies*, Vol. 43, No. 4, pp. 700–720.

Loyaza, N. (1996) 'The Economics of Informal Sector: A Simple Model and Some Empirical Evidence from Latin America', Carnegie Rochester Series in Public Economics, Vol. 45, pp. 129–162.

Mattos, E., F. Marques and S. Maia (2008) 'Oferta de trabalho e transferências: evidências do efeito das condições impostas pelo programa Bolsa-Família', in ANPEC, *XXXVI Anais do XXXVI Encontro Nacional de Economia [Proceedings of the 36th Brazilian Economics Meeting]*.

Medeiros, M., T. Britto and F. Soares (2008) 'Targeted Cash Transfer Programmes in Brazil: BPC and the Bolsa Família', IPC Working Paper No. 46 (Brasilia: IPC).

Mello, L., N. Menezes-Filho and L. Scorzafave (2006) 'Improving Labour Utilisation in Brazil', OECD Economics Department Working Papers, No. 533 (Paris: OECD).

Organisation of Economic Co-operation and Development (OECD) (2010) *Tackling Inequalities in Brazil, China, India and South Africa: The Role of Labour Market and Social Policies* (Paris: OECD).

Reinhart, C. and K. Rogoff (2009) *This Time is Different: Eight Centuries of Financial Folly* (Princeton and Oxford: Princeton University Press).

Resende, A. C. C. and A. M. Hermeto (2006) 'Avaliando Resultados De Um Programa De Transferências de Renda: O Impacto Do Bolsa-Escola Sobre Os Gastos Das Famílias Brasileiras', ANPEC, *Anais do XXXIV Encontro Nacional de Economia [Proceedings of the 34th Brazilian Economics Meeting]*.

Ribeiro, R. and A. Juliano (2005) 'Desemprego juvenil e impactos do Programa Nacional de Estímulo ao Primeiro Emprego', *Econômica*, Vol. 7, No. 1, pp. 47–76.

Scorzafave, L. and E. Lima (2010) 'Inequality Evolution in Brazil: The Role of Cash Transfer Programs and Other Income Sources', in J. Bishop (ed.), *Studies in Applied Welfare Analysis: Papers from the Third ECINEQ Meeting, Research on Economic Inequality*, Vol. 18 (Bingley: Emerald Group), pp. 107–129.

Soares, F. V., S. Soares, M. Medeiros and R. G. Osorio (2006) 'Cash Transfer Programmes in Brazil: Impacts on Inequality and Poverty', IPC Working Paper No. 21, June (Brasilia: IPC).

Ulyssea, G. (2006) 'Informalidade no mercado de trabalho brasileiro: uma resenha da literatura', *Revista de Economia Política*, Vol. 26, No. 4, pp. 596–618.

5
The Tale of Two Labour Markets: The Resilience of the Indonesian Labour Market to the Global Financial Crisis versus Increasing Casualization of Jobs

5.1 Introduction

From the 1970s to the 1990s, Indonesia made incredible economic and social progress. During this period, Indonesians moved from rural to urban areas to take up better-paid jobs and, as a result, poverty fell from 40 per cent in 1976 to 11 per cent two decades later (Dhanani and Islam 2001). This rapid development trajectory was brought to a halt by the East Asian financial crisis of 1997–1998 and the subsequent political crisis, which sent the country into a deep recession leaving millions in poverty. Despite this tragic reversal of fortunes, the labour market appeared to be rather stable at the aggregate level – the impact of this crisis was more evident in transitions across different types of employment rather than a fall in the number of jobs, along with a sharp fall in real wages. In particular, the massive economic contraction in 1998 resulted in an increase in agricultural and informal sector employment and a rise in female labour force participation as a household coping mechanism (Fallon and Lucas 2002; Islam and Chowdhury 2009; Manning 2000).

The period following the East Asian financial crisis has been described as one of 'jobless growth', which has been variously attributed to public sector downsizing, slower industrial growth, the failure of the service sector to take up the slack, and the excessive regulation of the Indonesian labour market (World Bank 2010). In terms of the last factor, many commentators have blamed the Manpower Law (No.13/2003) for the poor labour market outcomes, especially with respect to the rise in unemployment from 2003, which persisted despite the pick-up in economic growth at that time.[1] However, although this law has been widely cited as a major constraint to formal sector job creation, compliance with the legislation is very low (Dhanani et al. 2009; World Bank 2010). Moreover, the unemployment rate peaked at 11.2 per cent in 2005 before falling strongly over the following years (along with rising employment), in spite of the high severance pay and restrictions on temporary work mandated by the Manpower Law. Therefore, although there has been considerable discussion on this issue, the relationship between labour market regulation and outcomes in Indonesia is far from straightforward.

In late 2008, the global financial crisis spread across the globe, hitting many emerging economies hard, particularly as a consequence of the unprecedented contraction in world trade flows. Indonesia was no exception: exports fell by almost 18 per cent from 2008 to 2009. However, in contrast to the devastating effects of the East Asian crisis of a decade ago, the impact of the global financial crisis on the domestic Indonesian economy has been relatively mild. Moreover, there is little indication at both the aggregate and micro-level that the latest crisis has had any major implications for labour market and employment trends. Indeed, the unemployment rate has continued to fall, reaching 7.9 per cent in 2009 (and 7.1 per cent in 2010), which is the lowest level since 2001.

Taking into account these key developments in the Indonesian labour market over the last few decades, the main objective of this chapter is to dig deeper into trends and determinants of employment status since 1996. More specifically, this chapter uses micro-data from the national labour force survey (Sakernas) over the period 1996–2009, which covers both the East Asian financial crisis of 1997–1998 and the global financial crisis of 2007–2009. This allows for a broader perspective on stability in and determinants of employment status in terms of both longer-term trends and adjustments to large external shocks. The focus is on employment status because the nature of employment is arguably the greater labour market challenge in Indonesia than unemployment itself. This chapter focuses in particular on the increasing casualization of wage employment in the 2000s.

The findings of this analysis show that much of the recent developments in the Indonesian labour market seem to have been part of a longer-term trend since around the mid-2000s. More specifically, the share of wage employment for both men and women rose in the 2000s. However, this was accompanied by an increased casualization of wage employment, which resulted in less protection for workers. Indeed, formal employment growth remained limited, once casual employment is taken into account. Moreover, since about the mid-2000s, there has been an increase in transitions in the labour market, which could reflect greater job insecurity for a large proportion of the workforce. These labour market trends coincided with the adoption of the Manpower Law of 2003 and a hike in the inflation rate in 2005 (due to the reduction in the fuel subsidy); however, it is difficult to identify a causal relationship, particularly due to the number of policy and institutional changes during this period such as the push to decentralization. Finally, the recent global financial crisis did not significantly affect the Indonesian economy. Nonetheless, the failure for the economy to generate sufficient regular formal sector jobs, especially in the non-agricultural sector, continues to be a major challenge for the Indonesian government.

Therefore, with respect to the overall framework proposed in the Introduction, this chapter focuses on comparing outcomes during the global financial crisis (that is, 2009) with the previous decade or so. In addition, the chapter focuses on the main labour legislation, the Manpower Law and minimum wages, in terms of their impact on outcomes in the labour market.

The remainder of the chapter is structured as follows. Section 5.2 reviews the broad macroeconomic developments over 1996–2009, while section 5.3 examines labour market trends in more detail. Turning to the micro-econometric results, section 5.4 focuses on the trends and determinants of employment status, notably casual employment, over the last decade or so to highlight longer-term issues and the impact of both the East Asian financial crisis of 1997–1998 and the global financial crisis of 2007–2009. Section 5.5 reviews in more detail the nature of labour market policies and institutions, with specific focus on the Manpower Law 13/2003. Finally, section 5.6 concludes.

5.2 Reviewing over a decade of growth, crisis and recovery in Indonesia

Prior to the East Asian financial crisis of 1997–1998, Indonesia belonged to the group of 'tiger' economies in the region that had grown rapidly and made major inroads into tackling poverty over the previous decades. The Indonesian economy grew by 6 per cent on average from 1976 to 1986, before accelerating to 6.9 per cent over the following decade (1987–1996). This period of strong growth resulted in an impressive fall in the headcount poverty ratio (based on the US$1/day poverty line), from 40 to 11 per cent between 1976 and 1996 (Dhanani and Islam 2001). This remarkable achievement was propelled by gradual trade liberalization and a policy orientation towards manufacturing and exports.

This success story was interrupted by the crisis of 1997–1998, which began in Thailand in July 1997 and led to an unexpectedly severe downturn in Indonesia. The economy contracted by over 13 per cent in 1998, by 14 per cent in per capita terms (Figure 5.1). Following an emergency loan from the International Monetary Fund (IMF), the Government of Indonesia reined in government spending – though the crisis was largely driven by unsustainable external lending to the private sector – and let the rupiah (Rp.) float. Consequently, the rupiah fell from Rp. 2450/US$ in June 1997 to Rp. 14,900/US$ a year later, while interest rates were ratcheted up to defend the currency (from 19 per cent in June 1997 to 36 per cent in September 1998). In addition, external capital flows swiftly reversed, leaving businesses facing a severe credit crunch. Government debt rose from negligible levels prior to the crisis to US$72 billion (Dhanani et al. 2009; Islam and Chowdhury 2009). The crisis also triggered a political crisis, which resulted in the end of the 33-year Soeharto era.

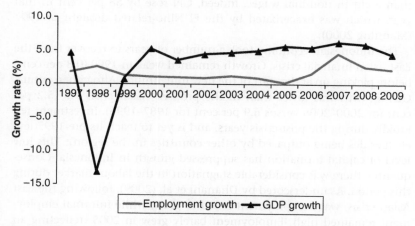

Figure 5.1 Trends in GDP and employment growth rates in Indonesia, 1997–2009

Notes: Authors' calculations from Sakernas, 1996–2009; IMF World Economic Outlook database, April 2010.

Source: For the employment growth rate, 2005 refers to the November round. 2006–2009 refers to the August rounds.

During this period of economic turmoil, the Indonesian labour market appeared to be remarkably resilient at the aggregate level. In spite of the magnitude of the shock witnessed during the East Asian crisis, total employment in Indonesia continued to grow by 2.7 per cent in 1998 (Figure 5.1). As a result, the employment–population ratio remained relatively static over this crisis period, rising in fact very slightly from 63.2 in 1997 to 63.3 per cent in 1998. At the same time, the unemployment rate (excluding discouraged workers) increased from only 3.1 per cent in 1997 to 3.7 per cent in 1998, before reaching 4.3 per cent in the following year.

However, beyond this aggregate view of the labour market, the downturn in 1997–1998 translated into considerable transitions in the labour market. In this respect, the literature on this painful period of Indonesian history stresses that, following the fall in male wage employment, there was an increase in agricultural employment and unpaid family work, particularly among women (Dhanani et al. 2009; Fallon and Lucas 2002; Islam and Chowdhury 2009; Manning 2000). Furthermore, the most deleterious outcome of the East Asian financial crisis was, in fact, a severe deterioration in real wages. In 1998, real wages in Indonesia fell by a massive 44 per cent (Fallon and Lucas 2002). This was due, however, to a surge in consumer price inflation rather than a cut in nominal wages. Indeed, CPI rose by 58 per cent in that year, which was exacerbated by the El Niño-related drought of 1997 (Manning 2000).

The Indonesian economy took a number of years to recover from the East Asian financial crisis. Growth remained weak in 1999 (0.8 per cent) before picking up at the start of the new millennium. Altogether, annual GDP growth was lower than in the pre-East Asian crisis era (5.2 per cent for 2000–2008 versus 6.9 per cent for 1987–1996). Investment fell rapidly during the post-crisis years, and is yet to reach its pre-1997 levels (besides being outpaced by other countries in the region). This low level of capital formation has suppressed growth in Indonesia. Consequently, there was considerable stagnation in the labour market during this period. As underscored by Dhanani et al. (2009), following the East Asian crisis, wage employment failed to grow, while informal employment remained high. Employment barely grew in 2005 (reflecting an employment elasticity of growth of close to zero [0.04 per cent]). Overall, the structural transformation that had taken place in the 1980s and the first half of the 1990s stalled: the share of employment in manufacturing fell from 12.9 per cent in 1997 to 12.4 per cent in 2007, while the share in agriculture remained at 41.2 per cent over this period. This was partly due to a fall in the export share of labour-intensive manufactured goods (electrical machinery and textiles, garments, footwear and leather products). The World Bank (2010) argues that the period of jobless growth following the crisis of 1997 was actually due to a fall in the employment elasticity of the service sector (over the period 1999–2003). Finally, in 2007, the level of real wages was no higher than in 1997 (Dhanani et al. 2009; Islam and Chowdhury 2009).

Benefiting from the global boom, growth in Indonesia started picking up after 2005, reaching 6.4 per cent in 2007 – the highest figure for over a decade. Investment reached 27.8 per cent of GDP in 2008.[2] Consequently, total employment grew by 4.7 per cent from 2006 to 2007 (Figure 5.1), which was largely due to growth in the wholesale and retail trade, agriculture and the public sector. These three sectors accounted for 1.4, 1.1, and 0.7 percentage points of the total employment growth, respectively. In comparison, the manufacturing and construction sectors accounted for only 0.5 and 0.6 points.

Interrupting this more positive trend, the global financial crisis sent shockwaves around the world in 2008 as advanced economies slid into deep recession. Like most developing countries, the impact of this most recent crisis in Indonesia was transmitted through the trade channel (Patunru and von Luebke 2010; Patunru and Zetha 2010). Indeed, as a consequence of the fall in global demand, Indonesian exports collapsed by almost 10 per cent from 2008 to 2009 (in constant 2000 US$ terms). Imports fell by an even greater 15 per cent over the same period; this was driven partly by the high import content of Indonesian exports (Patunru and von Luebke 2010). Due to strong demand for commodities, the recovery in trade in 2010 and 2011 was swift with exports growing by over 14 per cent per annum.[3]

Despite the relatively large trade shock emanating from the global financial crisis, the Indonesian labour market came out looking relatively unscathed, despite early fears that the economy would be hard hit by the worldwide downturn.[4] A number of reasons have been proposed as an explanation for this resilience, including the large domestic market and the relatively small share of exports in GDP (at around 30 per cent). In addition, the Indonesian economy was in a strong position as reflected by a budget surplus and low level of government debt (and hence fiscal space), current account surplus, large foreign currency reserves and low inflation (Patunru and Zetha 2010).

As a consequence of these good 'initial conditions', Indonesia was able to react to the downturn of 2008 and 2009 with a fiscal stimulus package and loosening of monetary policy, in stark contrast to the

East Asian financial crisis. On the fiscal side, the government focused efforts on tax cuts for individuals and businesses, which amounted to Rp. 43 trillion or 58.7 per cent of the total package (ILO 2009b; Patunru and Zetha 2010). According to official figures, the 2009 stimulus helped create over 1.07 million jobs (ILO 2009b). Nonetheless, though the stimulus package clearly played an important role in supporting the Indonesian economy, it is difficult to claim that it was the main reason behind this fortuitous outcome. As suggested by Patunru and Zetha (2010), it was the nature of Indonesia's trade structure, in particular the low share of exports to GDP, that helped to protect the country from a more severe downturn, as witnessed in other more open Southeast Asian economies such as Malaysia and Singapore. Due to the shallow impact of the global financial crisis, the Indonesian economy recovered strongly late in 2009. Growth continued to strengthen in 2010, moving from 5.7 per cent in the first quarter to 6.2 per cent in the second quarter.[5] The growth rate hit 6.5 per cent (year-on-year) in the first quarter of 2011.[6]

Therefore, by all accounts, this aggregate macroeconomic picture suggests a turnaround from the disastrous outcome of the 1997–1998 crisis, reflecting in part the improved capacity of the Indonesian economy to cope with a large external shock. However, the question remains as to whether the impact of the most recent crisis of 2008–2009 on the labour market is more subtle, as witnessed during the East Asian crisis, especially in regard to changes in employment status. Furthermore, the growth experience of the last decade, which was characterized by the stagnation of the manufacturing sector, may have set off longer-term labour market trends. These issues are the focus of the remainder of the chapter, which reviews aggregate trends and presents findings from a micro-econometric analysis of the determinants of labour supply and employment status.

5.3   The Indonesian labour market 1996–2009: what do the aggregates tell us?

Moving to the labour market, Figure 5.2 shows the gradual increase in the unemployment rate after the East Asian crisis, which reached a peak in 2005 (11.2 per cent). However, due to changes in the national labour force survey (Badan Pusat Statistik's Sakernas), it should be noted that data before and after 2001 are not strictly comparable.[7] The unemployment rate subsequently fell from the 2005 highpoint, even during the global financial crisis, reaching 7.9 per cent in 2009 (before falling

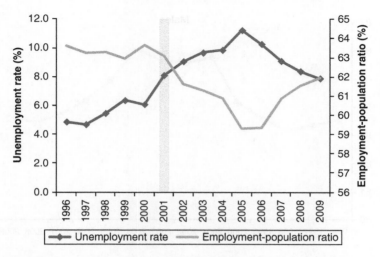

Figure 5.2 Unemployment rate and employment–population ratio, 1996–2009
Notes: For the unemployment rate, the series before and after 2001 are not comparable (indicated by the vertical grey bar).
Source: Authors' calculations from Sakernas, 1996–2009. 2005 refers to the November round. 2006–2009 refer to the August rounds.

further in 2010 to 7.1 per cent). The movement in the employment–population ratio mirrors the trends in unemployment: the ratio fell from 2000, arriving at a low of 59.3 per cent in 2005, before improving over the recent years (surpassing 62 per cent in 2009).

As illustrated in Figure 5.3, the rise in the female labour force participation rate in 1998 captures the much discussed added-worker effect evident during the East Asian financial crisis (see, for example, Manning (2000)). Figure 5.3 also suggests that much of the trend in unemployment since 2001 was driven by flows into and out of unemployment, since labour force participation rates for men were declining from 2004 and that of women had been declining since 2001. Interestingly, while the male labour force participation rate continued to decline up to 2008, there was a rise in the supply of labour by women during 2007 and 2008. This relationship is examined in more detail in the next section.

Though unemployment is a serious challenge for the Indonesian government, it is arguably less of a problem than poor conditions of work and low productivity of employment, particularly in the informal sector. For this reason, it is important to analyse trends in employment across sectors and by status.

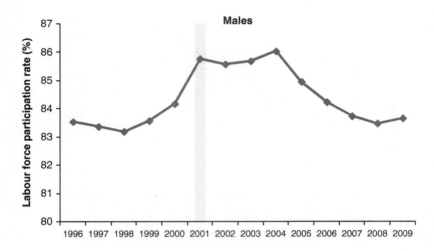

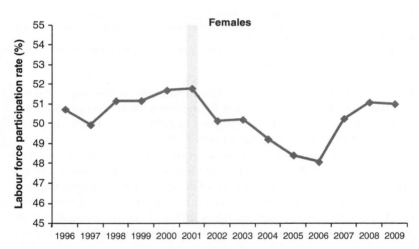

Figure 5.3 Labour force participation rates by gender, 1996–2009

Notes: Due to a change in the definition of the unemployed, the figures before and after 2001 are strictly not comparable (indicated by the vertical grey bar). Also, the figure may be capturing changes in sampling errors over time. For example, the unweighted sample size of the labour force is notably small in 2001, and notably bigger between 2007 and 2009 due to the district-level representation of the data.

Source: Authors' calculations from Sakernas 1996–2009. August rounds for 2006 to 2009.

Firstly, the East Asian crisis negatively affected employment across a wide range of industries for both men and women, especially mining, manufacturing, electricity, gas and water, construction, trade, finance, and public and social/private services sectors. In the 2000s, employment recovered in most sectors (in terms of absolute numbers), except manufacturing. Indeed, between 2001 and 2009, manufacturing wage employment fell by 0.2 per cent per annum for men, while it increased by 0.1 per cent per annum for women. At the same time, the share of casual employment in total employment more than doubled in manufacturing, utilities and construction for men and in manufacturing and construction sectors for women.

Though it is important to review trends in informality and informal employment, changes in definitions in the labour force survey (Sakernas) does not allow a comparison with the 1990s and the 2000s. Data from the past decade, however, show that informal employment increased during the mid-2000s before decreasing: informal employment as a share of total employment stood at 61.5 per cent in 2001, while it reached 64.7 per cent in 2003 (Figure 5.4). By 2009, the share had fallen to 61.6 per cent. This decline was mostly driven by a fall

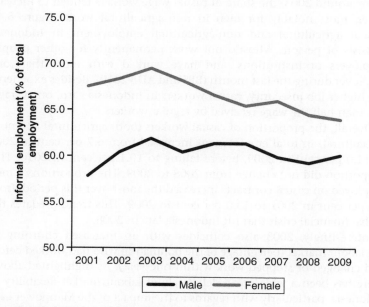

Figure 5.4 Informal employment over the past decade
Source: BPS Sakernas, authors' calculations.

in female informal employment, which dropped from 69.5 per cent in 2003 to 64.0 per cent in 2009 (though the female share remains higher than for males, which was 60.1 per cent in 2009).[8]

Looking in more detail at employment status over the peried 1996–2009, there have been some pronounced changes for both Indonesian men and women (Figure 5.5). Firstly, as noted by many studies, a fall in the share of wage employment is evident for Indonesian males during the East Asian financial crisis, which was accompanied by an increase in own-account employment that continued until 1999.[9] In comparison, there was only a moderate change to female wage employment in the late 1990s, accompanied by an increase in the share of unpaid work in 1998. The share of wage employment for both men and women began to increase around 2003 as the Indonesian economy started growing more strongly (the shares increased by approximately five percentage points between 2003 and 2009). For men, this was accompanied by a declining share of employers, while for women it was associated with a lower proportion of unpaid family workers.

It is important to note that, while wage employment has increased since around 2003, the share of casual wage workers tended to increase faster, most notably for men in non-agricultural work (Figure 5.6). Casual agricultural and non-agricultural employment in Indonesia consists of persons who do not work permanently for other people, employers or institutions, and have worked with more than one employer during the last month (BPS and ADB 2010). Besides experiencing higher job insecurity, casual workers in Indonesia earn, on average, less than half the wage received by regular workers.[10]

Overall, the proportion of casual workers (both agricultural and non-agricultural) in total employment increased from 6.7 per cent in 2001 to 11.0 per cent in 2009, before falling to 10.1 per cent in 2010. This proportion did not change from 2008 to 2009. The proportion of men employed on casual contracts increased the most over this period: from 7.3 per cent in 2001 to 13.0 per cent in 2009. This trend predates the global financial crisis that hit Indonesia late in 2008.

Interestingly, 2003 also coincides with an increased churning in the labour market (percentage of the population who had worked before and changed or stopped work within one year). As highlighted above, there has been a widespread debate about labour market flexibility in Indonesia, particularly with regards to the impact of the Manpower Law, which was enacted in 2003. This law, if enforced, could bring about a substantial increase in severance pay and restrictions on temporary

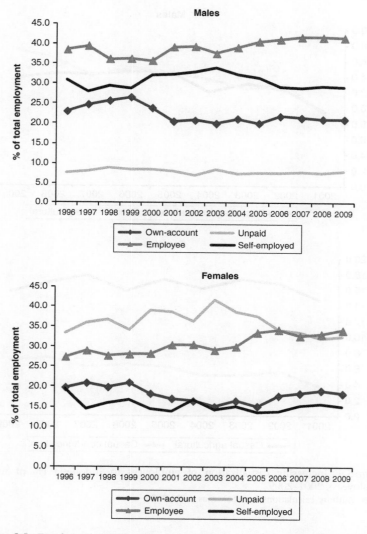

Figure 5.5 Employment status of men and women in Indonesia, 1996–2009 (% of total employment)

Notes: 2005 refers to the November around. 2006 to 2009 refer to the August rounds. Vulnerable employment corresponds to own-account and unpaid family workers; employee corresponds to wage employment; and employer refers to those with permanent or temporary paid or unpaid helpers. Since 2001, employment status was refined by additional two categories: agricultural and non-agricultural casual workers. The casual workers were counted as employees for 2001–2009.

Source: Authors' calculations from Sakernas, 1996–2009.

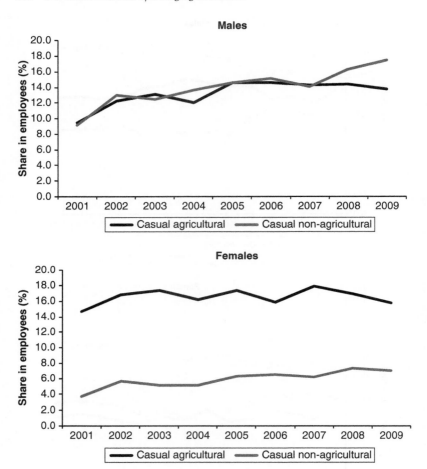

Figure 5.6 Increasing casualization of employees in Indonesia (% of total employees), 2001–2009
Source: Authors' calculations from Sakernas, 1996–2009.

employment (Manning and Roesad 2007). While it is very difficult to establish causality (many policies and pieces of legislation were changed around the same time), it could be argued that the enactment of the Manpower Law has played a role in the increase in casual employment as a consequence of the high level of severance pay afforded to permanent workers (and hence in the segmentation in the Indonesian labour market).

However, such a causal effect of the Manpower Law is far from obvious. Firstly, the data from the national labour force survey (BPS Sakernas) shows that, until 2007, regular wage job holders were more likely to have changed their jobs or stopped work during the past year than were casual job holders. Secondly, it is important to note that the increasing share of casual wage workers began between 2001 and 2002, and thus the Manpower Law on its own is unlikely to account fully for such a trend. Thirdly, as reported by the World Bank (2010), compliance with the Manpower Law is low: 66 per cent of laid-off workers received no severance pay, 27 per cent obtained less than the amount stipulated under the law, and only 7 per cent were given the full entitlement. Thus, the law is not providing de facto protection to workers. Finally, looking at employers' perceptions as reported in the IFC's Enterprise Survey reveals that, in 2003, when the Law was introduced, 26 per cent of firms identified that labour regulations were a major constraint to doing business (which was only exceeded by corruption).[11] By 2009, this proportion had fallen to only 2.5 per cent despite being in the midst of the global financial crisis with its implications for retrenchments, particularly in export-oriented firms. In anticipating the implementation of the Law, employers may have shifted their demand from regular workers to temporary employees or outsourced their work to formal or informal entities in the short run. However, given the Law's weak implementation, such a shift is unlikely to have continued in the longer run.

Based on these aggregate labour market trends, it is possible to come up with some preliminary insights. Firstly, the global financial crisis (2008–2009) did not severely impact the Indonesian economy or labour market. In comparison, the East Asian financial crisis had a much greater impact, reflected by a fall in male wage employment and a sharp contraction in real wages. The labour market outcomes witnessed over 2008–2009 seem to relate to much longer-term trends that started to appear in the early 2000s, rather than as an outcome of the global financial crisis. More specifically, between the mid-2000s and 2009, there was an increase in male wage employment, especially in terms of casual employment, and in the share of individuals who had changed work within the previous year. The unemployment rate continued to increase in the 2000s before peaking at 11.2 per cent in 2005 and then starting on a downward trajectory. Given weak enforcement, the Manpower Law of 2003 alone is unlikely to explain the trend in the labour market in the 2000s. Around the same period, other major policies were implemented, including the move to decentralization that could have affected the labour market through its impact on local public investment initiatives, changes in administrative procedures and input sourcing across districts.[12]

5.4   Further insights from the micro-data: drivers of employment status

To provide sharper contours to the impact over the longer term, this section examines how individual and household characteristics drive employment status, which, in this context, consists of four states: own-account workers (self-employed), unpaid family workers, employers and employees. The first two categories make up what the International Labour Organization (ILO) defines as vulnerable employment, and thus acts as a proxy for informal employment. The category 'employees' represents workers receiving a wage/salary and, therefore, is more aligned with the notion of formal employment (though this is confounded by the inclusion of casual workers before 2001), while the other category ('employers') is probably a mixture of the two. The last subsection checks the relevance of these four employment states by expanding the status to include casual workers for a shorter period covered by the data.

5.4.1   Determinants of employment status between 1996 and 2009: summary statistics

This analysis utilizes the micro-data from the national labour force (Sakernas) files of Statistics Indonesia (Badan Pusat Statistik). As a first step, it is useful to reflect on the sample summary statistics in order to identify key differences across employment states by individual and household characteristics. To this effect, Table 5.A2 in the Appendix presents averages for the entire period (1996 to 2009), which provides a comparison of long-term cross-sectional traits that distinguishes between male and female workers for each employment state.[13] Table 5.A1 in the Appendix provides a description of the key variables from Sakernas used in the empirical analysis.

These sample statistics indicate that the average age of male employers tends to be much higher than for other employment states, at around 44 years old, followed by own-account workers (39 years old). Similarly for women, both own-account workers and employers tend to be older than those in other employment states.

In terms of educational attainment, the best educated workers are, unsurprisingly, wage and salaried employees: 18.9 per cent of females and 12.7 per cent of males have a tertiary education compared to less than 2 per cent for the other employment categories. Conversely, own-account workers and unpaid family workers are the worst educated. In the case of males, 54.1 per cent of own-account workers have, at most, a primary level of education (54.4 per cent for unpaid family workers). A similar picture is evident for females. As expected, Indonesian men tend to be better educated than women. Looking at the trends in educational attainment confirms that both men and women in Indonesia have been getting better educated. However, the share of men without schooling or with incomplete primary education remained stubbornly high over this period at around one quarter, while it decreased for females from 37.1 per cent in 1996 to 32.0 per cent in 2009.

In general, the agricultural sector represents the largest share of working men and women (44.2 per cent and 44.9 per cent, respectively), particularly in the case of unpaid family workers and employers (for females). The next most important sector in terms of employment shares is the wholesale and retail trade, which accounts for 25.7 per cent of women and 15.7 per cent of men. Employment in both these sectors is typically informal and unprotected; 9.9 per cent of working men and 12.7 per cent of working women are employed in the manufacturing sector. Reflecting the stagnation of this sector, the share of employment in manufacturing has fallen for both sexes: from 10.4 per cent in 1996 to 7.5 per cent in 2009 for men and from 14.0 per cent in 1996 to 9.9 per cent in 2009 for women.

Turning to the area of residence, the share of urban workers increased, most notably for women (from 30 per cent in 1996 to 40 per cent by 2009). This rising share of urban workers among women was led by an increase in the share of urban own-account workers and employers. For men, the increasing urban share in total workers was dominated mainly by own-account workers, whose share increased by 16 percentage points between 1996 and 2009. As a result, while wage employment is still predominantly an urban phenomenon, own-account work has become increasingly urbanized, particularly for men.

5.4.2 Determinants of employment status from 1996 to 2009: findings from a multinomial logit model

In order to examine the importance of individual and household characteristics in explaining differences in employment status, this section briefly presents estimates for various waves over the period 1996–2009, capturing both crises and periods of recovery. The model of employment status is estimated using a multinomial logit specification. The dependent variable consists of four employment states: own-account workers, unpaid family workers, wage employees and employers. The reason for choosing these four states stems from their comparability since the 1990s. The employer category is used as the normalized outcome (i.e., $J = 3$). However, because of a rising incidence of casualization, notably in non-agricultural employment for men (see Figure 5.6), a five-state model is examined in greater detail in the next subsection.[14] The model is conditioned on age, education, marital status, sector of employment, household size excluding the individual in question, urban location and province. Due to differences in labour force participation, the model is estimated separately for women and men. To ease interpretation of the results, this section focuses on the predicted probabilities and the marginal effects of specific characteristics on the predicted probabilities of employment status.[15] A Wald test is also carried out to indicate whether the relationship between individual characteristics and employment outcomes has changed over time.[16]

Given that average predicted probabilities depend on the composition of workers' characteristics, the equality of coefficients compared to a baseline year are tested after fitting the model to examine whether the relationship between the predicted probabilities of employment status and its determinants changed. Predicted probabilities can differ over time not only because of changes in returns to the worker characteristics and exogenous shocks, but also as a result of changes in the composition of the sample. In this respect, testing the equality of coefficients can be considered as a way of analysing whether the return to workers' characteristics changed over time. The main variables examined in this section are basic educational attainment[17] and urban-rural location, which provides some insights into the evolution of the Indonesian labour market since 1996.

On the whole, the coefficients across the years are (jointly) significantly different from each other, whichever baseline year is used. Focusing on the key issue of educational attainment, Table 5.1 presents the average predicted probabilities for individuals with primary education and less. The figures for males reveal that, ceteris paribus, the likelihood of own-account work for those with, at most, a primary education increased from 1996 to 1997 before decreasing (notably in 2005). At the same time, the probability of wage employment for less educated Indonesian men increased throughout the 2000s. Though representing a very low likelihood, the probability of unpaid family work increased for men over the period. In comparison, there is less evidence of a changing

Table 5.1 Average predicted probabilities of employment status: men and women with primary education or less

Year	Male: average predicted probabilities			Female: average predicted probabilities		
	Own-account	Unpaid	Wage	Own-account	Unpaid	Wage
1996	0.3323	0.0158	0.3503	0.2552	0.3164	0.2095
1997	0.3583**	0.0257***	0.3555**	0.2824	0.3333	0.2159
1998	0.3866	0.0269	0.3108**	0.2708	0.3422*	0.2000
1999	0.3736	0.0239***	0.3118***	0.2764	0.3071	0.2149*
2002	0.2820	0.0212***	0.3932***	0.1993	0.3430	0.2640**
2005	0.2729**	0.0217**	0.4033***	0.1695	0.3986	0.2652***
2007	0.2968	0.0292***	0.3917***	0.2191	0.3438*	0.2501***
2008	0.2815	0.0283***	0.3946***	0.2130	0.3369***	0.2684***
2009	0.2814*	0.0284***	0.3974***	0.2159	0.3490***	0.2648***

Note: The dependent variable for the multinomial logit model consists of four employment states: own-account workers; unpaid family workers; employers; and employees. The predicted probabilities derived from the multinomial logit model estimates are for education dummy (= 1 with primary education or less and = 0 otherwise), holding all other variables at their means. *, **, *** indicate that the underlying coefficient on education dummy is significantly different from the 1996 coefficient at 10 per cent, 5 per cent and 1 per cent levels respectively.
Source: Authors' calculations from Sakernas, 1996–2009.

role for educational attainment in the case of women. Overall, the predicted probabilities suggest that females with primary education or less are more likely to be in wage employment, a trend that has continued through the 2000s. The likelihood of unpaid family work has increased for women over the last few years.

Thus, this empirical analysis reveals that having low education is associated with better chances of wage employment than was the case previously. This can be considered a positive labour market development, reflecting the expansion of employment opportunities for the less educated, if the type of wage employment is regular or formal in nature. Yet, as discussed above, there has also been an overall increase in the incidence of casual employment amongst wage employees in the 2000s. Whether or not the labour market increasingly offers better and more job opportunities for the less educated is further examined below.

5.4.3 What determines casual employment?

A four-state conceptualization of employment status is important for distinguishing different trends across workers over a long period of time (1996–2009). However, as highlighted above, there have been changes within the category of wage and salaried employees as a consequence of an increase in casual employment.

Moving to the results of an expanded multinomial logit model with five employment states (own-account workers, unpaid family workers, employers, employees and casual workers) amongst non-agricultural workers reveals a number of trends over the period 2001–2009 (Figure 5.7). Firstly, the probability of engaging in non-agricultural casual employment decreases significantly with the level of education.[18] Educational attainment plays a greater role in explaining the probability of casual employment for men than for women. Compared to those with incomplete primary education, attending junior secondary school decreases the probability of non-agricultural casual employment by around 4–5 percentage points for working-age men and women. Having tertiary education decreases the same probability by more than 9 percentage points, respectively, for men (and by more than 6 points for women). Most notably for men, there has been divergence in the disparities in the likelihood of casual employment: Indonesians with tertiary education are increasingly less likely to have such work compared to those with lower levels of education. For women, however, having tertiary education seems to do little to keep well-educated women away from casual employment. In contrast to their male counterparts, the marginal effects of women's senior secondary and tertiary education do not show a large difference in terms of their influence on taking up casual employment. Therefore, though attaining higher education clearly matters for ensuring that workers can find permanent employment, this effect seems to be more limited for women than for men.

In contrast to the case of casual employment, education is positively correlated with the likelihood of having regular wage employment, reflecting that better-educated Indonesians are more likely to work in more permanent and better jobs. In this respect, having tertiary education increases the probability of regular wage employment by more than 40 and 30 percentage points respectively for working-age men and women (Figure 5.8). The probability of regular employment for Indonesians with tertiary education declined after 2007 for both men and women. At the same time, while senior secondary education plays an important role in increasing the likelihood of having regular wage employment, its impact tended to decline in the late 2000s.

Looking at the probabilities of employment status by sector shows that, for Indonesian males, there is only evidence of a large increase in the likelihood of casual employment for those working in construction

167

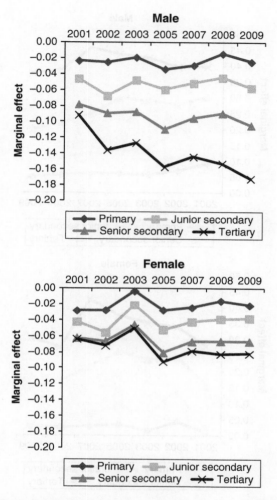

Figure 5.7 Marginal effects of education on predicted probabilities of non-agricultural casual employment by gender, selected years

Notes: The dependent variable for the multinomial logit model consists of five employment states: own-account workers; unpaid family workers; employers; regular wage employees; and casual employees. Base educational level is 'incomplete primary'.

Source: Authors' calculations from Sakernas, 2001–2009.

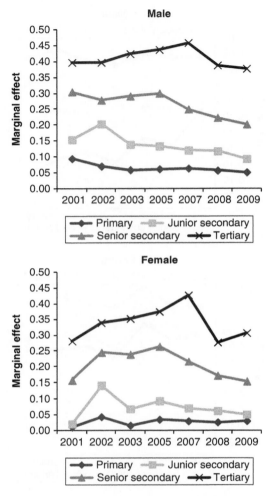

Figure 5.8 Marginal effects of education on predicted probabilities of non-agricultural regular wage employment by gender, selected years

Notes: The dependent variable for the multinomial logit model consists of five employment states: own account workers; unpaid family workers; employers; regular wage employees; and casual employees. Base educational level is 'incomplete primary'.

Source: Authors' calculations from Sakernas, 2001–2009.

(from 9.8 per cent in 2001 to 29.5 per cent in 2009). For females, the predicted probability increased from 1.9 per cent in 2001 to 8.7 per cent in 2009. Overall, the probability of casual employment has increased the most for those in the construction sector. By 2009, the marginal effect of being in the construction sector on the probability of casual employment reached 35 percentage points for men and 27 points for women.[19] In terms of the manufacturing sector, the predicted probability of being in casual employment increased for Indonesian men from 1.3 per cent in 2001 to 4.0 per cent in 2009.

With regard to non-agricultural regular wage employment, all selected industries show negative effects compared to the base industry of public, social and private services (including education and health). Compared to the base industry, being in the trade sector decreases the likelihood of regular wage employment by 37 and 46 percentage points for men and women, respectively. For manufacturing, the negative marginal effects associated with regular wage employment are 2 and 11 percentage points respectively for men and women. This suggests that the public, social and private services sector tends to be the dominant provider of wage employment, both regular and casual. Casualization of wage employment takes place unambiguously in the construction sector, while in the other sectors workers tend to resort to alternative employment states, such as unpaid contributing family work for women and own-account work for men.

5.5 Labour market policies and institutions in Indonesia: does the Manpower Law 13/2003 hinder job growth?

One of the most contentious issues debated in the context of the Indonesian labour market is the impact of labour market institutions, namely the Manpower Law 13/2003 and the high severance payments and restrictions on the use of fixed-term contracts it imposes on employers. As noted above, in 2003, when the Law was introduced, 26 per cent of firms identified labour regulations as a major constraint to doing business (which was only exceeded by corruption).[20] The World Bank's Indonesian Jobs Report stresses that the 'Manpower Law substantially increased the rigidity of Indonesia's labour regulations...which are now among the most rigid in East Asia and the world' (World Bank 2010, p. 13). However, as underlined above, the relationship between these regulations and labour market outcomes are far from obvious. For example, while the unemployment rate increased in the years immediately following the enactment of the Law, the rate subsequently has fallen (despite the effects of the global financial crisis) even though the regulations have remained the same.

The remainder of this chapter focuses on the Manpower Law in more detail and how these regulations compare with those in other emerging economies and countries in the same region. Labour market policies are less utilized in Indonesia than in other middle-income countries such as South Africa – for this reason, this section concentrates more on regulations, but some space is devoted to the nature of public works programmes and training schemes. Ultimately, the lack of labour market schemes along with insufficient coverage of social protection systems is a major gap in the policy environment in Indonesia.

5.5.1   Labour market regulation in Indonesia: the Manpower Law 13/2003

Following the demise of the Soeharto regime, a range of labour legislation was enacted to improve protection of workers: the Trade Union Law (21/2001), the Manpower Law (13/2003), the Industrial Disputes Law (4/2004), the Migrant Worker Law (39/2004) and the Social Security Law (40/2004) (Manning and Rosead 2007). The Manpower Law in particular has received considerable attention because of the costs it imposes on employers and the subsequent association of the legislation with deteriorating labour market outcomes during 2003–2005. The Manpower Law (13/2003) is a wide-reaching piece of legislation that includes clauses on severance pay, restrictions on the use of fixed-term contracts and sub-contracting, minimum wages, working hours and female and child labour. The first three sets of clauses are the most controversial elements of the legislation.

Prior to the enactment of the Manpower Law, severance pay in Indonesia was low by international standards: the average severance pay was two months' wages in 1996 (World Bank 2010). With the introduction of the legislation in 2003, severance pay owing to workers has increased considerably for those with three or more years of service. Moreover, the applicability of the law to workers has become more complicated with varying rates of severance pay (along with different eligibility for long-service pay) depending on the type of separation/dismissal. As outlined in the Law (and summarized in Manning and Roesad 2007 and World Bank 2010), the regulation of severance pay and long-service leave depends on the reason for dismissal or separation. In particular, the number of months of severance pay owed to workers dismissed for economic reasons is doubled in the case of

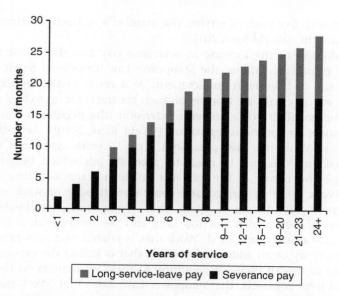

Figure 5.9 Severance and long-service-leave pay according to years of service – for dismissals due to economic reasons (Manpower Law 13/2003)
Sources: ILO NATLEX database available at: www.ilo.org/dyn/natlex/natlex_browse.home?p_lang=en; Manning and Roesad (2007).

firms that remain in operation (in comparison to the basic rate that is paid, for example, to workers dismissed as a result of the closure of the firm).

Figure 5.9 summarizes how severance pay and long-service pay varies for workers dismissed for economic causes. Severance pay in this case reaches a maximum of 18 months' pay for workers with service of 8 years of more, while the long-service leave component continues to increase (to a maximum of 10 months for service of 24 years or more). The total package owed to dismissed workers, therefore, reaches 28 months' pay for those with service of 24 years or more, up from around 20 months according to the 1996 law. However, it should be noted that the absolute change in severance pay rates resulting from the enactment of the Manpower Law (13/2003) is the greatest for workers with long periods of service. For example, for workers with 10 years of tenure, pay owing increased from around 12 months' wages according to the 1996 law to 22 months' under the Manpower law. For workers with 20 years of tenure, the rate increased from 15 to 25 months. In comparison, for workers with five years of service, the increase was much less (from 12 to 14 months) (World Bank 2010).

In addition to the increase in severance pay and the added complexity of pay regulations, the Manpower Law introduced restrictions to the use of fixed-term employment. As a result of the legislation, employers may only use workers on such contracts for up to two years with the possibility of a one-year extension (the maximum was five years under the previous legislation [World Bank 2010]). As outlined in Article 59 of the Law, paragraph (1):[21] 'A work agreement for a specified time can only be made for a certain job, which, because of the type and nature of the job, will finish in a specified time, that is: a. Work to be performed and completed at once or work which is temporary in nature; b. Work whose completion is estimated at a period of time which not too long and no longer than 3 (three) years; c. Seasonal work; or d. Work that is related to a new product, a new activity or an additional product that is still in the experimental stage or try-out phase.' In addition to these restrictions on the use of fixed-term contracts, the Manpower Law states that 'Work may be subcontracted as mentioned under subsection (1) must meet the following requirements: a. The work can be done separately from the main activity;...c. The work is an entirely auxiliary activity of the enterprise...' (Article 65). Thus, sub-contracting is allowed only for non-core activities.

As argued in the literature on the Manpower Law, the introduction of this legislation has considerably increased the 'rigidity' of labour market regulations in Indonesia, which now exceeds that of most countries in the region (see Manning and Roesad 2007; World Bank 2010). As highlighted in Chapter 3, according to the OECD EPL Index, Indonesia receives a high score, notably for the regulation of permanent workers (the highest score in the sample of OECD and non-OECD countries), which, in turn, is driven by high severance pay. The OECD scoring on this dimension of employment protection ranges from 1.49 in Brazil and 1.91 in South Africa (the least restrictive in this sub-sample of emerging economies) to 3.65 in India and 4.29 in Indonesia.

However, these rigidities are based on a de jure interpretation of the legislation. In practice, as stressed above, Indonesian employers appear to easily avoid the sanctioned severance pay rates. As reported by the World Bank (2010), compliance with the Manpower Law is low: 66 per cent of laid-off workers received no severance pay, 27 per cent obtained less than the amount stipulated under the law, and only 7 per cent were given the full entitlement. In terms of the fixed-term regulations, drawing on data from the Indonesian Family Life Survey (2007), the World Bank (2010) show that 15 per cent of workers on fixed-term contracts have been working for the same employer for more than three years, and hence, are not compliant with the Manpower Law clause on the limit for such contracts.

Thus, the law does not provide de facto protection to workers, which indeed is a stronger argument for the need to carry out reform of the legislation than criticisms of its costs or rigidities.

As highlighted in Chapter 3, minimum wages present another controversial issue; they have been widely blamed for many poor outcomes in labour markets and Indonesia is no exception. As highlighted above, during the East Asian financial crisis, real wages in Indonesia fell by a massive 44 per cent, which was propelled by the depreciation of the rupiah and high inflation (Fallon and Lucas 2002). Following the end of the Soeharto regime, democratic reforms strengthened the bargaining power of trade unions. In response to the demands of unions, the government increased real minimum wages, which grew, on average, by 9.6 per cent from 1999 to 2003 (Manning and Roesad 2007; World Bank 2010). This growth in minimum wages varied across provinces (in 2000, minimum-wage setting was decentralized to the provincial level): for example, the total growth rate was 65.2 per cent from 2000 to 2003 in Jakarta, while it reached 90.8 per cent in Bandung.

According to Saget (2008), the ratio of the monthly minimum wage to GDP per capita per month stood at 0.66 (2002/2004) compared to 0.13 in Malaysia, 0.55 in China, 0.74 in Vietnam and 0.90 in the Philippines. As discussed in Chapter 3 of this book, the ratio of minimum wages to average wages (also known as the Kaitz Index) in Indonesia reached over 60 per cent in 2008, which exceeds the ratio in all other emerging economies covered in this book apart from Argentina. According to Damanyanti (2011), there has been an increasing trend in the Kaitz Index and the ratio has exceeded 60 per cent (relative to the average wage) since 2005.

The Manpower Law 13/2003 sought to provide a comprehensive approach to minimum-wage setting, which had been decentralized in Indonesia. Since the enactment of the Law, minimum wages in Indonesia are set at the provincial and district level on an annual basis, based on recommendations by wages councils and local administrations (minimum wages can also be set at the sectoral level) (Article 89 of the Manpower Law 13/2003). These wage councils base their decisions on what is known as the 'decent living standard' or Kebutuhan Hidup Layak (KHL). The majority of provinces, however, set minimum wages below the KHL (ratio of the minimum wage to the KHL was around 85 per cent in 2009) (Damanyanti 2010). Prior to the enactment of the Manpower Law, minimum wages were set through ministerial decrees. Thus, as argued by Manning and Roesad (2007), the reforms of 2003 provided greater flexibility in the minimum-wage setting process (in terms of aligning the minimum wage with local labour market conditions). Moreover, the 2003 legislation allows firms that are unable to pay the minimum wage to postpone payment (that is, pay lower wages) (Article 90 of the Manpower Law 13/2003). It should be noted that minimum wages have grown more slowly (less than real wages) since the Manpower Law was enacted (World Bank 2010).

As is evident in the literature on labour market regulations in general, empirical studies on the impact of the minimum wage on outcomes in the Indonesian labour market come up with mixed findings. Earlier studies such as Islam and Nazara (2000) find little evidence to support the hypothesis that minimum wages had negatively affected the formal sector. More recent papers, however, hint at some stronger findings. According to results presented in Comola and de Mello (2011), the increase in the real minimum wage over this period is associated with a net increase in employment, which is due largely to a rise in informal sector employment. The World Bank (2010) concludes that, while the minimum wage increases are not correlated with aggregate employment or unemployment rates, they are linked to informality rates and the (temporary) shift of workers out of industrial employment (especially for skilled workers) and into agricultural employment (particularly for women). The findings of this study suggest that these effects of the minimum wage increases are stronger over the short term (in the year following) and are no longer statistically significant after two years following the increase.

It is crucial to look beyond the pernicious effects of labour market regulations such as minimum wages: after all, their objective is to protect workers; in this case, protect the wages of workers at the lower end of the distribution. In this respect, the results of Chun and Khor (2010) suggest that the minimum wage legislation has helped reduce wage inequality in Indonesia.

Like the provisions of the Law covering severance pay rates and fixed-term restrictions, non-compliance is a major issue for the coverage of the minimum wage in Indonesia. According to World Bank estimates based on Sakernas data, 40 per cent of workers were receiving wages below the minimum wage in 2007 (World Bank 2010). Non-compliance is the highest in the case of poor workers: almost 55 per cent of wage employees in the bottom quintile report receiving less than the minimum wage (World Bank 2010).

The issue of non-compliance goes to the crux of the issue: despite the strict protection provided by the legislation, few workers are afforded the protection that has been legislated for. The World Bank (2010) argues that the Law has resulted in an increase in rigidity in the Indonesian labour market (see above quote), but the 'predominance of non-compliance potentially explains why increases in severance pay have not led to increased job rigidity'. Ultimately, the argument is not that this piece of legislation does not influence hiring and firing decisions of Indonesian employers; clearly, enterprises have either internalized the costs or adopted methods to evade the legislated benefits for workers (through the use of casual labour, for example). This is borne out by the figures on perceptions from 2009 highlighted above. As a result, the debate needs to shift to asking the following question: are Indonesian workers receiving adequate and effective income and employment protection? Is the burden of protection being adequately shared between employers, workers and government?

5.5.2 Labour market policies in Indonesia

Compared to other countries considered in this book such as South Africa, the use of labour market policies in Indonesia remains rather limited. That said, one key institution is the Balai Latihan Kerja (BLKs) or public vocational training centre. There are 162 BLKs across the country and are mainly funded through government budgetary allocations. By 2007, most of the BLKs had shifted to the responsibility of regional/local governments. As outlined in Di Gropello et al. (2011), these training centres offer four types of training: 1) institutional training, which focuses on increasing skills of job-seekers; 2) non-institutional training, which reaches out to people in remote areas through mobile training units; 3) apprenticeship programmes; and 4) demand-based training, which is adapted to the needs of industry. In 2003–4, 34,759 trainees went through regional/local BLKs, while an additional 7,873 trainees undertook courses offered by the BLKs run by the Ministry of Manpower and Transmigration (MoMT). Participants receive a certificate upon completing the course.

In the stimulus package announced in 2009, there was some provision for increased training offered to laid-off workers through the BLKs. As reported in the ILO's country report to the G20 meeting of ministers of labour in Washington, DC in 2010, the Indonesian Ministry of Manpower and Transmigration allocated the additional training funds among regions using three criteria: 1) severity of unemployment; 2) the number of laid-off workers; and 3) and the capacity of BLKs. Each region then allocated the extra funding to BLKs. These extra resources resulted in nearly 3,000 additional courses being offered and about 50,000 job-seekers received training across the country (ILO 2010). In addition to these training programmes, the package aimed to create jobs through investment in infrastructure. In this regard, the Ministry of Economic Affairs estimates that investment in public works created around 950,000 jobs at a cost of 6,601 billion rupiah.

5.6   Concluding remarks

As one of the star performers of the Asia region, Indonesia had grown rapidly during the 1980s and 1990s, resulting in a significant fall in poverty. However, when the East Asian financial crisis hit in 1997–1998, the country suffered a major blow to this economic and social progress. This earlier crisis did not result in a large fall in employment and a commensurate rise in unemployment; rather, the economic contraction was accompanied by considerable transitions within employment, namely, from formal sector to informal and agricultural employment, particularly among women. The years following the East Asian crisis were characterized by slow growth, stagnant investment, inadequate economic diversification and weak formal job creation, which have often been attributed to such factors as rigid labour regulations, especially the enactment of the Manpower Law in 2003. The economic and labour market situation in Indonesia only began to consistently improve over the following five years, notably during the boom years leading up to the global financial crisis. During this period, unemployment fell from its 2005 peak and employment increased. When the global financial crisis spread in late 2008 to emerging economies such as Indonesia, it was expected that these countries would be severely affected. However, in contrast to previous crisis episodes, Indonesia proved to be rather resilient despite the fact that exports collapsed by almost 18 per cent from 2008 to 2009. Thus, for Indonesia, the most recent crisis turned out to be a short-lived temporary shock to export-oriented sectors.

The results presented in this chapter both confirm the findings of previous studies and show that much of the recent developments in the Indonesian labour market seem to have been part of a longer-term trend since the mid-2000s, particularly regarding the increasing casualization of the workforce. There appear to be more changes by employment type than across sectors, as the sectoral shares of employment for both men and women remained remarkably steady for more than a decade. The findings of the chapter also point towards the underlying changes in the relationship between educational attainment and employment status in the late 2000s. More specifically, the lack of education is clearly associated with worse outcomes in the labour market, especially in terms of likelihood of casual employment, and for this reason, much more needs to be done to improve enrolments in secondary education and above. Amongst the selected industries examined, casualization takes place unambiguously in the construction sector, while the public, social and private services sectors remain dominant providers of both regular and casual wage employment. In response to the increased casualization of the labour market, efforts are needed to promote formalization and the creation of regular jobs which, in turn, require both the right pull factors (strong economic growth, the right sectoral composition of growth) and push factors (increasing incentives for formalization and regularization of employment). In this process, the trade unions play an important role in ensuring that workers' rights are not curtailed, particularly in sectors where casualization is prevalent, such as construction.

Despite the apparent resilience of Indonesia to the impact of the global financial crisis, the country, therefore, continues to face a number of substantial challenges at the macroeconomic, sectoral and labour market levels. In particular, the Indonesian economy has failed in recent years to generate sufficient regular formal sector jobs, notably in the manufacturing sector. While there are some arguments that the introduction of new labour market regulations in 2003 (the Manpower Law) has deterred further investment from taking place and prevented creation of jobs in the formal sector, this chapter argues that it is unlikely to be the main driver of observed trends in the data. While overly protective labour market regulation can potentially deter employers from hiring, there is no obvious indication that labour market rigidities are the main concern for employers. This may be due to the low level of compliance with the regulations, as well as the existence of more serious deterrents to investment.

Overall, it is difficult to empirically isolate the impact of changes in labour market regulations vis-à-vis other important institutional and regulatory changes that took place in the 2000s; and a nuanced and careful analysis is necessary before embarking on further policy reforms. It has to be remembered that much of the change that took place in the labour market during the 2000s apparently occurred with very little cross-sectoral redistribution of workers and economic activities. In this respect, the stagnant levels of investment and lack of diversification over the economy of the last decade are likely to be more influenced by supply-side factors such as insufficient infrastructure, high transport and logistics costs, excessive costs of capital, inadequate education and training, and weak governance. Nonetheless, the fact that the few workers are afforded protection under the legislation indicates an opportunity to look at changing the law to improve legal effectiveness, while improving implementation through increased awareness of the laws and strong labour inspection (see, for example, the proposals of Lee and McCann 2008).

Ultimately, the Indonesian government should aim to develop more effective labour market regulations that increase coverage and protection for workers and an unemployment benefit system that provides adequate income to dismissed workers. Thus, a broader approach to social protection than that which currently exists would ensure that the burden of unemployment and underemployment is shared between the government and social partners. This, in turn, requires effective social dialogue in order to reach an agreement that is sustainable, equitable and, most importantly, politically viable. These institutions should be accompanied by effective labour market policies, particularly a permanent public works programme and training schemes, that can help further cushion economic and other shocks.

Appendix

All data used in this chapter is sourced from Statistics Indonesia's (Badan Pusat Statistik) national labour force survey (Sakernas) for the period 1996–2009.

Table 5.A1   Description of key variables

Variable	Description
Employment status	Employment status consists of four states: Own-account workers Unpaid family workers Employees Employers This categorization is refined further to include two separate states for employees: wage and salaried employees and casual employees

Educational attainment	Educational attainment is defined as follows: No education or incomplete primary Primary school Junior high school (general and vocational) Senior high school (general and vocational) Tertiary (diploma or university degree)
Sector	Employment status is classified across nine sectors: Agriculture, forestry, hunting and fishery Mining and quarrying Manufacturing industry Electricity, gas and water Construction Wholesale trade, retail trade, restaurants and hotels Transport, storage and communication Financing, insurance, real estate and business services Public administration (community, social, and personal services)
Province	Geographical location is classified by urban/rural and provincial dimensions. Province is defined as:

Nanggroe Aceh Darussalam	Nusa Tenggara Barat
Sumatera Utara	Nusa Tenggara Timur
Sumatera Barat	Kalimantan Barat
Riau	Kalimantan Tengah
Jambi	Kalimantan Selatan
Sumatera Selatan	Kalimantan Timur
Bengkulu	Sulawesi Utara
Lampung	Sulawesi Tengah
Kepulauan Bangka Belitung	Sulawesi Selatan
Kepulauan Riau	Sulawesi Tenggara
DKI Jakarta	Gorontalo
Bogor	Sulawesi Barat
Jawa Tengah	Maluku
DI Yogyakarta	Maluku Utara
Jawa Timur	Papua Barat
Banten	Papua
Bali	

Source: Sakernas, authors' compilation.

Table 5.A2 Summary statistics of individual and household characteristics driving employment status by gender, average 1996–2009

Variable	Employment status (average)				
	Own-account	Unpaid	Employee	Employers	Total
Female					
Age (years)	41.9	37.3	33.1	42.9	37.7
Educational attainment					
No school/incomplete primary (%)	35.1	33.3	17.2	36.7	29.3
Primary school (%)	37.4	44.2	26.1	39.0	36.7
Junior high school (%)	15.2	14.7	14.9	13.7	14.7
Senior high school (%)	10.7	7.1	25.6	9.0	13.6
Tertiary (%)	1.6	0.7	16.2	1.7	5.8
Marital status					
Single (%)	8.0	13.5	33.5	6.2	17.5
Married (%)	66.7	82.7	54.7	67.7	69.1
Divorced/widowed (%)	25.2	3.8	11.8	26.0	13.5
Household size (persons)	4.0	4.4	4.5	4.2	4.3
Rural (%)	55.1	82.8	40.1	71.2	63.1
Sector					
Agriculture (%)	17.0	73.4	21.3	48.2	43.6
Mining (%)	0.5	0.4	0.4	0.2	0.4
Manufacturing (%)	12.5	7.5	26.2	9.8	14.5
Electricity, gas and water (%)	0.01	0.004	0.1	0.01	0.05
Construction (%)	0.2	0.1	1.0	0.2	0.4
Wholesale and retail trade (%)	58.2	17.5	11.5	38.6	26.2
Transport, storage and communication (%)	1.0	0.2	1.2	0.5	0.7
Financial interests, real estate (%)	0.3	0.05	2.5	0.3	0.9
Public administration (%)	10.3	0.9	35.7	2.3	13.4
Male					
Age (years)	39.2	25.3	35.4	44.6	38.2
Educational attainment					
No school/incomplete primary (%)	20.7	14.5	11.2	29.2	19.1
Primary school (%)	40.8	40.1	29.0	42.9	36.8
Junior high school (%)	21.2	28.8	19.7	15.3	19.4
Senior high school (%)	15.4	15.4	29.0	10.8	19.3
Tertiary (%)	1.8	1.3	11.1	1.8	5.4
Marital status					
Single (%)	13.4	73.9	24.7	5.3	20.3

Married (%)	82.7	23.2	73.4	92.0	77.0
Divorced/widowed (%)	3.9	3.0	1.9	2.7	2.7
Household size (persons)	4.3	5.1	4.5	4.3	4.5
Rural (%)	57.3	82.3	44.2	78.3	60.8
Sector					
Agriculture (%)	32.5	76.7	19.0	71.2	42.8
Mining (%)	1.2	0.6	1.8	0.6	1.2
Manufacturing (%)	4.6	6.3	20.3	6.5	11.4
Electricity, gas and water (%)	0.1	0.01	0.6	0.1	0.3
Construction (%)	2.8	0.8	14.9	2.0	7.1
Wholesale and retail trade (%)	30.2	13.2	9.4	15.1	16.0
Transport, storage and communication (%)	20.5	0.7	7.2	2.4	8.1
Financial interests, real estate (%)	0.4	0.1	2.9	0.2	1.3
Public administration (%)	7.7	1.7	23.9	2.0	11.8

Source: BPS Sakernas, authors' calculations.

Notes

1. See, for example, OECD (2008).
2. World Development Indicators online database, at: data.worldbank.org/data-catalog/world-development-indicators
3. World Development Indicators online database.
4. See, for example, ODI (2009) for a discussion on the expectation of a further deterioration in 2009.
5. See dds.bps.go.id/eng/brs_file/eng-pdb-10mei10.pdf
6. See Statistics Indonesia (BPS), http://dds.bps.go.id/eng/
7. In 2001, the definition of unemployment was broadened to include discouraged workers and future starts, which were previously considered inactive. This change in definition resulted in higher unemployment rates after 2001. Suryadarma et al. (2005) attempt to construct almost-comparable unemployment rates between 1994 and 2003 by excluding the discouraged.
8. Authors' calculations based on BPS Sakernas data.
9. Since the Sakernas questionnaire changed its methodology in 2001, it is not possible to calculate a consistent series for formal and informal employment between 1996 and 2009. In general, wage employees are mostly formal workers, while own-account is mostly informal, and unpaid work is entirely informal. The employer category represents a mix of formal and informal employers. To avoid confusion, employment status is used in most of the discussions in the chapter to proxy informal work. From this perspective, a large majority of women were engaged in informal work throughout the period examined.
10. Based on data compiled by Professor Chris Manning (ANU) for the Indonesia Study Group Presentation, ANU, December 2010.
11. See www.enterprisesurveys.org.
12. See for instance Kuncoro (2004) and Bardhan (2005).

13. These averages are also compared to changes over the entire period where relevant (not presented in Table 5.A2 but are available upon request).
14. Due to data constraints, an analysis of determinants of casualization is only possible from 2001.
15. The coefficients of a multinomial logit model are not easily interpreted. Standard errors take into account the survey nature of the sample. The predicted probabilities and the marginal effects are generated from the estimated coefficients.
16. To test the equality of coefficients across the years, the model was fitted for each year. Then, seemingly unrelated estimations were conducted on the obtained estimates between the baseline year and selected years for examination (1997, 1998, 1999, 2002, 2005, 2007, 2008 and 2009) in order to test the equality of coefficients across the years. In STATA, the post-estimation command suest was used after mlogit. A number of waves of the national labour force survey (Sakernas) were used as 'baseline' years in order to help identify changes over the two crisis periods: 1996 for the East Asian financial crisis of 1997–1998 and 2007 for the global financial crisis that hit Indonesia in 2008. Moreover, 2002 and 2005 are examined to help detect changes in the relationship between individual characteristics and employment status as a result of the enactment of the Manpower Law in 2003.
17. In this section, educational attainment was simplified into a dummy which is equal to 1 for individuals with primary education or less and 0 otherwise.
18. In each year, the coefficients on educational dummies are significant at the 1% level for both men and women.
19. This is in relation to base industry of public, social and private services (including health and education).
20. See www.enterprisesurveys.org.
21. English translation available in ILO's NATLEX database available at: http://www.ilo.org/dyn/natlex/natlex_browse.home?p_lang=en

References

Asian Development Bank (ADB), International Labour Organization (ILO) and Islamic Development Bank (IDB) (2010) *Indonesia: Critical Development Constraints* (Mandaluyong City: Asian Development Bank).

Basri, M. C. and S. Rahardja (2010) 'The Indonesian Economy Amidst the Global Crisis: Good Policy and Good Luck', *ASEAN Economic Bulletin*, Vol. 27, No. 1, pp. 77–97.

Bardhan, P. (2005) *Scarcity, Conflicts, and Cooperation: Essays in the Political and Institutional Economics of Development* (Cambridge, MA: MIT Press).

Blundell, R. and T. Macurdy (1999) 'Labour Supply: A Review of Alternatives', in O. Ashenfelter and D. Card (eds), *Handbook of Labour Economics*, Volume 3 (Amsterdam: North-Holland), Chapter 27.

BPS (Badan Pusat Statistik) and ADB (Asian Development Bank) (2011) *The Informal Sector and Informal Employment in Indonesia. Country Report 2010* (Jakarta: BPS).

Chun, N. and N. Khor (2010) 'Minimum Wages and Changing Wage Inequality in Indonesia', Asian Development Bank Economics Working Paper Series, No. 196 (Manila: ADB).

Comola, M. and L. de Mello (2011) 'How Does Decentralised Minimum-Wage Setting Affect Employment and Informality? The Case of Indonesia', *The Review of Income and Wealth, Special Issue: The Informal Economy in Developing Countries: Analysis and Measurement*, Vol. 57, Issue Supplement s1, S79–S99, May.

Damanyanti, A. (2011) 'Low-paid Workers in Indonesia', paper presented to 'The 2nd Conference on Regulating for Decent Work' conference, 6–8 July, ILO, Geneva.

Dhanani, S. and I. Islam (2001) 'Poverty and Vulnerability in a Period of Crisis: The Case of Indonesia', *World Development*, Vol. 3, No. 7, pp. 1211–1231.

Dhanani, S., Islam, I. and A. Chowdhury (2009) *The Indonesian Labour Market: Changes and Challenges*. Routledge Studies in the Modern World Economy (Abingdon: Routledge).

Di Gropello, E., A. Kruse and P. Tandon (2011) *Skills for the Labour Market in Indonesia: Trends in Demand, Gaps and Supply* (Washington, DC: World Bank).

Fallon, P. R. and R. E. B. Lucas (2002) 'The Impact of Financial Crises on Labor Markets, Household Incomes, and Poverty: A Review of Evidence', *The World Bank Research Observer*, Vol. 17, No. 1, pp. 21–45.

International Labour Office (ILO) (2010) *G20 Country Briefs: Indonesia's Response to the Crisis* (Geneva: ILO).

International Labour Office (ILO) (2009a) 'Indonesia: Higher Informal Employment during the Economic Slowdown', *G20 Statistical Update* (Geneva: ILO).

International Labour Office (ILO) (2009b) 'Indonesia's Response to the Crisis', *G20 Country Update* (Geneva: ILO).

International Labour Office (ILO) (2009c) *Labour and Social Trends in Indonesia 2009: Recovery and Beyond through Decent Work* (Jakarta: ILO Office for Indonesia).

International Labour Office (ILO) (2006) *Implementing the Global Employment Agenda: Employment strategies in Support of Decent Work, 'Vision' Document* (Geneva: ILO). Also available at: www.ilo.org/gea.

International Labour Office (ILO) (2003) *Working Out of Poverty*, Report of the Director-General, International Labour Conference, 91st Session, Geneva, 2003 (Geneva: ILO). Also available at: www.oit.org/public/english/standards/relm/ilc/ilc91/pdf/rep-i-a.pdf.

International Labour Office (ILO) (2001) *Reducing the Decent Work Deficit: A Global Challenge*, Report of the Director General, International Labour Conference, 89th Session, Geneva, 2001 (Geneva: ILO). Also available at: www.ilo.org/public/english/standards/relm/ilc/ilc89/rep-i-a.htm.

International Labour Office (ILO) (1999) *Decent Work*, Report of the Director-General, International Labour Conference, 87th Session, Geneva, 1999 (Geneva: ILO). Also available at: www.ilo.org/public/english/standards/relm/ilc/ilc87/rep-i.htm.

Islam, I. and A. Chowdhury (2009) *Growth, Employment and Poverty Reduction in Indonesia* (Geneva: ILO).

Islam, I. and S. Nazara (2000) 'Minimum Wages and the Welfare of Indonesian Workers', Occasional Discussion Paper Series, No. 3 (Jakarta: ILO Office for Indonesia).

Kuncoro, A. (2004) 'Bribery in Indonesia: Some Evidence from Micro-level Data', *Bulletin of Indonesian Economic Studies*, Vol. 40, No. 3, pp. 329–354.

Lee, S. and D. McCann (2008) 'Measuring Legal Effectiveness: Lessons from Tanzania', Presentation to the IIRA 2009 Study Group on Labour Market Regulations, Sydney, 24 August 2009.

Matsumoto, M. and S. Verick (2010) 'Employment Trends in Indonesia over 1996–2009: Casualization of the Labour Market during an Era of Crises, Reforms and Recovery', ILO Employment Working Paper No. 99 (Geneva: ILO).

Manning, C. (2000) 'Labour Market Adjustment to Indonesia's Economic Crisis: Context, Trends and Implications', *Bulletin of Indonesian Economic Studies*, Vol. 36, No. 1, pp. 105–136.

Manning, C. and K. Roesad (2007) 'Manpower Law of 2003 and Its Implementing Regulations: Genesis, Key Articles and Potential Impact', *Bulletin of Indonesian Economic Studies*, Vol. 43, No. 1, pp. 59–86.

Overseas Development Institute (ODI) (2009) *The Global Financial Crisis and Developing Countries: Preliminary Synthesis of Ten Draft Country Reports* (London: Overseas Development Institute).

Organisation of Economic Co-operation and Development (OECD) (2008) *OECD Economic Surveys: Economic Assessment of Indonesia* (Paris: OECD).

Patunru, A. A. and C. von Luebke (2010) 'Survey of Recent Developments', *Bulletin of Indonesian Economic Studies*, Vol. 46, No. 1, pp. 7–31.

Patunru, A. A. and E. Zetha (2010) 'Indonesia's Savior: Fiscal, Monetary, Trade or Luck?', *Public Policy Review*, Vol. 6, No. 4, pp. 721–740.

Saget, C. (2008) 'Fixing Minimum Wage Levels in Developing Countries: Common Failures and Remedies', *International Labour Review*, Vol. 147, No. 1, pp. 25–42, March 2008.

Suryadarma, D., A. Suryhadi and S. Sumarto (2005) *The Measurement and Trends of Unemployment in Indonesia: The Issue of Discouraged Workers*, SMERU Working Paper, July (Jakarta: SMERU).

Titiheruw, I. S., H. Soesastro and R. Atje (2009) *Paper 6: Indonesia*, Global Financial Crisis Discussion Series, Overseas Development Institute and the Centre for International Strategic Studies.

World Bank (2010) *Indonesia Jobs Report: Towards Better Jobs and Security for All* (Washington, DC: World Bank).

6
The South African Labour Market: Long-term Structural Problems Exacerbated by the Global Financial Crisis

6.1 Introduction

The segregation policies of the Apartheid era in South Africa resulted in low levels of education, suppressed entrepreneurialism and spatial inequalities among the African population. Though Apartheid was dismantled in 1994, economic and social outcomes in this country continue to be heavily influenced by its historical legacy. This is no more apparent than in the labour market, which is characterized by some of the highest unemployment rates and lowest employment–population ratios in the world. At the same time, the informal sector is relatively small, which can be argued to be a manifestation of Apartheid policies that stymied entrepreneurship.

In addition, labour demand in South Africa has become increasingly skills-biased and, subsequently, the formal part of the economy has failed to absorb the large rise in labour supply that has accompanied the transition to democracy (most notably among African women). Moreover, since the 1990s, there has been a structural shift as reflected by the declining numbers of jobs in the mining and agricultural sectors, which were major employers of poorly educated South Africans. On top of these characteristics, real wages have either remained stagnant or fallen over the post-Apartheid period, above all for low-skilled workers.

In terms of the persistent inequalities present in the labour market, black Africans in this country are much more likely than other racial groups to be employed in the informal sector, unemployed or to have given up job search altogether and exited the labour force. Youth, the less-skilled and women which are, of course, not distinct categories, also

185

experience considerable barriers to participating in the labour market, especially with respect to finding jobs in the formal economy. Youth have faced particular barriers to accessing the labour market: according to the September 2007 Labour Force Survey, the (narrowly defined) unemployment rate of young South Africans aged 20 to 24 stood at 44.7 per cent even before the global financial crisis hit in 2008.

These issues, especially the failure of young South Africans to make a successful transition from school to work, continue to be key policy concerns for the government of South Africa as they are a major factor behind (and a cause of) the insufficient economic growth and sharp inequalities that drive social unrest and crime. The latest policy initiative, labelled the 'New Growth Path', is a reflection of the government's commitment to engineer significant change that would overcome these persistent barriers.[1] Over recent decades, this situation in the South African labour market has also attracted considerable attention from academics, which has played an important role in shaping the policy response. In this respect, a broad range of studies have investigated these labour market dimensions in depth, including Banerjee et al. (2008), Bhorat et al. (2001), Bhorat and Kanbur (2006), Devey et al. (2008), Kingdon and Knight (2004, 2006, 2007), OECD (2008), Padayachee (2006), Valodia et al. (2005) and Valodia (2007).

One of the key references, Banerjee et al. (2008), finds that unemployment in South Africa is more structural than transitional, while demand has shifted towards skilled workers, which has exacerbated the barriers faced by the unskilled. Overall, the problem of unemployment has been driven by both the fall in demand for less-skilled workers and increase in supply of those with lower levels of education (mostly African women). Banerjee et al. (2008) outline three key reasons why unemployment has remained high among the African population: firstly, less effective job search due to spatial separation between business centres and rural areas, lack of affordable transport and, potentially, discrimination; secondly, the failure for the informal sector to act as an 'absorber' of excess labour supply; and finally, high reservation wages.

Similarly to Banerjee et al. (2008), Kingdon and Knight (2007) argue that the rise in the unemployment rate from 1995 to 2003 was due to inadequate economic growth and thus insufficient labour demand relative to the rapid expansion in labour supply over this period.[2] Indeed, the labour force grew at over 4 per cent per annum from 1995 to 2003, mainly due to population growth and an increase in labour force participation among women (from 47.8 per cent in 1995 to 62.8 per cent in 2003) and black Africans (from 51.8 per cent to 65.9 per cent over the same period). This study also attributes the high South African unemployment rate to labour market inflexibility, though this hypothesis is not tested through the empirical analysis. Kingdon and Knight (2007) cite evidence that informal sector workers have both higher incomes and subjective well-being than the unemployed. For this reason, the authors conclude that the bulk of unemployment in South Africa is involuntary, reflecting the barriers to not only formal sector employment but also to jobs in the informal sector. Hurdles to informal sector employment include crime, lack of access to credit, inadequate infrastructure and services, and insufficient skills and training opportunities (Kingdon and Knight 2007).[3] Informal sector workers in South Africa are disproportionately black, female and uneducated, and are mostly operating in the wholesale trade and retail sector (Devey et al. 2008; Valodia 2007; Valodia et al. 2005).

One of the main themes of this chapter is the difference between the narrow definition of unemployment, which includes only individuals who are actively searching for a job, and the broad classification that also counts the discouraged as unemployed (that is, adding individuals who are able to work but are not currently searching for a job). In 1994, the difference between the narrow and broad unemployment rates stood at 11.5 percentage points (20.0 versus 31.5 per cent) (Kingdon and Knight 2006). Over the last decade and a half, this gap narrowed and, prior to the onset of the recession, it amounted to only 4.8 points (23.5 versus 28.3 per cent). Therefore, while unemployment remained high even in years of stronger growth, a greater percentage of unemployed South Africans were searching, which reflects the higher expected benefits of job search. Going beyond just the differences between aggregate rates, Kingdon and Knight (2006) investigate the nature of searching and non-searching unemployment. Using different tests, this study finds that discouraged workers are more deprived and no happier (in terms of self-reported subjective well-being) than the searching unemployed, while local wage determination takes into account both types of joblessness. As demonstrated by the results presented below, the conclusion of Kingdon and Knight (2006) continues to be highly relevant for South African policymakers: 'our findings imply that the non-searching unemployed deserve no less policy attention than do the searchers, and that the broad unemployment measure should be estimated alongside the narrow measure and given credence in South Africa...' (Kingdon and Knight 2006, p. 311).

During the global economic boom years of 2002–2007, unemployment in South Africa began to finally fall as economic conditions further improved. In this respect, the unemployment rate stood at 25 per cent in 2007 (it reached a low of 21.9 per cent in the third quarter of 2008), down from 31.2 per cent in 2003. Owing to its strong trade and financial links, South Africa was hit hard by the global financial crisis, which has come on top of the longer-term structural problems in its economy and labour market. Consequently, the country fell into a recession in the fourth quarter of 2008 and the economy contracted by 1.7 per cent in 2009.[4] This severe slump was largely driven by a contraction in the manufacturing sector, along with a fall in output in the mining, financial, real estate and business services, and wholesale and retail trade sectors (Statistics South Africa 2009; South Africa Reserve Bank 2009). The South African government recognized the severity of the downturn and responded with a fiscal stimulus package that aimed to support demand and create jobs, while the South African Reserve Bank loosened monetary policy.[5]

In spite of the response of the government of South Africa, the ensuing recession of 2008–2009 decimated the labour market resulting in a drop in employment of over 800,000 (difference in the average in 2010 over 2008). As shown in this chapter, this massive loss of jobs resulted in a number of outcomes that may appear to external commentators as unexpected but are, in fact, entirely consistent with the findings presented in the literature highlighted above. Nonetheless, they serve as a reminder of the continuing sclerotic state of the labour market in South Africa and the need for policymakers to take action on addressing the structural factors driving these processes. In this respect, the main effect of the downturn on the labour market has been a rise in the number of discouraged individuals, from an average of 1.12 million in 2008 to 1.98 million in 2010. In comparison, narrowly defined search unemployment increased over the same period by only 214,000 (from 4.08 to 4.29 million). Drawing on the estimates from the micro-data, discouragement has increased more for uneducated black Africans.

As also indicated in Chapter 2, the government of South Africa has made increasing efforts to tackle these challenges through labour market policies such as the Expanded Public Works Programme and the Training Layoff Scheme. Nonetheless, the findings presented in this chapter underscore the need for policymakers to further reduce barriers to job search through such measures as investing in training, infrastructure and transport subsidies.

Thus, in the context of the framework presented in Chapter 1 on the key dimensions of this book, this chapter highlights the connection between longer-term labour market challenges, which mostly stem from the era of Apartheid, and the impact of the global financial crisis, which exacerbated the problems that existed before the onset of the downturn in late 2008. The chapter also presents the policy landscape in terms of labour market and social policies, which have gained importance in the government's response to these challenges.

The remainder of this chapter is structured as follows: section 6.2 reviews the aggregate statistics, while section 6.3 presents the data, empirical strategy and micro-estimates of the determinants of labour market status before the crisis (2008) and after (2009–2010), including the role of gender, race, education and spousal labour market status in driving vulnerability to poor outcomes in the labour market. Focusing in more detail on the issue of discouragement and job search, section 6.4 analyses differences between individuals classified as unemployed and discouraged, and how the decision to undertake job search changed during the recession of 2009. Section 6.5 explores the nature of labour market policies in South Africa before section 6.6 concludes.

6.2 What the aggregates tell about the impact of the global financial crisis on the South African labour market

During the recession of 2008–2009, the impact on labour market status in South Africa was multifaceted and, in some respects, unexpected. Overall, the number of South Africans employed decreased from 13.7 million in 2008 to 12.9 million in 2010 (a drop of 5.8 per cent), which had been driven by layoffs, particularly in the wholesale and retail trade, manufacturing and agricultural sectors. This dramatic fall in employment represents a partial destruction of the gains made during the 2000s when total employment grew by 3.8 million from 2001 to 2008 (from 10.9 million to 13.7 million). Already among the lowest in the world, the employment–population ratio in South Africa subsequently dropped from 44.6 per cent in 2008 to 40.7 per cent in 2010.

In addition to considering the total adjustment, it is also important to look at changes to formal versus informal sector employment.[6] In this sense, it is usually assumed that the urban informal sector absorbs workers who are unable to find a job in the formal sector, though the literature increasingly views the sector as consisting of both survivalists and entrepreneurs who choose to operate informally.[7] During a downturn, particularly one that is driven by an external shock, it is generally expected that employment in a developing country will fall in the formal sector, accompanied by a rise in employment in the informal

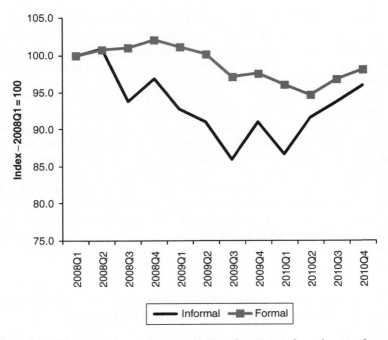

Figure 6.1   Adjustment in employment during the crisis: informal versus formal sector, 2008Q1–2010Q4
Source: Statistics South Africa Quarterly Labour Force Survey, 2008Q1 to 2010Q4; authors' calculations. All figures are population-weighted.

sector (see, for example, the impact of the Asian Financial Crisis on Indonesia in Fallon and Lucas 2002).

In contrast to this stylized fact, informal sector employment in South Africa, surprisingly, fell during the recession of 2008–2009 (Figure 6.1). The share of informal sector employment declined from 17 per cent in 2008Q1 to 15.5 per cent in 2009Q3. From 2008 to 2009, annual employment losses in this sector accounted for 36.1 per cent of the fall in employment (despite its share being below 20 per cent) compared to 37.3 per cent for the formal sector. However, this has since reversed: from 2009 to 2010, 64.2 per cent of the fall in total employment was due to losses in the formal sector. All in all, informal sector employment declined by 14 per cent from 2008Q1 to 2009Q3, while formal sector employment fell by 5.3 per cent from 2008Q1 to 2010Q2. Over 2010, employment in the informal sector has recovered much more rapidly than in the formal sector. Altogether, these figures reveal that adjustment in the informal sector has been more rapid both in terms of job losses during the recession and employment growth once recovery was under way. In general, this could be explained by differences in labour adjustment costs: hiring and firing are more expensive in the formal sector and thus employers are slower to adjust employment over the business cycle. Moreover, these trends also underscore that the service sector, where informal enterprises are located, recovered faster.

Despite this loss of jobs, the narrowly defined unemployment rate for the whole population only increased from an average of 22.9 per cent in 2008 to 24.0 per cent in 2009, before peaking at 25.0 per cent in 2010 (maximum of 25.3 per cent in the second quarter of 2010) (Figure 6.2). As expected, the narrowly defined unemployment rate for youth increased by a greater amount (5 percentage points from an annual average of 45.5 per cent in 2008 to 50.5 per cent in 2010). In terms of

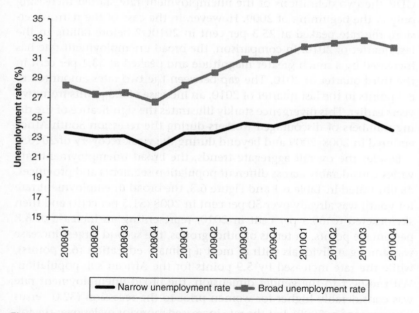

Figure 6.2 Rising divergence between the narrow and broad unemployment rates during the recession and beyond, 2008Q1–2010Q4

Notes: The narrow unemployment rate is the ratio of the unemployed who are searching for a job to the labour force (U/E+U); the broad unemployment rate is the ratio of the sum of the narrowly defined unemployed and discouraged workers to the broad labour force, which includes these discouraged workers (U+D/U+D+E).

Source: Statistics South Africa Quarterly Labour Force Survey, 2008Q1 to 2010Q4; authors' calculations. All figures are population-weighted.

variation within the population, the rate rose by 2.9 percentage points for prime-age men (from 15.5 per cent in 2008 to 18.4 per cent in 2010), which stems from the male bias in manufacturing employment, while it increased by only 1 point for prime-age women (from 21.5 per cent to 22.5 per cent).[8] Reflecting the long-term inequalities present in the labour market, searching or narrowly defined unemployment has increased more for black and coloured South Africans.

The fall in employment during the recession translated to a larger increase in discouragement, and hence a rise in the broad unemployment rate, which includes this labour market category. In this regard, Figure 6.2 clearly illustrates the divergence between the narrow and broad unemployment rates (see also Table 6.1). Both rates reached a low in the fourth quarter of 2008, 21.9 and 26.7 per cent, respectively (a gap of 4.8 percentage points). Reflecting a lag of one quarter with respect to GDP, the two definitions of the unemployment rate started increasing only at the beginning of 2009. However, in the case of the narrow version, the rate peaked at 25.3 per cent in 2010Q2 before falling in the last quarter of 2010. In comparison, the broad unemployment rate has increased by a much greater magnitude and peaked at 33.1 per cent in the third quarter of 2010. The gap between the two rates amounted to 8.4 points in the last quarter of 2010, an increase of 3.6 points from two years earlier. This divergence starkly illustrates the significance of the rising numbers of discouraged workers during the recession South Africa endured in 2008–2009 and beyond during the weak recovery of 2010.

Besides the overall aggregate trends, the broad unemployment rate varies considerably across different population segments and provinces. As illustrated in Table 6.1 and Figure 6.3, the broad unemployment rate for youth was already over 50 per cent in 2008 (51.5 per cent) and then skyrocketed to 60.3 per cent in 2010, representing an increase of 8.8 percentage points. In terms of other groups, the second largest increase was among individuals with at most a primary education (6.9 points), while the rate increased by 5.9 points for the African sub-population. With respect to the gender dimension, the broad unemployment rate was considerably higher for women prior to the recession (32.0 versus 23.5 per cent in 2008), but the rate increased more for males over the following two years (5.9 versus 4.5 points). This reflects the sectoral nature of the recession (there were larger contractions in the manufacturing and mining sectors, which are male-dominated).

Turning to geographical diversity, prior to the crisis the broad unemployment rate was highest in the provinces of Limpopo (38.1 per cent in 2008), Eastern Cape (35.1 per cent) and North West (31.5 per cent)

Table 6.1 Evolution of the narrow and broad unemployment rates in South Africa, annual averages 2008–2010

	Annual average			Difference – 2008 to 2010 (percentage points)
	2008	2009	2010	
Narrow unemployment rate (%)				
Total	22.9	24.0	24.9	2.0
Broad unemployment rate (%)				
Total	27.5	30.1	32.7	5.2
Male	23.5	27.1	29.4	5.9
Female	32.0	33.4	36.5	4.5
Youth	51.5	56.2	60.3	8.8
African/black	32.5	35.5	38.4	5.9
Primary education or less	28.3	31.2	35.2	6.9
Western Cape	19.7	21.8	23.2	3.5
Eastern Cape	35.1	38.1	39.7	4.6
Northern Cape	28.7	32.3	34.1	5.4
Free State	28.6	32.4	33.5	4.9
KwaZulu-Natal	26.3	29.5	31.7	5.4
North West	31.5	34.6	36.4	4.9
Gauteng	24.2	26.6	30.5	6.3
Mpumalanga	29.4	32.4	38.0	8.6
Limpopo	38.1	37.5	39.1	1.0
GDP growth rate (Y on Y-1) (%)	3.6	−1.7	2.8	–

Notes: All figures are population-weighted; figures may vary from published sources due to revisions and sample selection.
Source: Statistics South Africa Quarterly Labour Force Survey, 2008Q1–2010Q4, authors' calculations for annual averages; Statistics South Africa, Gross Domestic Product, Fourth Quarter 2010.

(Table 6.1 and Figure 6.3). These provinces have a high proportion of former 'homelands' or 'Bantustans', which were reservations created by the Apartheid regime. These areas are the poorest in South Africa and have the highest rate of discouragement, particularly among rural women, which is captured by the broadly defined unemployment rate. Households in these regions are highly dependent on social transfers, especially the old-age pension and child support grant. Moreover, local markets are undeveloped, while producers face barriers to accessing the national economy (Makgetta 2010). As noted by Kingdon and Knight (2006), the chances of finding a job in the former homelands is low and the costs of job search are prohibitive, particularly due to unaffordable transport costs, which all contribute to the persistent and high levels of discouragement. Indeed, the role of spatial mismatch and impact

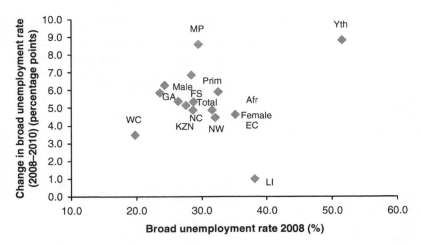

Figure 6.3 Changes in the broad unemployment rate across groups and provinces, annual averages 2008–2010

Notes: EC = Eastern Cape province; FS = Free State province; KZN = KwaZulu-Natal province; LI = Limpopo province; MP = Mpumalanga; NC = Northern Cape province; NW = North West province; WC = Western Cape province; Afr = African population; Prim = primary education or less; and Yth = youth aged 15–24.

Source: Statistics South Africa Quarterly Labour Force Survey, 2008-2010; authors' calculations. All figures are population weighted.

of geography on job search behaviour is one of the most crucial issues driving the situation in the South African labour market, and is, therefore, discussed further in the context of the econometric results in section 6.3.

Reflecting both long-term disparities and the nature of the shock, the broad unemployment rate increased the most during the recession of 2008–2009 in Mpumalanga (8.6 points), Gauteng (6.3 points) and KwaZulu-Natal (5.4 points). Mpumalanga and KwaZulu-Natal are provinces that have a high proportion of former homelands. In terms of sectoral composition, Gauteng is reliant on manufacturing, financial services and mining, while Mpumalanga is dominated more by mining and KwaZulu-Natal by manufacturing.

6.3   Drivers of labour market status: insights from the micro-data for 2008–2010

6.3.1   Data and definitions

The micro-data used in this chapter is sourced from Statistics South Africa's Quarterly Labour Force Survey (QLFS), which is a household-based survey of individuals aged 15 years or older.[9] Statistics South Africa revised its previous biannual survey (LFS) and launched the QLFS in 2008. The QLFS is conducted as a rotating panel with households remaining in the panel for four consecutive quarters. The sample size for the QLFS is approximately 30,000 dwellings and these are divided equally into four rotation groups, that is, 7,500 dwellings per rotation group. The sampling weights take into account the original selection probabilities, adjustment for non-response, and benchmarking to known population estimates from the Demographic Division of Statistics South Africa. The sample used in this chapter for both deriving preliminary statistics and estimating the multinomial logit model consists of all individuals aged between 15 and 64 (the working age population, including those in agriculture). All figures and estimates presented below are population-weighted.

The analysis below focuses on five labour market states: formal sector employment; informal sector employment; unemployment; discouragement; and other out-of-the-labour force. As per Statistics South Africa, the definition of informality is based on the size of the firm and whether the employer is registered for VAT and income tax. In addition, employment in a private household is also categorized as informal sector employment. A person is narrowly defined as unemployed if they: a) were not employed in the reference week; b) actively looked for work or tried to start a business in the four weeks preceding the survey interview; and c) would have been able to start work or would have started a business in the reference week. A discouraged individual is jobless but has given up job search (that is, does not satisfy criterion b)). Those classified as other out-of-the-labour force include individuals in education, retirement or those with caring responsibilities.[10]

Table 6.2 summarizes the key individual and household variables used in the econometric analysis. These figures indicate that there are significant disparities in labour market status by gender, household size, education, marital status and race, which have been well documented in the literature (see, for example, Banerjee et al. 2006, 2008, Kingdon and Knight 2004, 2007). In particular, those working in the formal sector tend to be older, male, better educated and have a smaller family. Black/Africans are over-represented in informal sector employment, unemployment, discouragement and other forms of inactivity. In terms of spousal employment status, there is a strong relationship between spouses' job search status. Finally, formal sector workers are over-represented in such provinces as Gauteng and Western Cape, while informality is more uniformly distributed. A greater proportion of individuals in Gauteng are considered to be searching unemployed

Table 6.2 Summary statistics by labour market status, average 2008Q1–2010Q4

Variable	Sample statistics by labour market status					
	F	I	U	D	OLF	Total
Age (years)	38.1	39.6	30.7	31.8	31.0	34.0
Female (% of sample)	42.4	58.6	52.2	60.8	61.6	54.4
Number of household members	3.6	3.8	4.6	5.0	4.8	4.3
Primary school or no education (% of sample)	14.2	39.3	17.3	30.4	31.4	25.4
Less than year 12 education (% of sample)	28.9	41.4	44.7	46.2	53.1	43.3
Year 12 education (% of sample)	33.8	16.5	32.6	21.2	13.5	22.6
Tertiary education (% of sample)	23.1	2.9	5.4	2.3	2.0	8.7
Black/African (% of sample)	64.6	87.6	86.1	93.5	82.8	79.0
Coloured (% of sample)	15.5	9.0	10.9	5.0	9.7	11.2
Indian/Asian (% of sample)	4.0	1.1	1.2	0.6	2.4	2.5
White (% of sample)	15.9	2.3	1.9	0.9	5.1	7.3
No spouse (% of sample)	50.8	61.9	79.2	79.5	80.3	69.7
Spouse employed in formal sector (% of sample)	26.9	11.9	9.5	8.0	7.7	13.9
Spouse employed in informal sector (% of sample)	4.6	9.7	3.7	4.0	2.5	4.1
Spouse unemployed (% of sample)	4.4	4.4	3.7	1.1	1.1	2.7
Spouse discouraged (% of sample)	1.4	1.8	0.4	3.1	0.5	1.0
Spouse OLF (% of sample)	11.8	10.3	3.5	4.3	8.0	8.6
Western Cape (% of sample)	17.3	9.1	11.4	2.8	8.8	11.3
Eastern Cape (% of sample)	8.2	11.1	9.6	16.3	13.3	11.3
Northern Cape (% of sample)	5.4	4.9	5.6	4.8	5.5	5.4
Free State (% of sample)	8.6	10.2	10.4	8.0	8.3	8.9
KwaZulu-Natal (% of sample)	15.2	17.0	12.8	19.2	19.9	17.3
North West (% of sample)	7.7	7.2	8.8	11.4	9.2	8.6
Gauteng (% of sample)	23.0	17.5	22.8	10.0	11.0	16.7
Mpumalanga (% of sample)	8.2	11.8	10.1	11.5	9.6	9.6
Limpopo (% of sample)	6.2	11.4	8.6	15.9	14.6	11.1

Notes: All figures are population-weighted. F = Employed in the formal sector; I = Employed in the informal sector; U = Unemployed; D = Discouraged; OLF = Other out-of-the-labour force. Sample covers the working-age population (15–64).

Source: Statistics South Africa Quarterly Labour Force Survey, average based on quarterly data for 2008Q1–2010Q4; authors' calculations.

compared to the total sample. At the same time, a higher share of discouraged workers is found in Eastern Cape, KwaZulu-Natal, North West, Mpumalanga and Limpopo, which in turn is driven by the higher proportion of former homelands as noted above.

6.3.2 Estimates from a model of labour market status

To identify the labour market impact in the South African context, this section estimates a model of labour market status separately for before and after the onset of the crisis. The Quarterly Labour Force Survey data is pooled providing four quarters of data for the pre-crisis period (2008Q1 to 2008Q4) and eight quarters covering the crisis (2009Q1 to 2010Q4). In the context of this chapter, the dependent variable consists of five labour market states $(J = 5)$: formal sector employment; informal sector employment (including private households); unemployment; discouraged workers; and other forms of inactivity. Formal sector employment is used as the normalized outcome. The model is conditioned on age, education, marital status, spousal labour market status, household size, population group and province. Due to differences in labour force participation, the model is estimated separately for women and men. To ease interpretation of the results, average partial effects (APEs) are estimated, which provide more consistent estimates than marginal effects at the mean (Bartus 2005).[11]

Using this empirical strategy, the pre-crisis average partial effects indicate that a range of individual and household characteristics drive the labour market status of South African women (Table 6.3). Firstly, based on the average partial effect at the mean age (34.6 years), an additional year would increase the probability of employment, unemployment and discouragement, while it would lead to a decrease in the likelihood of other forms of inactivity.[12] As expected, educational attainment plays a dominant role in differences across labour market status of South African women. In particular, the less education a woman has, the less likely she is to be employed in the formal sector and the more likely she is to be employed in the informal sector or discouraged. Most striking is the situation for females with at most a primary education: the probability of formal sector employment for these individuals in the pre-crisis period was 40.2 percentage points lower than those with a tertiary education. The relationship between educational attainment and the probability of narrowly defined unemployment is non-linear. In fact, the likelihood increases the most for females who have completed high school (in comparison to tertiary-educated individuals), while it is lower for those with less education.

Table 6.3 Multinomial logit estimates (average partial coefficients) – female labour market status, 2008 versus 2009–2010

Variable	Formal sector employment		Informal sector employment		Unemployment		Discouragement		OLF	
	2008 (1)	2009/10 (2)	2008 (3)	2009/10 (4)	2008 (5)	2009/10 (6)	2008 (7)	2009/10 (8)	2008 (9)	2009/10 (10)
Age	0.006***	0.007***	0.003***	0.003***	0.003***	0.003***	0.001***	0.001***	-0.013***	-0.014***
Primary school or none (ref: tertiary)	-0.498***	-0.470***	0.115***	0.099***	0.003	-0.007*	0.042***	0.045***	0.337***	0.332***
Less than Year 12	-0.425***	-0.402***	0.096***	0.088***	0.029***	0.020***	0.028***	0.037***	0.271***	0.256***
Year 12	-0.241***	-0.230***	0.056***	0.053***	0.063***	0.050***	0.023***	0.029***	0.098***	0.098***
Black/African (ref: white)	-0.078***	-0.101***	0.088***	0.081***	0.110***	0.102***	0.036***	0.048***	-0.157***	-0.129***
Coloured	0.031***	0.007	0.023***	0.023***	0.068***	0.063***	0.017***	0.027***	-0.139***	-0.121***
Indian/Asian	-0.035***	-0.035***	-0.028***	-0.011**	0.051***	0.022***	0.001	0.003	0.011	0.021**
Household size	-0.010***	-0.005***	-0.008***	-0.006***	0.005***	0.003***	0.002***	0.003***	0.011***	0.006***
Spouse employed in formal sector (ref: no spouse)	-0.021***	-0.021***	-0.034***	-0.029***	-0.024***	-0.041***	-0.003	-0.011***	0.081***	0.103***
Spouse employed in informal sector	-0.087***	-0.079***	0.057***	0.054***	-0.013**	-0.036***	-0.004	0.004	0.047***	0.057***

Table 6.3 (Continued)

Spouse unemployed	-0.042***	-0.018***	0.009	0.019***	0.045***	-0.015***	-0.024***	0.009
Spouse discouraged	-0.038**	-0.020*	0.003	0.008	-0.100***	0.134***	0.129***	-0.008
Spouse OLF	-0.058***	-0.056***	-0.025***	-0.022***	-0.053***	0.002	-0.012***	0.151***
Western Cape (ref: Gauteng)	0.003	0.013***	-0.007	0.016***	-0.036***	-0.014***	-0.025***	0.028***
Eastern Cape	-0.044***	-0.029***	-0.020***	-0.011***	-0.052***	0.023***	0.030***	0.091***
Northern Cape	-0.042***	-0.039***	-0.028***	-0.016***	-0.023***	0.021***	0.018***	0.072***
Free State	-0.028***	-0.017***	-0.017***	-0.008***	-0.023***	0.012***	0.017***	0.056***
KwaZulu-Natal	-0.010**	-0.006*	0.006	0.000	-0.073***	-0.004*	0.027***	0.080***
North West	-0.041***	-0.044***	-0.044***	-0.038***	-0.053***	0.023***	0.025***	0.088***
Mpumalanga	-0.038***	-0.026***	0.005	0.015***	-0.054***	0.017***	0.033***	0.124***
Limpopo	-0.088***	-0.071***	-0.026***	-0.009***	-0.060***	0.017***	0.036***	0.151***
Observations	113,222	213,406	113,222	213,406	113,222	213,406	113,222	213,406

Notes: *** $p < 0.01$, ** $p < 0.05$, * $p < 0.1$. The average partial effects (APEs) are based on a multinomial logit regression where the dependent variable is labour market status. The APEs are presented as percentage point changes in the probability of an outcome.

Source: Statistics South Africa Quarterly Labour Force Survey; authors' calculations.

Turning to different population groups, the estimates confirm the disparities that have long been present in the South African labour market. In comparison to white women, black African women are more likely to be informally employed, unemployed and discouraged, while they are less likely to be formally employed or inactive for other reasons. Coloured women are more likely to be employed, unemployed, discouraged and less likely to be out-of-the-labour force than white women. Finally, Indian/Asian women have a lower probability of being employed in the formal sector and in the informal sector (both periods). At the same time, Indian/Asian women have a higher probability of unemployment.

The specification used in Table 6.3 also includes two variables reflecting household status. First, formal sector employment is less likely for individuals without spouses. Having a spouse working in the informal sector is associated with a 5.7 percentage point higher probability of working in the same sector in 2008 (compared to having no spouse). Moreover, the likelihood of job search for unemployed females is very much linked to the job search status of their spouse (the effect is over 4 percentage points for narrowly defined unemployment and 13 points for discouragement). Second, there is a significant correlation between household size and labour market status: a larger household is associated with a lower probability of employment for women (in both the formal and informal sectors) but a higher chance of being unemployed, discouraged or out-of-the-labour force. This result suggests that intra-household transfers potentially have an impact on labour market status, an issue discussed in Section 6.4 when investigating the reasons behind discouragement.

In terms of the geographical dummies, the estimates suggest that females in provinces with a high proportion of former homelands, such as Limpopo, North West and Eastern Cape, are generally less likely to be employed (in both the formal and informal sectors) in comparison with Gauteng, which is of course also driven by the fact that these provinces have a higher proportion of black women. These women also have a lower probability of unemployment in these provinces, while they are more likely to be discouraged or out-of-the-labour force. Similarly to the findings for women, education has a large APE on the probability of being in a particular labour market state for men (Table 6.4). More specifically, having lower levels of schooling (compared with tertiary education) reduces the likelihood of formal sector employment, while it increases the likelihood of all other states. Like the estimates for females, this result is strongest for South African men who have at most a primary

201

Table 6.4 Multinomial logit estimates (average partial coefficients) – male labour market status, 2008 versus 2009–2010

Variable	Formal sector employment		Informal sector employment		Unemployment		Discouragement		OLF	
	2008 (1)	2009/10 (2)	2008 (3)	2009/10 (4)	2008 (5)	2009/10 (6)	2008 (7)	2009/10 (8)	2008 (9)	2009/10 (10)
Age	0.008***	0.008***	0.003***	0.003***	0.005***	0.005***	0.001***	0.002***	−0.017***	−0.018***
Primary school or none (ref: tertiary)	−0.326***	−0.338***	0.096***	0.089***	0.023***	0.034***	0.030***	0.048***	0.178***	0.167***
Less than Year 12	−0.271***	−0.275***	0.072***	0.068***	0.033***	0.050***	0.017***	0.028***	0.148***	0.129***
Year 12	−0.150***	−0.158***	0.034***	0.034***	0.050***	0.059***	0.014***	0.022***	0.052***	0.043***
Black/African (ref: white)	−0.096***	−0.114***	0.046***	0.042***	0.101***	0.101***	0.026***	0.033***	−0.078***	−0.061***
Coloured	−0.037***	−0.052***	0.031***	0.028***	0.094***	0.090***	0.009***	0.018***	−0.097***	−0.083***
Indian/Asian	−0.001	−0.018**	0.006	0.021***	0.061***	0.054***	0.003	0.002	−0.069***	−0.059***
Household size	−0.013***	−0.010***	−0.005***	−0.004***	0.007***	0.005***	0.002***	0.003***	0.009***	0.006***
Spouse employed in formal sector (ref: no spouse)	0.238***	0.238***	−0.015***	−0.008**	−0.070***	−0.054***	−0.016***	−0.020***	−0.135***	−0.155***
Spouse employed in informal sector	0.102***	0.111***	0.086***	0.082***	−0.038***	−0.030***	−0.013***	−0.018***	−0.138***	−0.145***

(Continued)

Table 6.4 (Continued)

Variable	Formal sector employment		Informal sector employment		Unemployment		Discouragement		OLF	
	2008 (1)	2009/10 (2)	2008 (3)	2009/10 (4)	2008 (5)	2009/10 (6)	2008 (7)	2009/10 (8)	2008 (9)	2009/10 (10)
Spouse unemployed	0.189***	0.205***	0.032***	0.035***	−0.019**	−0.009	−0.029***	−0.047***	−0.173***	−0.183***
Spouse discouraged	0.147***	0.144***	0.014	0.049***	−0.102***	−0.099***	0.043***	0.056***	−0.102***	−0.150***
Spouse OLF	0.148***	0.185***	0.021***	0.024***	−0.080***	−0.084***	−0.019***	−0.033***	−0.071***	−0.092***
Western Cape (ref: Gauteng)	0.022***	0.021***	−0.024***	−0.009***	−0.021***	−0.013***	−0.010***	−0.018***	0.033***	0.020***
Eastern Cape	−0.106***	−0.080***	0.010**	0.007**	−0.027***	−0.055***	0.032***	0.051***	0.090***	0.078***
Northern Cape	−0.027***	−0.025***	−0.005	−0.014***	−0.037***	−0.035***	0.010***	0.012***	0.058***	0.062***
Free State	−0.054***	−0.035***	0.006	0.015***	−0.017***	−0.023***	0.001	0.003*	0.064***	0.039***
KwaZulu-Natal	−0.033***	−0.023***	0.008**	0.006*	−0.051***	−0.091***	0.003	0.033***	0.072***	0.076***
North West	−0.028***	−0.014***	−0.020***	−0.025***	−0.022***	−0.039***	0.019***	0.025***	0.051***	0.054***
Mpumalanga	−0.033***	−0.021***	0.012***	0.009***	−0.033***	−0.033***	0.000	0.016***	0.054***	0.029***
Limpopo	−0.132***	−0.096***	0.011**	0.024***	−0.027***	−0.078***	0.016***	0.034***	0.133***	0.117***
Observations	96,544	182,280	96,544	182,280	96,544	182,280	96,544	182,280	96,544	182,280

Notes: *** $p < 0.01$, ** $p < 0.05$, * $p < 0.1$. The average partial effects (APEs) are based on a multinomial logit regression where the dependent variable is labour market status. The APEs are presented as percentage point changes in the probability of an outcome.
Source: Statistics South Africa Quarterly Labour Force Survey: authors' calculations.

education: for this vulnerable group, the probability of formal sector employment was more than 32 percentage points lower in 2008 than those with a tertiary education (in 2009–10, it increased to 33.8 points).

In general, the estimates of the effect of age and race on male labour market outcomes are broadly in line with the results for women. For example, being an African man reduces the probability (in comparison with white males) of formal sector employment and other forms of inactivity, while it raises the likelihood of informal sector employment, unemployment and discouragement. The results for coloured South African males are similar to those found for African males, though the APEs are mostly smaller.

While not as large in magnitude as found in the case of females, spousal labour market status also has a strong association with outcomes in the labour market for men. For example, having a spouse who is employed in the informal sector increases the probability of being in the same state for males by 8.6 percentage points in 2008 (in comparison with individuals without a spouse), which decreases to 8.2 percentage points in 2009–10. In contrast, search unemployment is more likely for individuals without spouses. Alternatively, having a spouse who is not actively searching is correlated with an increase in the probability of discouragement for males by 4.3 points in 2008, which then rises to 5.6 points in the crisis period. These findings confirm the importance of social networks and peers in driving the decision to give up job search, a topic that is investigated further in Section 4. The impact of household size on the probabilities is comparable with the findings for women.

In order to identify whether the results for South African men and women changed from 2008 to 2009–2010 during the recession, the equality of coefficients from the multinomial logit model over the two periods is tested using a Wald test. This exercise reveals that, for the male sub-sample, the coefficients on educational attainment significantly changed (in a statistical sense), along with the spouse variables and provincial dummies. For example, the coefficient on the dummy for primary education or less became more positive from 2008 to 2009–2010 in the case of narrowly defined unemployment (from 2.3 to 3.4 points). Similarly, the estimated APEs show that male high school dropouts had a higher probability of being unemployed than tertiary educated individuals (by 3.3 percentage points in 2008). This marginal effect rose to 5.0 points in 2009–10. There were a number of changes in the magnitude of coefficients on the provincial dummies. For instance, in the case of discouragement, the APE on the dummy for KwaZulu-Natal, a province hard hit by the crisis and one with a high proportion of former homelands, went from being insignificant in 2008 to 3.3 percentage points (in comparison with males in Gauteng).

In the case of females, the APEs also changed for the population, educational attainment and province dummies. For example, the estimated APEs suggest that African females were 3.6 percentage points more likely to be discouraged in 2008 than white females, which increased to 4.8 points in 2009–2010. Altogether, these Wald tests of coefficient equality show that the probabilities of being unemployed and discouraged increased most significantly for black Africans, the poorly educated and in provinces that were hit the hardest.

To further underscore the changes since the onset of the recession in South Africa, it is useful to view the predicted probabilities of discouragement for females and males in a graphical form and plotting them against age. Age is used because of the known disparities facing young

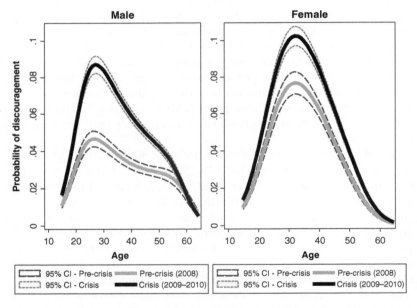

Figure 6.4   Predicted probability of discouragement rises for vulnerable men and women from 2008 to 2009–2010

Notes: The predicted probabilities derived from the multinomial logit estimates are graphed on age by gender for uneducated, black/Africans. All other variables are held at their means.
Source: Statistics South Africa Quarterly Labour Force Survey, 2008Q1–2010Q4; authors' calculations.

people in the labour market and the overall changes in employment status over the life-cycle. To highlight the strongest impact of the crisis, the effects of race and educational attainment (based on the multinomial logit estimates presented in Tables 6.3 and 6.4) are combined to underscore the situation for one of the most vulnerable groups in the South African labour market (uneducated African females and males). The change in predicted probabilities of discouragement displayed in Figure 6.4 illustrates that the likelihood of being in this state increased for both uneducated African men and women. Moreover, though discouragement is normally higher for women, the rise was larger for men. The maximum probability of discouragement for these vulnerable women increased from 7.8 per cent in 2008 (at age 32) to 10.2 per cent in 2009–2010. For men, the peak in the probability of discouragement rose by a greater amount, from 4.7 per cent prior to the crisis (at age 27) to 8.7 per cent in 2009–2010.

In summary, these estimates generated from the multinomial logit specification confirm that the impact of the crisis in South Africa is mainly evident in an increase in discouragement, which has important gender, education and racial dimensions.

6.4 Explaining rising discouragement during the recession – are these individuals different from those undertaking job search?

The findings above confirm that the main impact of the crisis in South Africa has been in terms of rising discouragement, particularly among less-skilled African males. This result resonates with the previous literature that has addressed the prominence of discouragement and the factors that hinder job search in the South African labour market (Kingdon and Knight 2006; Banerjee et al. 2006, 2008). The remainder of this chapter looks at three issues in this context: firstly, whether the unemployed and the discouraged are distinctive in terms of individual and household characteristics; secondly, the role of state transfers in driving the decision to undertake job search; and thirdly, differences in labour market transitions between the two categories.

6.4.1 Changes in job search over the crisis period

In a very simple theoretical setting, an individual chooses to participate in the labour market if the expected benefits from job search outweigh the costs (see, for example, Layard et al. 2005 and Blundell et al. 1998). More specifically, in job search theory, an individual will accept a job offer if it exceeds their reservation wage. In turn, the arrival rate of job offers depends on the intensity of job search, which itself is a function of the potential benefits of searching (net of costs). That is, it is assumed that individuals are maximizing expected utility through their decisions on search intensity. Thus, search will decrease with the costs of doing so, which would be driven in practical terms by the expenses incurred in finding and applying for vacancies. On the other hand, job search among the unemployed will increase with the expected benefits, which will be affected by the overall situation in the labour market (that is, whether the economy is growing or in recession). Theoretically, it is indeed expected that there is a strong relationship between the business cycle and job search. Most relevant for this chapter, discouragement is likely to increase during recessions, because when the job finding rate (exit rate from unemployment) decreases, fewer workers decide to participate in the labour market (Pissarides 2000). This describes the phenomenon of 'discouraged workers' that has periodically emerged as a major policy issue, as is the case with South Africa currently.

Another relevant issue is the problem of spatial mismatch. Kain (1986) first proposed that African-Americans residing in inner city areas of the United States were poorly connected to regions where jobs were being created. It was argued that this geographical distance was a major cause of higher unemployment rates among this sub-population. As discussed in Van Ham et al. (2001), this spatial mismatch reflects not only the costs of migration and commuting, but also the lower arrival rate of job offers in isolated areas. Ultimately, 'most people only search for jobs in the vicinity that would not necessitate a residential move' (Van Ham et al. 2001, p. 1737). In addition, discrimination forces individuals to rely on ethnic and social networks that provide access only to a limited set of job opportunities because these individuals are in a similar situation (Van Ham et al. 2001; Zenou 2011). Overall, discouragement would be higher because of both the costs of job search due to geography and the inability to use networks to increase the likelihood of receiving a job offer. These insights are pertinent to the situation evident in rural areas in South Africa, particularly in the former homelands, as stressed above.

In addition to these studies, there has been considerable discussion in the literature about the empirical robustness of any distinction between searching and non-searching unemployment. As cited in Jones and Riddell (1999, p. 147, fn2), 'As stated by the President's Committee to Appraise Employment and Unemployment Statistics (1962: p. 49): "When should a person not working but wanting to work be included in the labor force and thus counted as unemployed? This constitutes the most difficult question with which the Committee has had to deal."' From a definitional point of view, discouraged workers should be added to the unemployed if their characteristics and behaviour are similar (Jones and Riddell 1999). In terms of empirical studies on this topic, Jones and Riddell (1999) undertake an analysis of transition rates across four labour market states (employment, unemployment, marginal attachment, and non-participation or inactivity) in the United States, and find that unemployment, marginal attachment and non-participation are indeed distinct states. Moving to the South African context, Kingdon and Knight (2006) find that, for the pre-crisis period, discouraged workers are more deprived and no happier than the searching unemployed, while local wage determination takes into account both types of jobless.

To identify whether unemployment and discouraged individuals differ in terms of observable characteristics in the context of the 2008–2009 recession, a logit model is estimated for the sub-sample of individuals who are jobless but available for work (that is, excluding non-participants) (see Kingdon and Knight 2006 for a similar approach). Thus, the binary dependent variable equals one if an individual is not actively searching (discouraged), as opposed to being unemployed and actively searching for a job – the key difference being job search. As above, the estimates for 2008 are compared to 2009–2010 to identify changes during the crisis period.

As reported in Table 6.5 (males and females), a number of individual and household characteristics are associated with being discouraged in comparison with searching unemployment. Using the base specification (columns 1 and 2 of Table 6.5), the estimated odds ratios suggest that, prior to the start of the recession in South Africa, being poorly educated significantly increased the probability of discouragement over unemployment, particularly for women. For example, females with at most a primary education were over five times more likely to be discouraged in 2008 than individuals with tertiary education. Surprisingly, there is not a consistently strong impact of race (after controlling for age, gender, education and so on). Increasing the age by 1 year (from the mean) implies a marginal fall in the odds of discouragement over unemployment. In terms of household characteristics, individuals in large households have a higher probability of discouragement, while both males and females with discouraged spouses are much more likely to be inactive in terms of job search. In general, individuals in all provinces besides the Western Cape are less likely to be actively searching for jobs than those located in Gauteng. The odds of discouragement for females

Table 6.5 Drivers of discouragement among jobless males and females, odds ratios – 2008 versus 2009–2010

Variable	Males		Females	
	2008 (1)	2009/10 (2)	2008 (3)	2009/10 (4)
Age	0.906***	0.893***	0.918***	0.915***
Age-squared	1.001***	1.002***	1.001***	1.001***
Primary school or none (ref: tertiary)	3.751***	3.068***	5.089***	3.953***
Less than Year 12	2.520***	2.045***	3.013***	2.765***
Year 12	1.673***	1.335***	1.863***	1.616***
Black/African (ref: white)	1.480	0.896	1.714***	1.285*
Coloured	0.677	0.589***	1.197	1.049
Indian/Asian	0.550	0.420***	0.537*	0.661*
Household size	1.037***	1.044***	1.038***	1.034***
Spouse employed in formal sector (ref: no spouse)	0.885	0.792**	1.171**	1.267***
Spouse employed in informal sector	0.799*	0.723***	1.100	1.553***
Spouse unemployed	0.160***	0.140***	0.466***	0.494***
Spouse discouraged	5.818***	4.473***	18.472***	18.566***
Spouse OLF	0.782**	0.650***	1.778***	1.531***
Western Cape (ref: Gauteng)	0.667***	0.456***	0.735***	0.499***
Eastern Cape	3.149***	4.080***	2.611***	2.874***
Northern Cape	2.117***	1.932***	2.115***	1.941***
Free State	1.293**	1.371***	1.615***	1.862***
KwaZulu-Natal	1.741***	4.429***	1.604***	4.316***
North West	2.338***	2.461***	2.780***	2.789***
Mpumalanga	1.353***	1.934***	2.315***	2.694***
Limpopo	2.271***	4.055***	2.542***	4.901***
No. of observations	16,107	34,939	19,644	39,733

Notes: *** $p < 0.01$, ** $p < 0.05$, * $p < 0.1$. The odds ratios are based on a logit regression where the dependent variable is a binary variable that equals one for individuals reporting to be discouraged (not actively searching for a job). The sample is restricted to individuals who are ready and able to work (that is, excluding other forms of inactivity due to education, retirement, caring responsibilities and disability).

Source: Statistics South Africa Quarterly Labour Force Survey, 2008Q1–2010Q4; authors' calculations.

with discouraged spouses is more than 18 times higher than the case of individuals without spouses.

Moving to the crisis period (2009–2010), there are a number of changes in the odds ratios that are worth noting. For example, in terms of provincial dummies, the odds increased for males and females in the Eastern Cape, KwaZulu-Natal, Mpumalanga and Limpopo provinces, which are regions with a high proportion of former homelands. The higher odds of discouragement for females with spouses in the informal sector increased from 1.1 in 2008 (insignificant) to 1.6 in 2009–2010.

Another feature of the South African labour market that is particularly troublesome is the high proportion of jobless individuals who have never been employed. In 2008, prior to the onset of the recession in South Africa, 42.4 per cent of the unemployed had never had a job compared with 48.8 per cent of discouraged individuals. Adding a dummy to the specification used in Table 6.5, which indicates whether an individual has ever worked, shows, unsurprisingly, that this factor is positively associated with the likelihood of discouragement.[13] South Africans, in particular young people, who never gain work experience, have little hope of finding employment and, thus, do not actively search for a job. Looking at the changes over the crisis period, males who have never worked had a significantly higher odds ratio of discouragement in 2009–2010 than in 2008 (1.67 versus 1.39), reflecting how the deteriorating economy further impacted such marginalized individuals. For females who have never worked before, the odds ratio increased by a smaller margin (from 1.30 to 1.48).

6.4.2 What role for social transfers?

A hotly debated topic in many countries is the impact of social security transfers on labour force participation. In this regard, a large number of studies have investigated the effect of the South African old-age pension (OAP) on labour force participation within recipient households. Ardington et al. (2009) find that the OAP leads to increased employment among prime-aged adults as a consequence of relieving credit constraints to labour migration, a result that has been also found elsewhere (see, for example, Samson 2009). This more encouraging finding contrasts with some earlier findings, which suggested more perverse effects of the pension on labour force participation (for example, Bertrand et al. 2003).

As discussed later in this chapter, another important element of the South African social security system is the child support grant (CSG), which was first introduced in 1998 following the recommendation of the Lund Committee of Child and Family Support. The CSG has since become the most widespread social transfer in the country, accounting for 10.4 million recipients in 2010, which represented 68.1 per cent of all social security recipients, 37 per cent of all households and 34.8 per cent of social grants expenditure (National Treasury 2011; OECD 2011). Theoretically, the CSG, like the OAP, could increase job search if it alleviates the credit constraints that prevent individuals from migrating to urban centres or actively looking for a job further from their home, as was argued in the case of the OAP. For example, the grant may help mothers pay for child care that, in turn, allows them to work (Eyal and Woolard 2011). Alternatively, the transfer could decrease search due to an income/substitution effect (individuals are more likely to consume more leisure) or an increase in reservation wages (in a search theoretical setting). Given the relatively small size of the transfer (R260 in 2010), it was, however, not clear whether the CSG would have a major impact on labour force participation of recipients, particularly among female beneficiaries. As argued by Klasen and Woolard (2008), the relationship between transfers and labour outcomes can go the other way: unemployed individuals remain in rural households in order to access social transfers and remittances which, in turn, reduces their incentives for job search and the arrival rate of offers.

A few studies have investigated the potential labour market effects of the child support grant. In this regard, Williams (2007) finds that receiving the CSG is associated with an increase in broad labour force participation, while it has no effect on the narrow definition of participation or employment. Though Samson (2009) compares only raw figures on the likelihood of being in certain labour market states, this study concludes that the CSG is associated with a higher probability of job search and finding employment in poorer households, particularly among women. In a more recent study, Eyal and Woolard (2011) take advantage of changes in the cut-off age to identify the impact of the CSG on mothers' labour force participation. Using data from the October Household Survey (OHS) and General Household Survey (GHS), this study finds that receiving the grant is associated with a higher probability of labour force participation and employment (and a lower rate of unemployment conditional on participation).

Turning to the data utilized in this chapter (QLFS), the main form of income support for both the unemployed and discouraged is provided overwhelmingly by other persons in the household: in 2008, 77.7 per cent of the unemployed and 76.5 per of the discouraged reported receiving such transfers (Table 6.6). In 2009–2010, this proportion stayed approximately the same for the unemployed (77.4 per cent), while it increased for individuals who were not searching for a job

Table 6.6 Forms of income support for the discouraged and unemployed, both sexes

	Percentage receiving support (%)			
	Unemployed		Discouraged	
	2008	2009–2010	2008	2009–2010
Persons in the household	77.7	77.4	76.5	79.8
Persons not in the household	19.7	20.7	21.5	19.9
Child support/foster care grants	13.8	13.6	22.5	22.6
Savings	4.7	4.9	1.9	1.6
Unemployment Insurance Fund (UIF)	0.7	1.0	0.4	0.4
Pension	0.7	0.6	1.4	1.1
Charity	0.1	0.1	0.2	0.1

Source: Statistics South Africa Quarterly Labour Force Survey, 2008Q1–2010Q4; authors' calculations.

(to 79.8 per cent). Support from persons not in the household and child support/foster care grants are also important sources. At the same time, savings are a minor form of support for those without a job. Finally, despite the large increase in the number of beneficiaries of payments from the Unemployment Insurance Fund (UIF) during the crisis period (from 397,000 beneficiaries in 2007/08 to 529,000 in 2009/10),[14] a very small proportion of both unemployed and discouraged workers in our sample stated that they were being supported by such transfers (less than one per cent). This is far lower than the figure of five per cent quoted in a recent study by the National Treasury (2011). This under-scores that, though South Africa has established an unemployment benefits scheme (the Unemployment Insurance Fund – UIF), the lim-ited coverage means that most individuals without employment rely on other means for survival. The percentage stating that they receive sup-port from a pension is low, though this form of support may also be included in intra/inter-household transfers from relatives who receive the OAP.

Returning to the binary (logit) specification reported in Table 6.5, including dummies for the type of support received by individuals, this shows that there is some evidence of an association between receiving transfers and the decision to undertake job search (Table 6.7). The direc-tion of causality is, however, harder to establish unless using an identifi-cation strategy as adopted by Eyal and Woolard (2011). More specifically, receiving intra-household transfers is correlated with a lower probability

Table 6.7 The relationship between transfers and discouragement among jobless males and females, odds ratios – 2008 versus 2009–2010

Variable	2008 (1)	2009–2010 (2)
MALES		
Intra-household transfers	1.030	1.287***
Inter-household transfers	1.078	0.862***
UIF	0.903	0.541***
Savings	0.516***	0.447***
Pension	1.500	1.709***
Grants	1.626**	1.045
Observations	16,107	34,939
FEMALES		
Intra-household transfers	1.013	1.180***
Inter-household transfers	1.058	1.054
UIF	0.761	0.838
Savings	0.709**	0.583***
Pension	1.540**	1.196
Grants	1.350***	1.215***
Observations	19,644	39,733

Notes: *** $p < 0.01$, ** $p < 0.05$, * $p < 0.1$. The odds ratios are based on a logit regression where the dependent variable is a binary variable that equals one for individuals reporting to be discouraged (not actively searching for a job). The sample is restricted to individuals who are ready and able to work (that is, excluding other forms of inactivity due to education, retirement, caring responsibilities and disability). Other variables included in the logit regression are listed in Table 6.5.
Source: Statistics South Africa Quarterly Labour Force Survey, 2008Q1–2010Q4; authors' calculations.

of discouragement for females, but the odds ratio increased in magnitude over the crisis period. Inter-household transfers are associated with a higher probability of discouragement, which may reflect the role of support from spouses and other family members working away from the household. For males, the likelihood of discouragement increased during the South African recession for those receiving transfers from within the household, while it decreased for individuals receiving support from outside the household.

More specifically, Table 6.7 shows that receiving intra-household transfers is correlated with a higher probability of discouragement for females, but the odds ratio was only significant during the crisis period. Inter-household transfers are also associated with a higher probability of discouragement, but these ratios are not significant. For males, the likelihood of discouragement increased during the South African recession for those receiving transfers from within the household, while it decreased for individuals receiving support from outside the household (both are only significant in the crisis period).

The estimates reported in Table 6.7 also suggest that receiving UIF benefits (for males) and relying on savings is positively associated with job search among unemployed men and women. In terms of the more generous OAP, receiving this transfer was associated with a higher likelihood of discouragement for women prior to the crisis in 2008. In 2009–10, this likelihood for individuals receiving the pension increased significantly for males but not females. The dummy for child grants was positively and significantly correlated with the probability of discouragement for unemployed females (and for males in 2008), but there was not a major shift in the odds ratio for these variables over the crisis period.

6.4.3 Are transitions in the labour market different for the discouraged?

As highlighted above, the study by Jones and Riddell (1999) focused on transition rates to identify differences between the unemployed and discouraged workers. Though Statistics South Africa does not provide an identifier to link the various waves of the QLFS (which is sampled on the basis of a rotating panel as noted above), a panel can be created from the data using the household identifier and information on age, gender, population group, marital status and educational status. Using a similar approach taken by Ranchod and Dinkelman (2008) for the earlier Labour Force Survey (including dropping false matches on the basis of inconsistencies in marital status and educational attainment), this results in a sample of 181,372 observations for 2008–10; 60,624 observations were dropped from the full sample because individuals were present only in one wave; a further 20,421 observations were eliminated due to inconsistencies in marital status and educational attainment. This process resulted in a matching rate of 48.7 per cent (compared to 38 per cent for Ranchod and Dinkelman 2008 for the LFS). Attrition may not be random and, therefore, it is not possible to claim that figures from this data are representative of the South African working-age population.

Using this matched dataset, it is possible to compare the transitions across the five labour market states (formal sector employment, informal sector employment, unemployment, discouragement and out-of-the-labour force). To isolate the impact of the crisis, the transition rates for

Table 6.8 Labour market transitions rates in 2008 versus 2009

FEMALES	Period t+1									
Period t	Ft+1		It+1		Ut+1		Dt+1		OLFt+1	
	2008	2009	2008	2009	2008	2009	2008	2009	2008	2009
Ft	89.2	91.7	3.8	3.3	2.8	1.9	0.6	0.8	3.6	2.4
It	7.6	7.6	74.9	80.0	5.2	3.1	2.3	1.7	10.1	7.6
Ut	7.6	5.4	8.6	4.4	55.9	61.2	5.3	7.6	22.6	21.4
Dt	6.2	3.0	7.1	2.5	16.9	19.5	39.8	49.5	30.0	25.5
OLFt	1.7	0.7	2.4	1.9	6.2	5.5	2.4	3.3	87.3	88.9

MALES	Period t+1									
Period t	Ft+1		It+1		Ut+1		Dt+1		OLFt+1	
	2008	2009	2008	2009	2008	2009	2008	2009	2008	2009
Ft	90.6	92.8	3.7	2.9	3.2	2.3	0.5	0.7	2.0	1.2
It	17.5	12.9	67.1	74.3	8.1	6.7	2.9	1.6	4.4	4.6
Ut	13.7	9.7	7.7	4.0	60.4	67.7	4.2	7.6	14.0	11.1
Dt	3.8	3.6	7.0	8.2	22.7	24.6	43.2	46.4	23.2	17.3
OLFt	1.4	0.7	2.3	1.9	6.0	6.1	1.5	3.0	88.9	88.3

Notes: F = formal sector employment; I = informal sector employment; U = narrowly defined unemployment; D = discouragement; OLF = other out-of-the-labour force.
Source: Statistics South Africa Quarterly Labour Force Survey, 2008Q1–2009Q4; authors' calculations.

2008Q1–2008Q4 (that is, transitions from 2008Q1 to 2008Q2, 2008Q2 to 2008Q3 and 2008Q3 to 2008Q4) are compared to 2009Q1–2009Q4 (2009Q1 to 2009Q2, 2009Q2 to 2009Q3 and 2009Q3 to 2009Q4).

As displayed in Table 6.8, there is a general high degree of persistence in formal sector employment and inactivity (OLF), while there is considering churning across different states in the South African labour market, which is similar to findings for earlier periods (see, for example, Banerjee et al. 2006, 2008). Discouragement is the least absorbing state. At the same time, men are more likely to move into formal sector employment from informal sector employment and unemployment than from the state of discouragement (see the findings of Ranchod and Dinkelman 2008 for an earlier period).

Of particular interest is the high rate of transitions from discouragement into narrowly defined unemployment, which reflects that the decision to undertake job search changes over time, even from one quarter to the next. For example, in 2008, 22.7 and 16.7 per cent of discouraged males and females started actively searching for a job in the next quarter. As noted above (see also Kingdon and Knight 2006 and Makgetta 2010), the likelihood of finding employment in the former 'homeland' areas is very low, while the costs of job search to urban centres are high. A typical search strategy for individuals living in these regions is to wait for information about a specific job offer that they receive through their social network (especially through an employed relative or friend). This would partly explain the churning evident in the transitions between narrowly defined unemployment and discouragement.

In terms of changes in transition rates from 2008 to 2009, there is evidence that most states have become more absorbing during the recession; that is, individuals were less likely to move. For example, 60.4 per cent of males remained in informal sector employment from one quarter to the next in 2008, which increased to 67.7 per cent in 2009. Interestingly, these transitions from formal and informal sector employment into unemployment and discouragement largely decreased from 2008 to 2009 for both men and women. In contrast, the most visible impact of the crisis is the fall in the inflow rates for males, especially from informal sector employment and unemployment into formal sector employment, and from unemployment into informal sector employment. In 2008, 17.5 per cent of informal sector workers and 13.7 per cent of the unemployed moved to the formal sector in the next quarter. These transition rates fell in 2009 to 12.9 and 9.7 per cent, respectively. At the same time, there were lower inflow rates into informal sector work from unemployment (for both women and men). This is consistent with the decline in informal sector employment discussed above and displayed in Figure 6.1. Overall, the rise in narrowly defined unemployment during the recession of 2008–2009 was caused more by a fall in inflow rather than outflow rates. In addition to these changes to inflow rates, transitions from narrowly defined unemployment to discouragement, and vice-versa, increased for both sexes during the crisis period.

Given the low match rate, it is difficult to robustly identify the determinants of transitions (using the same individual and household variables employed above). Experimenting with different specifications (such as logit for entries into formal sector employment) reveals that there were no major significant changes during the recession. However, if a better matched panel was available, this type of analysis could be further explored.

6.5   Labour market policies and institutions in South Africa: increasing capacity to target the poor and respond to crises

As underscored in the above sections, the South African labour market continues to be characterized by high rates of unemployment and discouragement, notably for black Africans, youth and the poorly educated. This situation further deteriorated during the global financial crisis, eroding any gains made in the years leading up to the downturn. In response, the government of South Africa has sought to address both the entrenched levels of inequality and poverty, and the failure of the labour market to act as the mechanism to rectify these problems.

In the early post-Apartheid period, the government focused on macroeconomic stability through the Growth, Employment and Redistribution (GEAR) strategy of 1996–2000. While this approach did help generate some stability, policies were not able to stimulate growth and generate jobs for the large numbers of black Africans, particularly women, who joined the labour force at that time. To address these shortcomings, policymakers shifted their attention to the persistent problems of unemployment and poverty. As a result, the Accelerated and Shared Growth Initiative for South Africa (AsgiSA) was launched in 2006, covering six areas identified as binding constraints.[15]

Facing continuing challenges in the labour market as highlighted earlier in this chapter, the government of South Africa developed a new policy framework at the end of 2010, the New Growth Path (NGP), which seeks to promote economic transformation and inclusive growth that translates into sustained job creation. The NGP prioritizes job creation and aims to reduce unemployment by 10 percentage points by 2020, down from the current rate of 25 per cent, through the creation of five million jobs over the next decade. Stressing the importance of policy coherence, the NGP focuses on six key areas that have the potential to create jobs: infrastructure; the agricultural value chain; the mining value chain, the green economy; manufacturing sectors; and tourism and certain high-level services. For each of these 'jobs drivers', the framework outlines employment targets.[16] One of the key drivers identified is investment in infrastructure (energy, transport, water, communications) and housing, which is expected to create 250,000 jobs per year up to 2015. The implementation of the NGP would also rely on existing measures including the Expanded Public Works Programme (EPWP).

In addition to the EPWP, this section looks at recent labour market policy efforts to keep workers in jobs through the Training Layoff

Scheme and to establish an unemployment insurance scheme (the Unemployment Insurance Fund). In addition, the situation in the South African public employment service is discussed (although recipients of the UIF are not activated through job search assistance and other active labour market policies). Though not directly connected to the labour market, the section also covers social transfers, namely the Old Age Pension and Child Support Grant, which have played increasingly important roles in mitigating poverty.

The focus here, therefore, is not on labour market regulations. As underscored in Chapter 2 of this book, employment protection legislation in South Africa is not particularly stringent in comparison to other OECD (and non-OECD) countries (see also Benjamin et al. 2010). For example, the maximum severance pay is 5 months (only 2.5 months after 20 years of service). According to the World Bank Enterprise Surveys, less than 10 per cent of South African companies rate labour market regulations as a major constraint. As also highlighted in Chapter 2, minimum wages in South Africa constitute less than 20 per cent of the average wage. Overall, such institutions as employment protection legislation and minimum wages are neither a major barrier for South African employers nor a source of income/employment protection for workers in the country. However, industrial relations are an overall challenge in South Africa: union density is relatively high at 39.8 per cent (see Chapter 3).

6.5.1 The Expanded Public Works Programme (EPWP)

The Expanded Public Works Programme (EPWP) is a national programme which was established in 2004/05 with the aim of creating one million jobs in five years. The scheme aimed to create employment by increasing the labour intensity of government infrastructure projects, creating jobs in public environmental programmes such as Working for Water, and creating jobs in public social programmes. The EPWP is coordinated by the Department of Public Works, and consists of numerous key objectives, including drawing significant numbers of the unemployed into productive work, providing the unemployed with education and skills, and ensuring that beneficiaries are either able to find employment or are able to set up their own businesses once they exit the programme. Furthermore, this programme was meant to reduce and alleviate unemployment (HSRC 2007).

During 2007, the halfway point of the first phase of the EPWP, the Expanded Public Works Support Programme commissioned a mid-term review of the EPWP in order to assess the strengths and weaknesses of the programme and to elicit recommendations on the future of the programme (HSRC 2007). It was found that the EPWP was a complex public works programme which, unlike other successful programmes around the world, contained a range of different objectives including increasing employment, improving the skills base of participants to help them find employment in the future, and contributing to the government's social protection mandate (McCord 2007). The implementation model, however, 'offers only a single short-term episode of employment, and is therefore unlikely to have a significant social protection or employment impact in an economy that suffers from persistently high levels of unemployment and poverty' (McCord 2007, p. 8). Furthermore, both McCord (2007) and the HSRC (2007) findings suggest that the skills development aspect of the EPWP was inappropriate given the skills needs of the economy, and the nature of unemployment in South Africa. Recommendations included a clearer set of well-defined objectives for the programme, and delinking training for the unemployed from public works programme employment (McCord 2007; HSRC 2007).

In late 2008, the South African government agreed to the roll-out of the second phase of the EPWP, which was launched in April 2009 with the goal of creating 4.5 million jobs for poor and unemployed people in South Africa by 2014. From 1 April to 31 August 2009, the EPWP created a total of 223,568 work opportunities.[17] The performance of the EPWP improved in 2010: the programme generated 643,116 work opportunities from 1 April 2010 to 31 March 2011. The Community Works Programme (CWP) was responsible for 92,136 opportunities over this period.[18] A major challenge for the EPWP is the duration of work opportunities. Though the target is 100 days, the average reached so far is only 46 days.[19]

In general, it is not evident whether the problems encountered in the first phase of the EPWP have been dealt with in instituting the second phase. Though a large number of work opportunities were created, they were clearly dwarfed by the massive fall in employment during the recession highlighted above.

6.5.2   The Training Layoff Scheme

To mitigate the impact of the global financial crisis, the South African government, together with social partners, developed the 'Framework for South Africa's Response to the International Crisis', which included a number of interventions including the Training Layoff Scheme (TLS), which was announced and implemented in 2009. The objective of the

TLS was to subsidize employers to avoid firing workers. This scheme was specifically targeted at employers experiencing financial distress during the recession (employers had to demonstrate their financial difficulties or a drop in sales/revenue). According to the Department of Labour's 'A Guide to the Training Layoff Scheme' from 2009: 'A training layoff is a temporary suspension of work of a worker or group of workers that is used for training purposes'. Through the scheme, employers are able to reduce payroll costs since employees no longer earn a salary but are instead allocated training allowances, funded by the National Skills Foundation (NSF). In turn, workers are able to keep their employment contracts (though they earn a lower salary) and receive training. Importantly, participation in the scheme is voluntary, and is dependent on an agreement between an employer and trade union on behalf of workers, or between an employer and individual workers who may otherwise be dismissed due to operational requirements (DOL 2009). An initial amount of R2.9 billion was allocated to the scheme, consisting of R2.4 billion for training allowances for workers and R500 million for training costs (The Presidency 2009).

One of the main challenges (and criticisms of the TLS) has been the complexity of the scheme's implementation. Any employer, trade union or individual worker may apply for access to the training layoff scheme, either directly to the Commission for Conciliation, Mediation and Arbitration (CCMA) or as part of an alternative to retrenchment at a hearing at the CCMA. While the CCMA is responsible for facilitating and overseeing all training layoff agreements, if an agreement is entered into independently of the CCMA, the parties must ensure that the agreement complies with the terms of the training layoff scheme. Employees on the scheme may not earn more than R180,000 per annum, and must be within firms that are facing economic distress due to the recession, and thus contemplating retrenching these employees. The funds allocated to the NSF are used to pay training allowances to workers on the scheme, pegged at 50 per cent of their basic wage or salary, to a maximum of R6,239 per month. In turn, participating employers continue to carry the basic social benefit costs of employees during the period that workers are on the scheme, and this includes the costs of funerals, deaths and disabilities. Employers may also choose to combine the training layoff scheme with short-time work arrangements, though the employee would then be eligible for both the training allowance and short-time work pay.

The cost of the training is borne by the relevant Skills Education Training Authority (SETA), which should assist with the choice of training.

It is envisaged that the training should be linked as far as possible to skills needs of the employer, and may include 'learnerships', apprenticeships and skills development programmes. More generic training such as Adult Basic Education and Training (ABET) and other generic workplace training is also acceptable. Training should generally be NQF-aligned and bear credits. Employees can participate in the scheme for a maximum of three months per worker.

The figures presented in Table 6.9 reveal that take-up of the TLS was very low: applications for the scheme until 11 June 2010 represented just 44 cases involving 7,676 workers; 19 training layoff cases involving 5,992 workers cases were either being implemented, or were being processed by the NSF and SETAs. Therefore, 23 applications involving 1,646 workers were not completed either because the cases were withdrawn,

Table 6.9   Progress to 11 June 2010 with the Training Layoff (TL) Scheme

Cases in various stages of TL Scheme Process		No. of cases	No. of affected workers	Share of total workers affected
Training	TL approved by the DoL Committee and training in process	10	4,512	59%
SETA, NSF and DoL	TL at the stage of being processed by the SETA and NSF	9	1,480	19%
CCMA	TL being considered by the CCMA Advisory Committee	2	38	0%
Total cases that are in the TL Scheme process		21	6,030	79%
Cases in various stages of TL Scheme Process		**No. of cases**	**No. of affected workers**	**Share of total cases**
Withdrawn by parties		8	557	7%
Cases not recommended by the CCMA Advisory Committee		13	974	13%
Cases where eligibility could not be determined		1	12	0%
Cases where companies were liquidated		1	103	1%
Total cases that started the TL process, but did not proceed to training		23	1,646	21%
Total cases		44	7,676	100%

Source: CCMA (2010).

not recommended by the CCMA, eligibility could not be determined, or the companies were liquidated. Of these, the majority of cases (13 out of 23) involving 974 workers were cases where the CCMA Advisory Committee did not recommend the training layoff scheme, either because the CCMA did not find that the companies were experiencing financial distress due to the recession, or the CCMA found that the companies were not in distress at all.

In terms of geographical distribution, the uptake of the scheme in the Johannesburg area was low, accounting for a mere one per cent of all workers participating in the scheme, while it has been highest in the Tshwane area, accounting for 54 per cent of all workers involved in the scheme. Unsurprisingly, the uptake of the scheme has been highest in the three provinces which account for the highest share of employment – Gauteng, Western Cape and KwaZulu-Natal – together accounting for 92 per cent of all workers on the scheme. The only other provinces to feature were the Eastern Cape and Mpumalanga provinces, together accounting for eight per cent of all workers involved in training layoffs.

Turning to the sectoral distribution, uptake has been highest in the motor and motor components sector, accounting for more than half of all workers on the scheme, which was an industry hard hit by the downturn. In turn, the metal and engineering (15 per cent) and food and beverage (23 per cent) sectors also account for significant proportions of workers involved in the training layoffs. Together these three sectors account for almost 94 per cent of all workers on the training layoff scheme. These results appear to stem directly from the fact, noted above, that the tradable goods sector was one of the most visible casualties of the domestic recession.

The main factors that have hampered implementation of the TLS include: the programme was new and did not build on an existing programme; the complexity of the scheme and excessive bureaucratic procedures, which resulted in long delays; too many ministries and agencies were involved in its implementation; difficulty of proving financial distress; the inadequate training allowance (vis-à-vis severance pay); and finally, workers' concerns about losing severance pay benefits if they opted for participating in the TLS.

6.5.3 The Unemployment Insurance Fund

South Africa has built a comprehensive social security system since the end of Apartheid. As part of this architecture, the Unemployment Insurance Fund or UIF is an insurance fund to which employees and employers contribute,[20] and which offers short-term financial assistance to registered workers when they become unemployed or are unable to work because of illness, maternity or adoption leave. Thus, employees who are registered with the UIF and who have been paying contributions to the Fund can claim from the Fund if they lose their jobs or cannot work.[21] The UIF is thus the only component of South Africa's social security architecture that is specifically aimed at the unemployed.

Using available UIF data for 2010–2011 (Figure 6.5), the impact of the recession on UIF beneficiaries and total payments is clear. According to the National Treasury's Budget Review 2011, there were 397,000 UIF recipients in 2007–2008; by 2010–2011, this number increased substantially to 590,000. In terms of spending, UIF payments almost doubled from R2 billion in 2007–2008 to R4.3 billion in 2010–2011.

Provincial data indicates that the largest number of new claims emanated from Gauteng (27 per cent), the Western Cape (19 per cent)

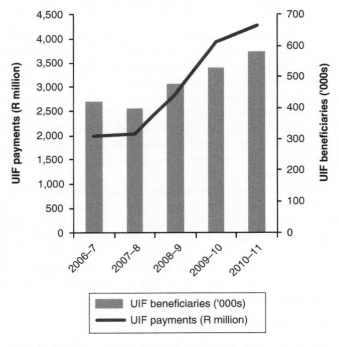

Figure 6.5 UIF payments and beneficiaries, 2008 and 2009
Notes: 2010–2011 is a revised estimate.
Source: National Treasury of the Republic of South Africa (2011).

and KwaZulu-Natal (19 per cent). While these results are not surprising since these provinces account for the largest relative shares of employment in South Africa, the data further show that monthly growth in new claims over the period was highest for the Eastern Cape. This result may be indicative, as noted above, of the economic shock to the local economy. Furthermore, when comparing the ratio of claims to employment across provinces, the data reveal that the UIF better serves those in metropolitan areas rather than rural areas with the claim share to employment share ratio being particularly low for the Eastern Cape, Free State and the North West.

In comparison to the UIF, other non-labour market social security payments have become much more widespread. As described in Box 6.1, the Old Age Pension and the Child Support Grant have become key pillars of the government's strategy to fight poverty.

Box 6.1 Social transfers compensating for underperforming labour market

In 1996, the Lund Committee of Child and Family Support recommended the introduction of the child support grant to target children in poor households that had been excluded under the Apartheid social security system. The scheme replaced the State Maintenance Grant which had a limited reach because of its strict eligibility conditions and the way these were applied to different racial groups.[22] The child support grant initially included several conditionalities. Applicants were expected to participate in 'development programmes' and have proof that the children were immunized.[23] Other conditionalities included proof of efforts to obtain private maintenance from the child's father, and of efforts to secure employment or join a development programme, but these were all subsequently dropped. This unconditional cash transfer was subsequently established in 1998 and has since become a crucial pillar in the government's approach to broadening access to social security. Initially, children under the age of seven were eligible for a monthly payment of R100 if the primary caregiver and his/her spouse jointly had R800 per month or less in income and lived in an urban area and formal house. For those who lived in rural areas or informal housing in urban areas, the income threshold was R1,100 per month.[24] The Department

Table 6.10   Grant beneficiaries in South Africa, 2010/11 (estimates)

Type of grant	Number of beneficiaries ('000s)	Expenditure (R million)
Old-age	2,647	33,797
War veterans	1	14
Disability	1,233	17,080
Foster care	554	4,898
Care dependency	121	1,582
Child support	10,336	30,594
Total	14,892	87,965

Source: National Treasury of the Republic of South Africa (2011) Budget Review 2011.

of Social Development is responsible for administering the grant, which is paid to the child's primary caregiver.

However, take-up of the CSG was initially low with only 21,997 beneficiaries in 1999 (Table 6.10). In 2000, the take-up rate was approximately just 10 per cent of eligible children.[25] Some of the key problems in rolling out the grant include the inadequate facilities for processing claims, lack of knowledge on how to apply, and missing documentation.[26]

In response, the South African Social Security Agency (SASSA) has continually expanded the programme over the last decade or so. To enlarge the scope of the transfer, the age cut-off was raised six times from 1998 and stood at 14 years in 2007 prior to the onset of the recession. During the crisis, the age cut-off was increased to 15 in 2009, 16 in 2010 and, finally, to 17 in 2011 (Figure 6.6). At the same time, the payment has increased from R100 to R260 as of 2011, while the government has conducted outreach campaigns in rural areas to encourage enrolment.[27] The means test threshold for the child support grant is now set at 10 times the value of the grant.

As a consequence of these reforms, the number of beneficiaries has increased rapidly, reaching almost 10.4 million in 2010, which represented 68.1 per cent of all social security recipients, 37 per cent of all households[28] and 34.8 per cent of social grants expenditure (Table 6.10). The take-up rate has surpassed 60 per cent. To further expand the scheme, the government has committed to further increasing the age cut-off to 18 in 2012.

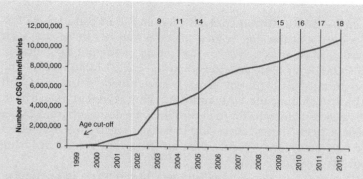

Figure 6.6 South Africa's Child Support Grant
Note: Figures for 2011 and 2012 are projected.
Sources: UNICEF South Africa and SAHRC (2011).

The South African child support grant scheme now reaches over 10 million children and, thus, has become an important part of the government's strategy to target poor households, and to improve, in particular, child outcomes. Despite the relatively small size of the cash transfer, the CSG has the potential to alleviate credit constraints which, in turn, supports investment in schooling (paying for school fees and uniforms) and nutrition of dependent children. Since its establishment in 1998, a range of evaluations has indeed indicated a positive impact of the CSG on school attendance, nutrition, weight and height z scores and child labour.[29]

Beyond the direct impact of the CSG on child outcomes, the grant, like all social transfers, has the potential to affect the labour market status of members of the recipient household, especially of the mother. As debated in the literature, the CSG could either increase labour force participation by reducing constraints to job search or decrease it because of a negative income/substitution effect. In the first case, an increase in household income would help household members, namely mothers, pay for transport to search for jobs or for child care that subsequently allows them to search in the first place. Conversely, it is often argued that such transfers reduce incentives to work because of the higher income. However, recent empirical studies do not find evidence that receiving the CSG reduces labour force participation.[30]

In the South African context, there has been considerable discussion about the effectiveness of social transfers in general, with particular attention given to the impact of the old age pension. The OAP is far more generous than the CSG (R1,080 versus R260 per month in 2010). In general, government grants in South Africa, including the OAP and CSG, now represent 73 per cent of household income for the lowest income decile, up from 15 per cent in 1993. Though these cash transfers have had less of an effect on inequality, they clearly play an important role in reducing poverty in South Africa.[31]

Due to its greater generosity, there have been a large number of evaluations of the labour market impact of the OAP. In this context, while some earlier studies find that the OAP is associated with lower labour force participation of adults in recipient households,[32] more recent investigations show that the transfer has had a positive impact on labour force participation and probability of finding employment.[33] The results of Ardington et al. (2009) indicate that the negative impact of labour force participation disappears once non-resident household members (that is, migrant workers) are included in the analysis.[34] Beyond the case of South Africa, evidence for other developing countries suggests that the labour market impact of cash transfers on labour market outcomes is less negative than that found in advanced economies.

6.5.4   The South African public employment service

Another major challenge in implementing labour market policies in South Africa is the inadequacy of the public employment services. The basic aim of most PES programmes is to reduce unemployment by matching the unemployed with vacancies in the economy. PES programmes thus do not create jobs, but contribute to filling jobs faster and better.

According to the most recent administrative data, South Africa has 135 labour centres spread throughout the country, employing some 5,806 staff with a total budgetary commitment of about R1 billion, including the UIF. This translates into a per capita expenditure of about R175,000 per staff member within the PES system. Gauteng captures the largest share of the department's allocation, at 22 per cent, followed by KwaZulu-Natal (16 per cent), the Eastern Cape (13 per cent) and then the Western Cape (11 per cent). It is not immediately clear, however, how these allocations are made within the budget process of the department, and whether they are simply related to historical allocation models or instead based on a more rigorous assessment of labour market conditions within each of the regions and provinces.

In a global comparison, there is a very high number of (narrowly defined) unemployed per individual PES staff member for South Africa. Hence, whilst Germany has approximately 42 unemployed individuals per PES staff member, and Hungary has 150, the estimate for South Africa is 483 unemployed individuals per PES staff member. These figures suggest that South Africa has too few PES staff (and indeed PES offices as well) per unemployed person in comparison to more developed countries (but has more staff than most emerging economies).

Given the difficult situation under which the South African PES functions in terms of funding, staff and technology, it is not expected that the PES would have a significant impact during the recession. Moreover, the Employment Services of South Africa (ESSA) IT system used at labour centres was not fully functional during the recession, which impacted on the ability of the labour centres to support the unemployed in finding work. An optimized ESSA system went live from 23 March 2010.

Ultimately, the effectiveness of the PES and labour market programmes in assisting the unemployed will not only depend on resources allocated to these schemes, but also whether they target regions and individuals who are in most need of assistance. As highlighted above in the empirical analysis, those hit hardest during the recession of 2009 were poorly educated black Africans, many of whom have not worked in the formal sector (many have never worked at all). The vast majority of these individuals have not been able to access UIF or be part of the TLS scheme.

6.6 Conclusion

In spite of the response of the government of South Africa, the recession of 2008–2009 decimated the labour market resulting in a drop in employment of over 800,000 (the difference in the average in 2010 compared to 2008). As shown in this chapter, the main effect of the downturn and loss in employment was a rise in the number of discouraged individuals, from an average of 1.12 million in 2008 to 1.98 million in 2010. In comparison, narrowly defined search unemployment increased over the same period by only 214,000 (from 4.08 to 4.29 million). Drawing on estimates from the micro-data, discouragement has increased more for uneducated black Africans, while individuals who have given up job search are statistically different from those who continue searching while jobless. At the same time, there are considerable transitions in the labour market, particularly between narrowly defined unemployment and discouragement. Thus, many individuals change their job search strategy over a period of months. Overall, the findings in this chapter strongly support the notion that a broader measure of the unemployment rate best captures the deterioration in the South African labour market during the recession of 2008–2009. As also argued by Kingdon and Knight (2006), it is, however, ultimately useful for policymakers to distinguish between both searching and non-searching states of joblessness and thus report on both the narrow and broad unemployment rates.

The response of policymakers to the first post-Apartheid recession indicates that the South African government is experimenting with new and more innovative measures, such as the Training Layoff Fund. However, apart from the fact that this intervention had limited impact on saving jobs in the formal sector, most measures did not specifically target the issue of discouragement and job search. In 2010, the Zuma government announced its latest policy initiative, the 'New Growth Path', which focuses on how and where to create jobs. Though addressing insufficient labour demand is indeed a critical task, this needs to be supplemented with policies that tackle the supply side, namely the problems of inadequate skills, work experience and spatial inequalities. This would require further interventions to reduce barriers to job search, such as improving the quality of and access to training, investing in infrastructure, and providing targeted transport subsidies.

The challenge is to establish the right conditions for long-term job creation, which requires the optimum mix of macroeconomic, sectoral and labour market policies. In terms of the last, the EPWP could be expanded into a true 'employer of last resort' scheme as is the case with the Mahatma Gandhi National Rural Employment Guarantee Scheme in India. However, policymakers need to also go beyond such approaches and focus on reducing barriers to job search through infrastructure investment (which, in turn, could use the EPWP as a deliverer of such infrastructure), subsidies for transport, and training and job search assistance schemes. At the same time, social protection coverage needs to be improved.

One particular challenge for the South African government is that both the training layoff scheme and the UIF exclude informal sector workers, and this is particularly problematic given that these workers saw a steeper fall in employment compared to formal sector workers and they represented almost 30 per cent of the total fall in employment after the crisis struck. Thus, given that informal sector workers are generally those in more vulnerable economic circumstances, it is necessary to reconsider the measures so far instituted to incorporate these workers as well. Finally, the role played by the PESs and the EPWP initiative has been limited, due mainly to challenges within these initiatives, which existed even prior to the onset of the recession. As far as the PESs are concerned, though, substantial effort is being expended to look again at the role of labour centres and make them more meaningful to the fight against unemployment in South Africa.

Notes

1. See, for example, www.agrisa.co.za/konferensie/Agrisa/30814_ngp_framework_for_public_release_final_1.pdf
2. Referring to the claim of mis-measurement of South African unemployment, Kingdon and Knight (2007) suggest that the high unemployment rate measured through household and labour force surveys could indeed be an underestimate.
3. For the situation of African entrepreneurs during the Apartheid period, see Rogerson (1992).
4. See IMF World Economic Outlook October 2010, available at: www.imf.org/external/pubs/ft/weo/2010/02/weodata/index.aspx
5. The Monetary Policy Committee (MPC) of the South African Reserve Bank started reducing interest rates in December 2008. The cumulative reduction in the repurchase rate over 2008–2009 was 5 percentage points (the rate reached a low of 7 per cent) (South Africa Reserve Bank 2009). The result of tripartite negotiations, the Framework for South Africa's Response to the International Economic Crisis, outlines the main pillars of the government's action plan to respond to the crisis, including major public investment programmes, see www.info.gov.za/view/DownloadFileAction?id=96381.
6. This is defined in terms of registration/licensing of enterprises, excluding the agricultural sector.
7. See, for example, Jutting and de Laiglesia (2009).
8. This impact on young men has been also found in the case of OECD countries as highlighted by Verick (2009).
9. See www.statssa.gov.za/qlfs/index.asp
10. See the ILO's Key Indicators of the Labour Market (KILM) for further details on definitions, at: www.ilo.org/empelm/what/lang–en/WCMS_114240/index.htm
11. For this reason, the STATA margins command was used to calculate the average partial effects. The svy command in STATA was employed to take into account the use of survey data (standard errors are adjusted accordingly).

12. The combined effect of age has to take into account the squared term used in the model. This can be calculated as: $\beta_{age} + 2 \times mean(age) \times \beta_{age2}$
13. Results available from author upon request.
14. See National Treasury (2011), Chapter 7.
15. See www.info.gov.za/asgisa/asgisa.htm
16. www.thepresidency.gov.za/pebble.asp?relid=2323
17. www.epwsp.co.za/archives/091109_01.htm
18. www.epwp.gov.za/Downloads/report_2010-11_q4_annex_ae.pdf
19. www.pmg.org.za/report/20110301-department-public-works-phase-two-expanded-public-works-programme
20. Specifically, employers must pay unemployment insurance contributions of two per cent of the value of each worker's pay per month to the UIF, with the employer and the worker contributing one per cent each. UIF contributions are applicable to all workers and employers except those working less than 24 hours a month, learners, public servants, foreigners working on contract, employees in receipt of an old-age pension, and workers who earn only commission.
21. There are five kinds of benefits covered by UIF: unemployment benefits, illness benefits, maternity benefits, adoption benefits and death benefits. The Fund also assists the dependents of a contributing worker who has passed on.
22. Leibbrandt et al. (2010).
23. Woolard, I. and M. Leibbrandt (2010), 'The Evolution and Impact of Unconditional Cash Transfers in South Africa', Paper presented to the ABCDE Conference, Stockholm, Sweden, May 2010.
24. Hall, K. (2010) *Income and Social Grants – Child Support Grants, Statistics on Children in South Africa*, Children's Institute and University of Cape Town.
25. Samson et al. (2004).
26. Eyal and Woolard (2011).
27. Samson et al. (2008).
28. OECD (2011).
29. Samson and Williams (2007); Williams (2007); Samson et al. (2008).
30. See Samson (2009).
31. Lebbrandt et al. (2010).
32. Bertrand, et al. (2000).
33. See, for example, Samson et al. (2004), endnote v.
34. Posel et al. (2006).

References

Ardington, C., Case, A. and V. Hosegood (2009) 'Labor Supply Responses to Large Social Transfers: Longitudinal Evidence from South Africa', *American Economic Journal: Applied Economics*, Vol. 1, No. 1, pp. 22–48.

Banerjee, A., S. Galiani, J. Levinsohn and I. Woolard (2006) 'Why Has Unemployment Risen in the New South Africa?', CID Working Paper No. 134, October (Cambridge, MA: Center for International Development).

Banerjee, A., S. Galiani, J. Levinsohn, Z. McLaren and I. Woolard (2008) 'Why Has Unemployment Risen in the New South Africa?', *Economics of Transition*, Vol. 16, No. 4, pp. 715–740.

Bartus, T. (2005) 'Estimation of Marginal Effects using margeff', *The Stata Journal*, Vol. 5, No. 3, pp. 309–329.

Benjamin, P., H. Bhorat and H. Cheadle (2010) 'The Cost of "Doing Business" and Labour Regulation: The Case of South Africa', *International Labour Review*, Vol. 149, No. 1, pp. 73–91.

Bertrand, M., S. Mullainathan and D. Miller (2003) 'Public Policy and Extended Families: Evidence from Pensions in South Africa', *World Bank Economic Review*, Vol. 17, No. 1, pp. 27–50.

Bhorat, H. and R. Kanbur (eds) (2006) *Poverty and Policy in Post-Apartheid SA* (Pretoria: Human Sciences Research Council Press).

Bhorat, H., M. Leibbrandt, M. Maziya, S. Van der Berg and I. Woolard (2001) *Fighting Poverty – Labour Markets and Inequality in South Africa* (Cape Town: UCT Press).

Blundell, R., J. Ham and C. Meghir (1998) 'Unemployment, Discouraged Workers and Female Labour Supply', *Research in Economics*, Vol. 52, No. 2. pp. 103–131.

Commission for Conciliation Mediation and Arbitration (CCMA) (2010) *CCMA Retrenchment Support and Training Layoff Project Office Report*, 11 June (Johannesburg: CCMA).

Devey, R., L. Lebani, C. Skinner and I. Valodia (2008) 'The Informal Economy', in A. Kraak and K. Press (eds), *Human Resources Development Review 2008: Education, Employment and Skills in South Africa* (Pretoria: Human Sciences Research Council Press).

Department of Labour, South Africa (DOL) (2009) *A Guide to the Training Layoff Scheme* (Pretoria: DOL).

Eyal, K. and I. Woolard (2011) 'Female Labour Force Participation and South Africa's Child Support Grant', paper presented to the CSAE's 25th Anniversary Conference 2011: Economic Development in Africa, 20–22 March 2011, Oxford.

Fallon, P. R. and R. E. B. Lucas (2002) 'The Impact of Financial Crises on Labor Markets, Household Incomes, and Poverty: A Review of Evidence', *The World Bank Research Observer*, Vol. 17, No. 1, pp. 21–45.

Human Sciences Research Council (HSRC) (2007) *Mid-term Review of the Expanded Public Works Programme, Synthesis Report* (Pretoria: HSRC).

International Monetary Fund (IMF) (2010) 'Unemployment Dynamics during Recessions and Recoveries: Okun's Law and Beyond', in IMF (2010) *World Economic Outlook Rebalancing Growth, April 2010* (Washington, DC: IMF), Chapter 3.

Jones, S. R. G. and W. C. Riddell (1999) 'The Measurement of Unemployment: An Empirical Approach', Notes and Comments, *Econometrica*, Vol. 67, No. 1, pp. 147–162.

Jutting, J. and J. R. de Laiglesia (eds) (2009) *Is Informal Normal? Towards More and Better Jobs in Developing Countries*, OECD Development Centre Studies (Paris: OECD).

Kain, J. (1968) 'Housing Segregation, Negro Employment, and Metropolitan Decentralization', *Quarterly Journal of Economics*, Vol. 82, No. 2, pp. 175–197.

Kingdon, G. and J. Knight (2004) 'Unemployment in South Africa: The Nature of the Beast', *World Development*, Vol. 32, No. 3, pp. 391–408.

Kingdon, G. and J. Knight (2006) 'The Measurement of Unemployment When Unemployment Is High', *Labour Economics*, Vol. 13, No. 3, pp. 291–315.

Kingdon, G. and J. Knight (2007) 'Unemployment in South Africa, 1995–2003: Causes, Problems and Policies', *Journal of African Economies*, Vol. 16, No. 5, pp. 813–848.

Klasen, S. and I. Woolard (2008) 'Surviving Unemployment without State Support: Unemployment and Household Formation in South Africa', *Journal of African Economies*, Vol. 18, No. 1, pp. 1–51.

Layard, R., S. Nickell and R. Jackman (2005) *Unemployment: Macroeconomic Performance and the Labour Market* (Oxford: Oxford University Press).

Lebbrandt, M. et al. (2010) 'Trends in South African Income Distribution and Poverty since the Fall of Apartheid', OECD Social, Employment and Migration Working Papers, No. 101 (Paris: OECD).

Makgetta, N. S. (2010) 'Synthesis Paper: South Africa', mimeo.

McCord, A. (2007) *Component 1: International PWP Comparative Study, EPWP Mid-Term Review* (University of Cape Town: SALDRU).

National Treasury of the Republic of South Africa (2010) *Budget Review 2010*, available at: www.treasury.gov.za/documents/national%20budget/2010/review/Budget%20Review.pdf.

National Treasury of the Republic of South Africa (2011) *Budget Review 2011*, available at: www.treasury.gov.za/documents/national%20budget/2011/default.aspx.

Okun, A. M. (1962) 'Potential GNP: Its Measurement and Significance', American Statistical Association, Proceedings of the Business and Economics Section, pp. 98–104.

Organisation for Economic Co-operation and Development (OECD) (2008) 'Realising South Africa's Employment Potential', in OECD, *Economic Assessment of South Africa 2008* (Paris: OECD), Chapter 3.

Organisation for Economic Co-operation and Development (OECD) (2011) *OECD Employment Outlook 2011* (Paris: OECD).

Padayachee, V. (ed.) (2006) *The Development Decade? Economic and Social Change in South Africa, 1994–2004* (Pretoria: Human Sciences Research Council Press).

Pissarides, C. A. (2000) *Equilibrium Unemployment Theory*, Second Edition (Cambridge, MA: MIT Press).

Posel, D., J. A. Fairburn and F. Lund (2006) 'Labour Migration and Households: A Reconsideration of the Effects of the Social Pension on Labour Supply in South Africa', *Economic Modelling*, Vol. 23, No. 5, pp. 836–853.

Ranchod, V. and T. Dinkelman (2008) 'Labour Market Transitions in South Africa: What Can We Learn from Matched Labour Force Survey Data?', Southern Africa Labour and Development Research Unit Working Paper No. 14 (Cape Town: SALDRU).

Reinhart, C. and K. Rogoff (2009) *This Time is Different: Eight Centuries of Financial Folly* (Princeton and Oxford: Princeton University Press).

Rogerson, C. M. (1992) 'The Absorptive Capacity of the Informal Sector in the South African City', in D. M. Smith (ed.), *The Apartheid City and Beyond* (London: Routledge).

Samson, M. (2009) 'Social Cash Transfers and Employment: A Note on Empirical Linkages in Developing Countries', in OECD, *Promoting Pro-poor Growth: Employment* (Paris: OECD).

Samson, M., U. Lee, A. Ndlebe, K. MacQuene, I. van Niekerk, V. Ghandi, T. Harigaya and C. Abrahams (2004) *The Social and Economic Impact of South*

Africa's Social Security System. Commissioned by the Department of Social Development (Cape Town: EPRI).

Samson, M. et al. (2008) *Quantitative Analysis of the Impact of the Child Support Grant, May 2008*, SASSA/South African Department of Social Development/Unicef (Cape Town: EPRI).

Samson, M. and M. Williams (2007) 'A Review of Employment, Growth and Development Impacts of South Africa's Social Transfers', Economic Policy Research Institute Working Paper No. 41 (Cape Town: EPRI).

South Africa Reserve Bank (2009) 'September 2009', *Quarterly Bulletin*, No. 253 (Pretoria: SARB).

South African Human Rights Commission (SAHRC) and UNICEF South Africa (2011) *South Africa's Children: A Review of Equity and Child Rights* (Braamfontein: SAHRC).

Statistics South Africa (2009) 'Gross domestic product – third quarter: 2009', Statistical Release, P0441, available at: www.statssa.gov.za.

The Presidency (2009) *Progress Report to the President of the Republic of South Africa on the Implementation of the Framework for South Africa's Response to the International Economic Crisis* (Pretoria: Presidency of South Africa).

South African Human Rights Commission (SAHRC) and UNICEF South Africa (2011) *South Africa's Children: A Review of Equity and Child Rights* (Braamfontein: South African Human Rights Commission/UNICEF).

Valodia, I. (2007) *The Informal Economy in South Africa: Issues, Debates and Policies: Reflections after an Exposure Dialogue Programme with Informal Workers in Durban, South Africa*, WIEGO Research Report No. 75, March (Cambridge, MA: WIEGO).

Valodia, I., L. Lebani and C. Skinner (2005) 'Low-waged and Informal Employment in South Africa', *Review of Labour Markets in South Africa* (Pretoria: Human Sciences Research Council).

Van Ham, M., C. H. Mulder and P. Hooimeijer (2001) 'Local Underemployment and the Discouraged Worker Effect', *Urban Studies*, Vol. 38, No. 10, pp. 1733–1751.

Verick, S. (2009) 'Who Is Hit Hardest During a Financial Crisis? The Vulnerability of Young Men and Women to Unemployment in an Economic Downturn', IZA Discussion Paper No. 4359 (Bonn: IZA).

Williams, M. J. (2007) 'The Social and Economic Impacts of South Africa's Child Support Grant', Economic Policy Research Institute Working Paper No. 40 (Cape Town: EPRI).

Wooldridge, J. M. (2002) *Econometric Analysis of Cross Section and Panel Data* (Cambridge, MA: MIT Press).

Zenou, Y. (2011) 'Spatial versus Social Mismatch: The Strength of Weak Ties', IZA Discussion Paper No. 5507 (Bonn: IZA).

7
Strengthening the Turkish Labour Market through More Efficient Regulations

7.1 Introduction

Turkey was directly affected by the great recession of 2008–2009, but showed considerable resilience thanks to a decade of sound macroeconomic policies and reforms implemented after several economic shocks. The large contraction in GDP (by 4.7 per cent in 2009) was largely due to the collapse in foreign demand and was amplified by domestic confidence effects. While unemployment reached 14 per cent in 2009, it soon went back to its pre-crisis level, falling to 10.8 per cent in March 2011. In addition to strong stability-oriented macroeconomic policy, employment and labour market policies were enhanced to support labour demand, develop non-agriculture employment and reduce informality, such as an overall reduction of social security contributions, hiring subsidies or VAT tax reductions. The recent crisis differs, however, from past episodes in Turkey in two ways: first, white-collar educated workers were hit and lost their jobs; second, informal manufacturing and service sector occupations were severely affected so there were proportionately lower formal sector job losses.

Overall, the Turkish labour market is still suffering from structural problems: high inactivity (labour force participation rates are the lowest among the OECD countries – 28 per cent for women) and serious skills mismatches. Those are, of course, linked to salient and interrelated characteristics of the labour market. Agriculture's share in total employment fell from over 30 per cent in 2004 to 24 per cent in 2008, but is still very largely due to important subsidies that went on between 1950 and 2000. These subsidies slowed down the flows of population from rural to urban areas that should have started after agricultural mechanization; rural–urban migration is hence still ongoing (the urbanization rate reached 50 per cent only in the mid-1980s). The level of average education is quite low as is the rate of labour productivity. Informal employment, defined as employment of workers not registered with any social security institutions, represents a sizeable share of 44.8 per cent in 2010, according to the Turkish Statistical Institute. Finally, Turkey does not have means-tested universal social assistance coverage. This must have caused the social impact to be severe, reducing household wealth.

The remainder of this chapter is structured as follows. Section 2 reviews the main labour market developments over the past decade, covering both the pre-crisis period (2000–2007) and the 2008–2009 global financial crisis. Section 3 then provides interesting insights about the main determinants of labour force participation, access to formal and informal employment, and crisis impact based on micro-data. Section 4 discusses the role of labour market institutions and policies in Turkey in terms of adequacy and efficiency, articulating both short-term and long-term challenges. Section 5 concludes with some policy recommendations.

7.2 Labour market developments in the 2000s

7.2.1 Main labour market indicators

Despite the severe banking crisis that hit the country in 2001, Turkey grew for six consecutive years between 2002 and 2007. This sustained economic growth did not, however, translate into an increase in labour force participation nor a decrease of unemployment, which remained around 10.5 per cent from 2002 to 2007. Actually, the labour force participation rate steadily declined between 2000 and 2007, mostly driven by the decrease of female participation rate (Figure 7.1). The same trend can be observed for the employment rate (both aggregate and female rates).

Shortly after the crisis hit, and despite the sharp contraction of output, employment was rather stable, reflecting large-scale labour hoarding facilitated by wage adjustments, including cuts in informal wage payments, and employment support measures (see the next section). Nevertheless, due to strong working-age population growth and increasing labour force participation, the unemployment rate increased by 3 percentage points to 14 per cent in 2009. In 2010, Turkey had almost returned to its pre-crisis labour market conditions (Table 7.1): the labour force participation rate reached 48.8 per cent (71 per cent for men and 28 per cent for women); the aggregate unemployment rate went down

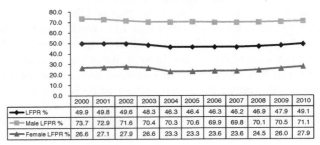

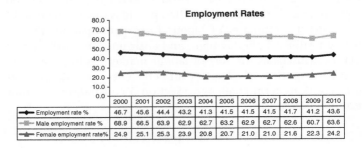

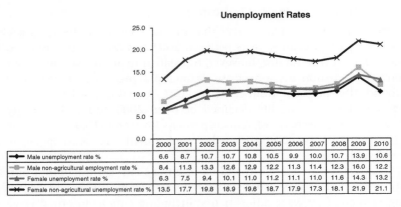

Figure 7.1 An overview of the Turkish labour market: labour force participation, employment and unemployment rates, 2000–2010, by gender

Notes: Non-agricultural unemployment rate = The ratio of job-seekers in non-agricultural occupations to non-agricultural labour force.

Source: Aggregate data from Turkstat website (www.tuik.gov.tr).

Table 7.1 Key indicators of the Turkish labour market

	Employment (thousand)	Unemployment (thousand)	LFP (%)	Unemployment rate (%)	Non-agriculture unemployment rate (%)	Employment rate (%)
2008	21,194	2,611	46.9	11.0	13.6	41.7
2009	21,277	3,471	47.9	14.0	17.4	41.2
2010	22,594	3,046	48.8	11.9	14.3	43.6

Source: Aggregate data from Turkstat website (www.tuik.gov.tr).

to 11.9 per cent in 2010 (almost at its 2008 level of 10.7 per cent) from 14 per cent in 2009. However, given the high proportion of unpaid family workers and the boost to informal self-employment during the crisis (see below), the non-agricultural unemployment rate is a more realistic indicator for international comparisons for Turkey. This rate went down to 14.3 per cent in 2010 from 17.4 per cent in 2009.

Unemployment statistics for youth (15–24 years) reveal a dire picture (Figure 7.2). Youth unemployment rates were still high in 2010: 21 per cent for the overall youth unemployment rate against 25 per cent in urban areas (respectively three and two points lower than the previous year's figures). Young women were specially hard-hit by the crisis, displaying particularly high unemployment rates: the female non-agricultural youth unemployment rate peaked at 33 per cent in 2009

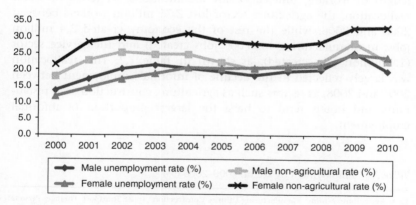

Figure 7.2 Youth unemployment (2000–2010)
Notes: Non-agricultural unemployment rate = The ratio of job seekers in non-agricultural occupations to non-agricultural labour force.
Source: Turkstat website (www.tuik.gov.tr).

and remained high in 2010, as did the overall female youth unemployment rate (25 per cent in 2009); for young men, the non-agricultural unemployment rate peaked in 2008 (28 per cent) and went down in 2009 to 22.8 per cent close to its 2006 level (22.3 per cent). These rates are quite high compared with the OECD average (16.4 per cent in 2009).

Finally, the duration of unemployment increased in Turkey in the first half of the decade. Long-term unemployed (more than 12 months) represented 21.1 per cent of the unemployed in 2000, a relatively good year for labour market indicators, as evidenced earlier. By 2005, however, the long-term unemployed constituted 39 per cent of the unemployed then went down to 28.6 per cent in 2010 (the weighted OECD average was 24 per cent in 2010). One possible explanation is that, although the trend in the proportion of long-term unemployed is upwards, during the crisis many of the longest term unemployed (2–3 years and above) dropped out of the labour force and became discouraged workers. They then returned to the statistics during the recovery and reported their total spell of joblessness in the HLFS.

7.2.2   Changing labour market trends over the 2000s

Important changes took place over the decade in the structure of employment by economic sector. Other general characteristics of employment, such as employment by status, type of contracts and length of working time, also saw modifications. In terms of sector reallocation, the agriculture sector lost 2.75 million workers between 2000 and 2008, while the rest of the economy created 2.4 million jobs, in manufacturing (630,000 jobs created) and the service sector (1.9 million jobs created), as shown in Table 7.2. This reallocation was largely reflected in the decline of informal employment between 2001 and 2008, as sectors such as agriculture, construction, and restaurants and hotels tend to have the largest proportion of informal employment.

Table 7.2   Employment by sector, 2000–2008 (%)

Year	Agriculture	Mining	Manufacturing	Utilities	Construction	Trade	Transport	Finance	Personal Services
2000	36.0%	0.4%	16.9%	0.4%	6.3%	17.7%	4.9%	3.3%	14.1%
2008	23.7%	0.5%	20.0%	0.4%	5.9%	21.6%	5.1%	5.5%	17.3%

Source: Aggregated Turkstat HLFS data.

Flexible forms of employment do exist in Turkey but display heterogeneous patterns. Temporary employment, for example, is rather widespread (the share of temporary employment as a percentage of total employment was 13 per cent on average for 2002–2007, at French or German levels) but was less and less used after the crisis; a rather small proportion of workers work part-time (around 9 per cent over the 2002–2007 period), but the proportion increased slightly during and after the crisis (part-time employment as a proportion of total employment reached 11.1 per cent in 2009, according to the OECD). Women's share in part-time employment was around 60 per cent in 2010.

As highlighted above, informal employment represents a high share of total employment. In 2010, 44.8 per cent of all workers had no social security coverage in their current job and thus registered as informal. Almost a half of these were individuals employed in the agricultural sector. In fact, the high incidence of informality in the agricultural sector (85.5 per cent in 2010) is an important factor contributing to the overall size of the informal sector in Turkey. Although relatively lower, informal employment also remains high in non-agricultural employment.

The cyclical behaviours of informal employment in total and in the non-agricultural sector does not display consistent patterns: while total informal employment is counter-cyclical over time-declining during the 2001–2008 period, from 52.9 per cent of total employment in 2001 to 43.5 per cent in 2008, then increasing from 2008 up to 44.8 per cent in 2010, non-agricultural informal employment shows a reverse pattern – increasing between 2001 and 2006, decreasing from 2006 to 2008 before stabilizing from 2008 to 2010 (Figure 7.3).

Self-employment represents about two-thirds of informal employment in Turkey; and agricultural self-employment about three-fourths. Disaggregating data by sex suggests an 'added worker' effect in addition to the increase of agricultural employment during hard times, that is, that self-employment was a coping mechanism for women during the crisis (female self-employment is 90 per cent informal; in agriculture, almost all self-employment is informal employment). So self-employment not only exhibited resilience throughout the crisis, but flourished especially for women.

Within the non-agricultural category, 80.6 per cent of women were unregistered in 2008, as against 85.7 per cent in the first quarter of 2010 (March). These women occupy the bottom level of the Turkish labour market, just above unpaid family workers in agriculture. They have no social protection at all. At best, some would qualify for health coverage through the so-called Green Card programme, a means-tested health care programme. Except municipal coal and food aid packages before

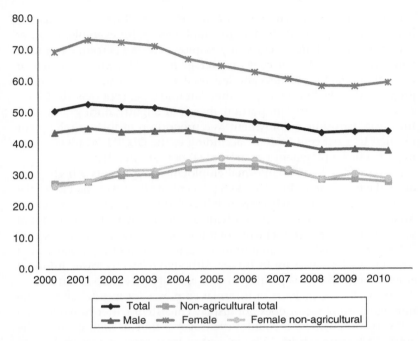

Figure 7.3   Share of informal employment in total employment, 2000–2010 (%)
Note: Turkstat reports unregistered work based on the survey question: 'Are you registered for social security coverage because of the job you are working now?'
Source: Ercan et al. (2010), based on LFS data.

elections, informal workers generally lack coverage of any public social assistance programme. Figure 7.3 illustrates the rise in self-employment between 2008 and 2010 for both men and women, and the agricultural and non-agricultural sectors.

7.3   An in-depth analysis of informal employment: Insights from the micro-data

This section examines the incidence of informality according to more detailed characteristics such as age, gender, sector and education (based on HLFS). Tables 7.3 and 7.4 below show, for example, that the incidence of informality is higher among younger and older workers compared to prime-working-age individuals (ages 25–54). At a given age, the prevalence of informality also differs considerably between men and women. Among younger men, informal employment in the non-agricultural sector is considerably higher than for females. For instance, in 2009, 52 per cent of 15 to 24-year-old men were employed without social security coverage in non-agriculture, against 38.6 per cent of young women.

It seems that a significant proportion of men start their working lives in the informal sector but manage to move to the formal sector as they reach their late 20s. As they get older, they make a transition back to the

Table 7.3 Incidence of informality, by sector and by sex

	2004	2005	2006	2007	2008	2009
All	49.0	47.1	45.9	44.3	42.2	42.6
Male	43.2	41.3	40.4	39.0	36.9	37.0
Female	65.9	63.8	62.0	59.6	57.3	57.3
Agricultural sector	89.9	88.0	87.6	87.7	87.3	85.1
Male	82.6	78.8	77.3	77.2	76.2	75.0
Female	98.5	98.4	98.7	99.0	99.1	96.1
Non-agricultural sector	33.6	34.1	33.8	32.0	29.4	29.8
Male	33.4	33.7	33.5	32.0	29.6	29.4
Female	34.5	35.8	35.1	32.0	28.8	31.1

Table 7.4 Incidence of informality, by sector and age

	2004	2005	2006	2007	2008	2009
All sectors			All			
Age 15–24	68.8	65.2	63.0	59.8	56.2	58.8
Age 25–54	42.0	40.4	39.5	38.0	36.2	36.2
Age 55–64	72.5	73.8	74.8	78.0	76.8	75.2
Non-agricultural sector			All			
Age 15–24	56.1	55.0	53.7	50.1	45.4	48.1
Age 25–54	27.9	28.3	28.2	26.7	24.7	24.9
Age 55–64	47.6	55.2	56.5	61.7	58.8	55.1
Non-agricultural sector			Men			
Age 15–24	61.0	59.1	57.2	54.1	49.0	52.0
Age 25–54	27.4	27.5	27.6	26.3	24.5	24.0
Age 55–64	46.3	54.1	55.7	61.4	58.7	54.8
Non-agricultural sector			Women			
Age 15–24	43.3	44.2	44.5	39.8	36.2	38.6
Age 25–54	30.5	32.0	31.1	28.7	25.8	28.3
Age 55–64	62.5	66.1	64.5	64.5	59.1	57.6

Note: All tables and figures in this section cover individuals aged 15–64.
Source: HLFS micro-data files for all tables and figures in this section.

informal sector in the form of self-employment. A smaller proportion of young women, on the other hand, start out in the informal sector. This may indicate that they are less willing to accept informal sector jobs outside agriculture, or that the type of jobs available to them is limited. The high incidence of informality in the non-agricultural sector among older women (aged 54–65) is, however, noteworthy.

Unlike the aggregate picture, micro-data by sector, age and sex show that non-agricultural informality actually increased from 2008 to 2009, possibly reflecting the effects of the crisis. Furthermore, based on the changes observed in the proportion of men and women employed without social security coverage by age, a higher proportion of prime-working-age women (25–55 years) than men seemed to be affected, while in the case of men, the most vulnerable group seems to be the

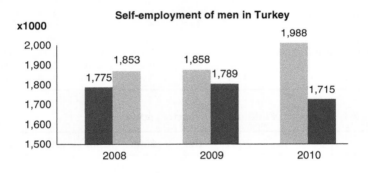

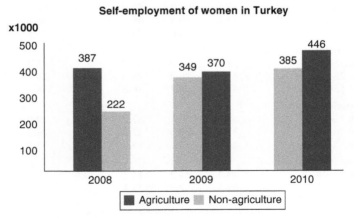

Figure 7.4   Self-employment in Turkey, 2008–2010
Source: Turkstat.

youngest age group (15 to 24-year-olds). The increase in informality among prime-working-age women might be indicative of the 'added-worker' phenomenon identified earlier.

The next sections analyse the main determinants of labour force participation rates according to individual and household characteristics; then they try to explain the participation in one of the five labour market states (formal sector employment, informal sector employment, unemployment, discouragement[1] and out-of-labour force), against individual and household characteristics. The objective is to identify any correlation between those factors and the way their effects changed between 2009, the crisis year[2] and 2006 (used as a benchmark).

7.3.1 Main determinants of labour force participation: a multivariate analysis

Logistic regressions are conducted separately for men and women (detailed results are shown in Appendix, Table 7.A1). The predicted probabilities indicate an increase in labour force participation between 2006 and 2009, from 82.4 to 83.7 per cent (for men) and 21.4 to 24.4 per cent (for women).

In terms of educational attainment, the results indicate that men and women with higher education[3] are more likely to participate in the labour market (Table 7.A1). For men, the positive association between education and labour force participation is not monotonous, although having some education makes the individual more likely to participate in the labour market compared to illiterates (the reference category): general high school graduates, for example, have a lower probability of participation. Above the high school level, the likelihood of participation increases sharply and the probabilities of university graduates, for instance, participating in the labour market are more than four times those of illiterates. For women, there seems to be a closer association between education and labour market participation,[4] the predicted participation rates increase sharply beyond secondary schooling: they are, for example, almost ten times higher for university graduate women compared to those for illiterate women.

Another important determinant of participation is age. The age-participation profiles for men are hump-shaped: labour force participation increases with age, reaches a peak around the mid-20s to 30s, and then declines (Table 7.A1 in the Appendix). From 2006 to 2009, the age effects generally increased (the predicted participation rates increased) by 1 to 3 percentage points, the highest increase being predicted for 46 to 50-year-old men at 2.7 percentage points. Although an increase can be observed for all age groups, the change is not statistically significant for older men (above age 50) and for 15–19- and 30–34-year-olds. Women's participation also increases with age, peaks around 30–35 years and declines thereafter. Even at its peak value, though, women's predicted participation rate (at mean values of covariates) does not exceed 35 per cent. The age effects in the two years are not found statistically to differ from each other except for 50 to 60-year-olds – whose odds of participation as compared to 15 to 19-year-olds actually declined in 2009 as compared to 2006. These findings indicate a slightly younger age structure of participation in 2009.

Finally, other determinants of labour force participation rates include marital status, children, household size and regions of residence. In summary, the crisis substantially reduced the 'negative' association between marriage and labour force participation among women. Compared to 2006, more married women participated in the labour force in 2009. However, the 'negative' effect of children on women's participation intensified in 2009. Therefore, it seems that the financial crisis mostly changed the participation behaviour of younger married women without children.

7.3.2   Main determinants of employment status, 2006 versus 2009

In this section, the choice among five mutually exclusive labour market states is discussed separately for men and women in 2006 and 2009, using a multinomial logit framework. Table 7.5 shows the distribution across the various labour market states. It shows that the proportion of men employed in the formal sector increased by less than 1 percentage point between 2006 and 2009 while in the informal sector the proportion went down by more than 3 percentage points.[5] This suggests that the economic crisis has mostly affected informal sector workers. The proportion of unemployed, on the other hand, increased among men by more than 3 percentage points. The proportion of discouraged workers registered a drop from 1.6 per cent to 0.8 per cent. The proportion that remained in the out-of-the-labour force (apart from discouraged workers) was about the same (at 24 per cent) in both years. Among women, similar changes (of different magnitude, however) can be observed between 2006 and 2009: the proportion of women employed in the formal sector increased (by 1.4 percentage points), the proportion employed in the informal sector declined (by 0.2 percentage points), while the proportion unemployed increased (by 1.3 percentage

Table 7.5 Distribution of men and women across five labour market states

	Men		Women	
	2006	2009	2006	2009
Formal sector	39.9	40.7	8.6	10.4
Informal sector	27.0	23.9	14.1	13.9
Unemployed	7.5	10.7	2.9	4.2
Discouraged workers	1.6	0.8	1.2	1.0
Out-of-the labour force	24.0	23.9	73.2	70.6

Source: HLFS micro-data, authors' calculations.

points). The proportion of discouraged workers went down slightly as well, while the out-of-the labour force category shrank by 2.6 percentage points.

The results of the multinomial logit model for the five labour market states for men and women are given in Appendix Tables 7.A2–7.A5, respectively. The base category in all estimations is the out-of-the-labour market category.[6]

Again, education is found to be an important predictor of formal sector employment for both men and women – the correlation is even stronger for women (background paper on Turkey). A similar conclusion can be drawn for unemployment, though university education does not generate such an important effect on unemployment than it does on formal sector employment. In contrast, the likelihood of informal sector employment decreases with schooling. It is interesting to compare how those marginal effects interact with the crisis. The top left panel of Figure 7.5, for instance, indicates similar effects on formal employment for the two years: the likelihood to be in formal sector employment did not change significantly for any educational group from 2006 to 2009. In contrast, the 'decreasing' effect of higher levels of schooling on informal sector employment diminished for men between 2006 and 2009: for instance, while the average marginal effect of university education on informal sector employment was –8.4 percentage points, it eventually declined to –1.8 percentage points. Hence, in 2009 it became more likely to observe more educated men engaged in the informal sector compared to 2006. The marginal effects of schooling on unemployment are higher in 2009 compared to 2006, though the effects are only significant for men with secondary schooling and less.

The same general patterns are found for women: the effect of education on formal sector employment is very similar in the two years (top panel of Figure 7.6). In the informal sector, on the other hand, the likelihood of observing more educated women in this state increased in 2009: while the average marginal effect of high school education on informal sector employment was –3.9 per cent in 2006, it was reduced to –1.9 per cent in 2009. The effect of education on unemployment did not change between the two years.

Age is another determinant of the likelihood of being in one of the five labour market states: for men, the highest marginal effects of age are observed for unemployment – almost 25 percentage points for the 25 to 29 age range. The effect on discouragement, on the other hand, is minimal and does not seem to vary much with age. For women, the highest effects are observed for informal sector employment: the average marginal effect increases with age peak at around 41 to 45 years of age and then declines. At the maximum, the marginal effect of age reaches 6.5 percentage points. This is quite a sizeable effect given that in 2009, 13.9 per cent of the women were employed in the informal sector. The average marginal effect of age on formal employment is also inverted-U-shaped: the highest marginal effects are observed for women aged 35 to 40 years at around 5 per cent. The marginal effect of age on unemployment, on the other hand, generally decreases with age. The marginal effect of age on discouragement, on the other hand, is minimal.

A comparison of 2006 and 2009 in terms of the marginal effects of age on formal employment among men reveals effects of similar magnitudes (Table 7.A2 and 7.A3 in the Appendix). Although the age effects look stronger in 2009 compared to 2006, the differences are not statistically significant, with the exception of the effects observed for the 25 to 29 age group. The average marginal effects of age on informal sector employment are generally weaker in 2009. These findings indicate that, in 2009, it became more likely to find older men engaged in informal employment compared to 2006. The marginal effects of age on unemployment, on the other hand, increased significantly among younger age groups from 2006 to 2009. For instance, while in 2006, the 25 to 29 age group was 16 percentage points more likely to be unemployed compared to the 15 to 19 age group, this figure increased to 25 percentage points in 2009.

Similar to what is observed for men, although the marginal effect of age on formal sector employment of women looks higher in 2009 as compared to 2006, the change is only statistically significant for the 20 to 24 and 41 to 50 age groups (Table 7.A4 and 7.A5 in the

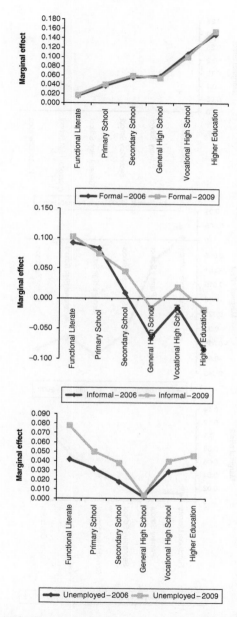

Figure 7.5 Marginal effects of education on predicted probability of formal employment, informal employment and unemployment, men (2006 versus 2009)

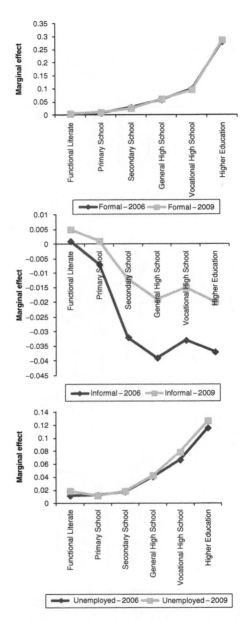

Figure 7.6 Marginal effects of education on predicted probability of formal employment, informal employment and unemployment, women (2006 versus 2009)
Source: Authors' calculations.

Appendix). In the case of informal employment, the age effects substantially weakened from 2006 to 2009 so that among prime-working-age women (30–55 years) the differences in the likelihood of informal employment reduced to less than two percentage points. In contrast, the age effects got stronger among the unemployed over time, so that it became even more likely for younger women to be unemployed in 2009 than in 2006.

Other determinants such as marital status, children and household size may have impacted the allocation of workers among the different labour market states, but their role over the crisis period mostly remained unchanged except for the region of residence.[7]

Based on the above findings, it may be concluded that the 2008–2009 crisis mostly affected informal sector workers and the unemployed. From 2006 to 2009, the unemployment rate increased for both men and women, though the most vulnerable groups were younger and less educated men, as well as younger women. Also, while on average the formal sector attracts the more educated workers, the 2009 crisis reduced the marginal effect of education, thus exposing more and more the most educated workers to the informal sector. To some extent, it is possible to say that there was some homogenization between the workforces of the formal and the informal sectors during the crisis. Finally, discouraged workers were not found to be very different from others in the out-of-the-labour force category.

7.4 Promoting efficient labour market regulations in Turkey

7.4.1 The labour market institution debate

One of the most divisive debates in the context of the Turkish labour market revolves around the economic impact of labour market regulations, such as their effect on job creation, productivity and scope of informality. The OECD's Economic Survey for Turkey stresses, for example, that the 'the growth of the high productivity and more competitive formal firms and their employment capacities are impaired by an unsupportive legal and regulatory framework'. The survey generally blames an 'excessively high' minimum wage, 'high compulsory social security contribution rates, which create a high wedge between gross employment costs and net worker incomes' and 'too restrictive employment protection'. The World Bank (2009, 2010) also points to Turkey's rigid labour regulations as the main suspects for the undesirable informal employment conditions.

In light of these calls for deregulation, it is important to check how Turkey compares to other emerging and OECD economies in terms of its institutional setting, as well as bringing in the main theoretical and empirical arguments on the economics of regulation. The cross-country overview provided in Chapter 3 of this volume brings important insights to the discussion. Actually, two institutional settings of the labour market emerge from the cross-country comparison: employment protection legislation and compulsory social security contributions. Turkey has one of the most protective labour legislation regimes. As evidenced in section 3.3.1 of Chapter 3, the OECD overall EPL index for Turkey was the highest of the OECD countries with a value of 3.5 (on a scale of 0–6) in 2008; the degree of employment protection ranges from 0.30 in Georgia to 3.9 in Nepal, with an OECD average of 2.19 and a value of 0.85 for the United States. This high score seems, however, mostly due to the strict legislation applying to temporary contracts (4.88 for temporary contract, 2.48 for regular permanent contract). Taymaz and Özler (2005) also identify the restrictions on the use of temporary forms of employment contract, as well as the lack of legal framework for temporary work agencies as the main culprits for the high score. This means that the utilization of temporary work is highly constrained or simply not enforced.

Compulsory social security contributions remain very high, despite various policy-targeted measures to reduce non-wage labour costs and a recent cut in them, creating a high wedge between gross employment costs and net workers' incomes (ILO G20 Brief 2011); this is high even by EU and OECD standards (the tax wedge in 2008 represented around 40 per cent of labour costs in Turkey, according to the OECD).

As also indicated earlier, there is an Unemployment Insurance Fund (UIF), which was set up in 1999 to cover unemployment benefits, health expenditures for the unemployed and their training and job placement expenses. In order to benefit from unemployment insurance, a worker must have contributed to the fund for the past 120 days and for at least a total of 600 days in the past three years; the other key features of the scheme (duration and replacement rate) are presented in Chapter 3. The key weakness of this institution is its low coverage rate (12.7 per cent of 2.61 million unemployed in 2008, 13.6 per cent in 2009), which can partly be explained by strict eligibility conditions. Table 7.6 presents the composition of unemployment insurance recipients by level of education (December 2010). It is interesting to note that the proportion of recipients reflects share of employment only for those with an elementary school background (around 55 per cent).

Table 7.6   Distribution of UI recipients by level of education and sex (2010)

Education level	Total	Men	Women	% in employment
No schooling	1.6%	1.4%	2.1%	4.5%
No diploma (functional literate)	1.1%	1.1%	1.3%	4.6%
Elementary (eight years)	54.6%	60.9%	36.3%	55.5%
Secondary	29.5%	27.4%	35.7%	21.5%
2-years college	5.3%	3.5%	10.6%	
College	7.6%	5.5%	13.3%	14.8%
Graduate degree	0.3%	0.2%	0.6%	

Note: College classification in Turkstat implies post-secondary, while ISKUR would break this down to show 2-year degrees.
Source: http://statik.iskur.gov.tr/tr/ark/ark/aralik.htm

In terms of educational attainment, Table 7.7 points to the general low levels of education and skills of labour resources. The median education level of those in employment is five years. More than a quarter of unpaid family workers have no diploma; 87 per cent have less than elementary (high school) education. Primary school graduates constitute more than half of the casual wage (daily or seasonal) workers and the self-employed. Wage-salary workers are the best educated; their median education is senior high school. They constitute more than half of the Turkish workforce. Table 7.7 also strongly suggests that the self-employed look more like casual wage workers in Turkey and not so much like employers. The last two rows of Table 7.7 show that the category with 'no diploma' is overrepresented in unemployment; as well, people with 'basic education/secondary' education have unemployment rates above the overall level (10.9 per cent). PISA results provided by the OECD also rank Turkey as one of the countries with the lowest results in terms of educational performance (OECD 2010).

Finally, as strongly advocated in Chapter 3, the relationship between labour market regulations and labour market outcomes is far from obvious. In relation to EPL, it is noteworthy that looking at subjective measures of labour regulations, such as firms' perceptions of major constraints to investment, the shortage of skills is perceived as a far greater obstacle by employers. This also suggests that EPL may actually not be binding for the larger segment of the labour market (Agénor et al., 2006). Moreover, even if some specific element of labour legislation may be assessed as 'too costly', such as severance payments for long-tenure workers, the relevance and opportunity to introduce any

Table 7.7 Education and job status in employment (2008)

15+ year-olds	No schooling	No diploma	Primary	Junior high	Senior high	Vocational high	College	Elementary (8 years)		Number (x1000)	(%)
Wage-salary	0.7%	2.0%	29.2%	10.4%	14.2%	14.6%	23.3%	5.7%	100.0%	11527	54.4%
Casual wage	7.6%	8.9%	54.3%	7.9%	6.2%	4.7%	1.4%	8.9%	100.0%	1409	6.6%
Employer	0.7%	1.8%	39.4%	14.1%	14.1%	10.2%	18.9%	0.8%	100.0%	1250	5.9%
Self-employed	7.4%	7.7%	58.5%	10.2%	6.5%	5.3%	3.5%	1.0%	100.0%	4325	20.4%
Unpaid family	16.5%	10.1%	44.2%	4.0%	6.7%	4.1%	1.6%	12.7%	100.0%	2683	12.7%
TOTAL	4.5%	4.6%	39.4%	9.6%	11.1%	10.4%	14.8%	5.5%	100.0%	21194	100.0%
U rate	7.0%	12.8%	9.4%	13.4%*	14.0%	11.5%	10.0%			10.9%	
Population (%)	9.1%	6.7%	39.1%	17.5%*	11.0%	7.9%	8.8%				

Notes: 'No schooling' corresponds to the proportion of people who are illiterate; 'no diploma' corresponds to the proportion of people who can read and write but who do not have a primary school education (eight years since 1997); 'junior high' corresponds to one year; 'senior high' to four years of schooling; 'elementary' to eight years of schooling; since this latest category was introduced after the 1997 denomination change, being part of this group implies that the person has graduated after the mandatory schooling level increase.
Source: Turkstat online database and micro-data.

legislative change would need to be considered within a policy package that should be balanced and negotiated among the social partners.[8]

7.4.2 Labour market policies in response to the crisis

As mentioned previously, a series of labour market policies were introduced in Turkey in addition to stability-oriented macroeconomic policy. These included a general reduction in social security contributions; targeted reductions in costs for hiring youth, women and the long-term unemployed; reductions for workers involved in training and research and development; and work-sharing schemes. Yeldan (2010) provides a comprehensive overview of the main labour market measures introduced in Turkey as well as their fiscal costs (Table 7.8). Training, wage subsidies (including work-sharing and social security reductions) and public work programmes have been the major measures, while job search assistance and entrepreneurship incentives have been negligible. In 2009, 508,000 persons benefited from short-time work compensation (Kısa Çalışma Ödeneği) and this was the major cash-injection crisis stimulus package for businesses during the crisis. According to Yeldan (2010), the fiscal cost of this measure reached 162 million TL (US$108 million). Various training programmes were also enhanced (in 2009, 214,000 individuals were trained – 120,000 men and 94,000 women). In addition, Turkey introduced broad hiring incentives by reducing employment costs for new hires in its May 2008 pre-crisis employment package. The measures reduced employers' social security contributions by five points and provided incentives for new women and youth hires by further reducing their social security contributions.

While no evaluations have been made of the various measures, serious weaknesses have been identified, including the weak capacity of ÝPKUR, the Turkish public employment agency (2,900 employees for approximately 3.8 million unemployed at the peak of the crisis in 2009), as well as extremely low government spending on ALMPs at less than 1 per cent of GDP (in 2008).

7.5 Concluding remarks

Based on both aggregate labour market statistics and labour force survey micro-data, this chapter has provided an in-depth review of the Turkish labour market over the past decade (2000–2010). The labour market policies and institutions have also been examined in light of the key labour market challenges facing the country. The Turkish labour market

Table 7.8   Main labour market measures and their estimated fiscal costs

	Estimated fiscal cost (million TL)			
	2008	2009	2010	2008–2010
5 percentage point reduction on employers' social security contributions (over a total of 19.5%)	17	3,726	4,327	8,070
Active Employment Programmes (IŞKUR's job training, apprenticeships, etc.)	–	152	343	495
Reduction of social security contributions for young and female workers (May 2008)	16	66	137	219
Increase in unemployment benefits	40	119	87	246
Increase of working time fund	–	162	106	268
Temporary public employment programme (infrastructure investment)	–	78	151	229
Total costs of employment-related measures	73	4,303	5,000	9,527
As a ratio to GDP (%)	0.01	0.45	0.49	–
General total including other measures	9,365	32,612	22,889	64,866
Total stimulus measures as a ratio to GDP (%)	0.99	3.42	2.23	–
Memo: GDP estimates (for 2010; last four quarters)	950,000	952,635	1,025,500	–

Source: Yeldan (2010) based on State Planning Organization, Pre-accession Economic Program Table 3.1 (for full text see www.spo.gov.tr); IŞKUR Bulletin, 2009, No. 41; IŞKUR (2009b) *Report to the Vth General Assembly Undersecretariat of Turkey.*

is still suffering from structural problems: rural–urban transition is still ongoing; the levels of education of the population and the workforce are still low; inactivity is high, especially for women; informal employment is still high; these features are just three facets of an ongoing transition. The upshot is that Turkey had ongoing structural labour market problems when it was hit by the global economic crisis.

During the crisis period in Turkey, agricultural employment rose, reflecting that the sector acted as a buffer to job losses in the informal and formal sectors. A more negative development was the increase in discouraged workers, which went up by 500,000 from the summer to the autumn of 2009. However, results from the micro-econometric analysis indicate that the crisis of 2009 did not change much in the labour market, and the longer-term issues are still very much evident, especially the lack of access to formal sector jobs for individuals with low levels of educational attainment. This chapter also underscores that, beyond the short-time working scheme, most labour market institutions and policies did not appear to be effective or have a wide coverage. There is a clear need to equip the future labour force with better skills, and to provide enough resources for active labour market policies. Moreover, given the serious gender gap identified throughout the analysis, there is a need for policies promoting equality of opportunity and social inclusion, with a focus on women and young people in particular. This would foster the transition of the informal economy to a formal one.

The long-term policy agenda for the country should, therefore, focus on establishing and promoting efficient labour market regulations, for example, a set of institutions and policies that will enhance job quality and satisfaction, without hindering economic efficiency and (formal) employment growth. In particular, Turkey must improve education standards to equip its labour force with better skills, extend social security coverage and review possibly the 'too-costly' segments of labour market institutions, such as employers' social contributions or high severance pay. Moreover, self-employment, which is still a key part of employment in Turkey, should be fostered as an important driver of entrepreneurship – and not a coping mechanism for the lack of primary segment jobs.

Finally, an important question linked to Turkey's transition and not addressed in this chapter concerns the way in which productivity and wages can be improved in the informal economy. Easing the borrowing constraints faced by informal economy firms and providing the owners and workers in these firms with training and education programmes are ways in which productivity and working conditions can be improved.

Appendix

Table 7.A1   Logit regression results for the likelihood of labour market participation of men and women in 2006 and 2009

	2006 Men	2009 Men	2006 Women	2009 Women
	Coeff (std error)	Coeff (std error)	Coeff (std error)	Coeff (std error)
Functional Literate	0.783***	1.099***	0.085***	0.141***
	[0.058]	[0.064]	[0.032]	[0.032]
Primary School	0.699***	0.916***	−0.099***	0.000
	[0.049]	[0.054]	[0.023]	[0.024]
Secondary School	0.606***	0.942***	−0.105***	−0.007
	[0.052]	[0.056]	[0.034]	[0.034]
General High School	0.284***	0.518***	0.315***	0.441***
	[0.053]	[0.057]	[0.033]	[0.034]
Vocational High School	0.895***	1.122***	0.831***	0.911***
	[0.056]	[0.060]	[0.035]	[0.036]
Higher Education	1.097***	1.410***	2.220***	2.266***
	[0.056]	[0.059]	[0.036]	[0.034]
Age 20–24	1.379***	1.494***	0.999***	1.022***
	[0.028]	[0.029]	[0.034]	[0.035]
Age 25–29	2.370***	2.573***	1.404***	1.420***
	[0.038]	[0.041]	[0.038]	[0.039]
Age 30–34	2.368***	2.468***	1.507***	1.519***
	[0.048]	[0.050]	[0.040]	[0.041]
Age 35–39	2.051***	2.241***	1.550***	1.502***
	[0.052]	[0.054]	[0.040]	[0.041]
Age 40–44	1.730***	1.897***	1.416***	1.363***
	[0.050]	[0.054]	[0.041]	[0.042]
Age 45–49	0.596***	0.745***	1.079***	0.989***
	[0.047]	[0.048]	[0.043]	[0.044]
Age 50–54	−0.327***	−0.238***	0.877***	0.699***
	[0.046]	[0.048]	[0.045]	[0.046]
Age 55–59	−0.955***	−0.897***	0.631***	0.471***
	[0.047]	[0.049]	[0.048]	[0.049]
Age 60–64	−1.440***	−1.373***	0.318***	0.214***
	[0.050]	[0.050]	[0.054]	[0.054]
Married	1.476***	1.460***	−0.946***	−0.728***
	[0.036]	[0.037]	[0.027]	[0.026]
Divorced	0.647***	0.898***	0.074	0.377***
	[0.085]	[0.088]	[0.049]	[0.046]
Widowed	1.247***	1.082***	−0.866***	−0.654***
	[0.104]	[0.102]	[0.047]	[0.046]

No. of children aged 0–4 in household	0.01 [0.020]	0.023 [0.020]	−0.285*** [0.016]	−0.399*** [0.017]
No. of children aged 5–11 in household	−0.003 [0.014]	0.049*** [0.015]	−0.096*** [0.012]	−0.147*** [0.012]
No. of children aged 12–15 in household	0.100*** [0.019]	0.109*** [0.020]	−0.016 [0.017]	−0.018 [0.017]
No. of adults aged 65 plus in household	−0.080*** [0.022]	−0.107*** [0.022]	0.018 [0.018]	−0.003 [0.018]
Household size	0.023*** [0.007]	0.011 [0.007]	0.080*** [0.006]	0.085*** [0.006]
West Marmara	0.148*** [0.041]	0.152*** [0.040]	0.325*** [0.036]	0.381*** [0.034]
Aegean	−0.115*** [0.029]	0.005 [0.029]	0.063** [0.028]	0.213*** [0.027]
East Marmara	−0.133*** [0.031]	0.054* [0.031]	0.096*** [0.030]	0.216*** [0.030]
West Anatolia	−0.170*** [0.033]	−0.033 [0.032]	−0.232*** [0.033]	0.054* [0.030]
Mediterranean	−0.029 [0.032]	0.300*** [0.031]	0.043 [0.030]	0.315*** [0.029]
Central Anatolia	−0.317*** [0.040]	−0.168*** [0.044]	−0.461*** [0.042]	−0.440*** [0.044]
West Black Sea	0.011 [0.034]	0.121*** [0.036]	0.455*** [0.031]	0.786*** [0.030]
East Black Sea	−0.012 [0.045]	0.123** [0.049]	0.962*** [0.039]	0.989*** [0.042]
North-East Anatolia	−0.115** [0.046]	0.091* [0.048]	0.031 [0.041]	0.247*** [0.041]
Mid-East Anatolia	−0.388*** [0.043]	−0.165*** [0.043]	−0.485*** [0.040]	−0.580*** [0.042]
South-East Anatolia	−0.667*** [0.036]	−0.484*** [0.037]	−1.722*** [0.047]	−1.113*** [0.044]
Rural	0.383*** [0.020]	0.479*** [0.021]	1.164*** [0.017]	1.144*** [0.018]
Constant	−1.319*** [0.065]	−1.721*** [0.068]	−2.262*** [0.052]	−2.442*** [0.052]
N	152,951	157,201	167,033	168,751
Pseudo R squared	0.264	0.270	0.171	0.177
Predicted participation	0.824	0.837	0.214	0.244
Observed participation	0.744	0.752	0.256	0.284

Notes: Robust standard errors in brackets. Covers men aged 15–64 years. * significant at 10%; ** significant at 5%; *** significant at 1%. Reference categories are illiterates for schooling level; ages 15–19 for age categories; single for marital status; and Istanbul for regions.

Table 7.A2 Multinomial regression results for men in 2006 (Base category: out-of-labour force)

	Formal	Informal	Unemployed	Discouraged
	Marginal effect	Marginal effect	Marginal effect	Marginal effect
Functional Literate	0.016***	0.093***	0.042***	0.002***
	[0.002]	[0.011]	[0.008]	[0.001]
Primary School	0.038***	0.084***	0.032***	0.001**
	[0.004]	[0.009]	[0.006]	[0.001]
Secondary School	0.056***	0.009	0.018***	0.000
	[0.005]	[0.007]	[0.005]	[0.000]
General High School	0.059***	−0.065***	0.002	0.000
	[0.005]	[0.005]	[0.004]	[0.000]
Vocational High School	0.107***	−0.015**	0.029***	0.000
	[0.009]	[0.007]	[0.006]	[0.001]
Higher Education	0.149***	−0.084***	0.033***	−0.001**
	[0.011]	[0.006]	[0.007]	[0.000]
Age 20–24	0.036***	0.153***	0.102***	0.004***
	[0.002]	[0.007]	[0.006]	[0.001]
Age 25–29	0.088***	0.242***	0.165***	0.005***
	[0.004]	[0.009]	[0.009]	[0.001]
Age 30–34	0.114***	0.200***	0.146***	0.004***
	[0.005]	[0.011]	[0.010]	[0.001]
Age 35–39	0.109***	0.139***	0.124***	0.004***
	[0.005]	[0.011]	[0.010]	[0.001]
Age 40–44	0.094***	0.078***	0.095***	0.001
	[0.005]	[0.010]	[0.008]	[0.001]
Age 45–49	0.030***	−0.029***	0.022***	0.001
	[0.002]	[0.007]	[0.005]	[0.001]
Age 50–54	0.004***	−0.090***	−0.013***	−0.001*
	[0.001]	[0.005]	[0.003]	[0.000]
Age 55–59	−0.003***	−0.125***	−0.032***	−0.002***
	[0.000]	[0.004]	[0.001]	[0.000]
Age 60–64	−0.006***	−0.146***	−0.042***	−0.003***
	[0.000]	[0.003]	[0.001]	[0.000]
Married	0.028***	0.276***	0.012***	0.000
	[0.001]	[0.009]	[0.003]	[0.000]
Divorced	0.002**	0.151***	0.054***	0.005***
	[0.001]	[0.021]	[0.009]	[0.002]
Widowed	0.016***	0.243***	0.016	−0.001
	[0.003]	[0.026]	[0.015]	[0.001]
No. of children aged 0–4 in household	−0.003	0.008***	−0.003*	0.000
	[0.002]	[0.003]	[0.002]	[0.001]
No. of children aged 5–11 in household	−0.005***	0.007***	−0.003***	0.000
	[0.002]	[0.002]	[0.001]	[0.000]

No. of children aged 12–15 in household	0.006** [0.003]	0.008*** [0.003]	−0.002 [0.002]	0.001 [0.001]
No. of adults aged 65 plus in household	−0.017*** [0.003]	0.006* [0.003]	0.003 [0.002]	0.000 [0.001]
Household size	−0.012*** [0.001]	0.010*** [0.001]	0.004*** [0.001]	0.001*** [0.000]
West Marmara	0.002*** [0.000]	0.038*** [0.008]	−0.005 [0.003]	0.014*** [0.003]
Aegean	−0.001*** [0.000]	−0.015*** [0.005]	−0.005** [0.002]	0.003** [0.001]
East Marmara	0.001* [0.000]	−0.040*** [0.005]	−0.007*** [0.002]	−0.001 [0.001]
West Anatolia	−0.001*** [0.000]	−0.028*** [0.006]	0.000 [0.002]	0.005*** [0.002]
Mediterranean	−0.002*** [0.000]	0.019*** [0.006]	0.012*** [0.003]	0.021*** [0.004]
Central Anatolia	−0.002*** [0.000]	−0.050*** [0.006]	−0.001 [0.003]	0.008*** [0.002]
West Black Sea	−0.001** [0.000]	0.021*** [0.007]	−0.009*** [0.002]	0.005*** [0.002]
East Black Sea	−0.001*** [0.000]	0.027*** [0.009]	−0.012*** [0.003]	0.009*** [0.002]
North-East Anatolia	−0.003*** [0.000]	0.051*** [0.009]	−0.018*** [0.002]	0.026*** [0.005]
Mid-East Anatolia	−0.005*** [0.000]	−0.004 [0.007]	−0.001 [0.003]	0.032*** [0.006]
South-East Anatolia	−0.005*** [0.000]	−0.030*** [0.006]	−0.004* [0.002]	0.065*** [0.009]
Rural	−0.000*** [0.000]	0.135*** [0.004]	−0.008*** [0.001]	0.003*** [0.000]
N	152,951			

Notes: Robust standard errors in brackets. Covers men aged 15–64 years. * significant at 10%; ** significant at 5%; *** significant at 1%. Reference categories are illiterates for schooling level; ages 15–19 for age categories; single for marital status; and Istanbul for regions. Base category is out-of-the-labour force.

Table 7.A3 Multinomial regression results for men in 2009 (Base category: out-of-labour force)

	Formal	Informal	Unemployed	Discouraged
	Marginal effect	Marginal effect	Marginal effect	Marginal effect
Functional Literate	0.018***	0.103***	0.078***	0.001**
	[0.002]	[0.009]	[0.010]	[0.001]
Primary School	0.041***	0.075***	0.050***	0.000
	[0.004]	[0.006]	[0.007]	[0.000]
Secondary School	0.060***	0.045***	0.038***	0.000
	[0.005]	[0.006]	[0.006]	[0.000]
General High School	0.055***	−0.016***	0.004	0.000
	[0.005]	[0.004]	[0.005]	[0.000]
Vocational High School	0.101***	0.019***	0.040***	0.000
	[0.008]	[0.005]	[0.007]	[0.000]
Higher Education	0.155***	−0.018***	0.046***	0.000
	[0.011]	[0.004]	[0.007]	[0.000]
Age 20–24	0.039***	0.100***	0.159***	0.001***
	[0.002]	[0.005]	[0.007]	[0.000]
Age 25–29	0.107***	0.160***	0.247***	0.002***
	[0.005]	[0.008]	[0.010]	[0.000]
Age 30–34	0.121***	0.125***	0.224***	0.002***
	[0.005]	[0.008]	[0.011]	[0.001]
Age 35–39	0.117***	0.102***	0.187***	0.001*
	[0.005]	[0.008]	[0.011]	[0.001]
Age 40–44	0.099***	0.072***	0.139***	0.001
	[0.005]	[0.007]	[0.010]	[0.001]
Age 45–49	0.030***	0.004	0.027***	0.000
	[0.002]	[0.005]	[0.005]	[0.000]
Age 50–54	0.003***	−0.035***	−0.021***	0.000
	[0.001]	[0.004]	[0.003]	[0.000]
Age 55–59	−0.004***	−0.057***	−0.042***	−0.000**
	[0.000]	[0.003]	[0.002]	[0.000]
Age 60–64	−0.007***	−0.066***	−0.054***	−0.001***
	[0.000]	[0.002]	[0.001]	[0.000]
Married	0.034***	0.192***	0.036***	0.001***
	[0.001]	[0.008]	[0.003]	[0.000]
Divorced	0.007***	0.108***	0.091***	0.002*
	[0.001]	[0.015]	[0.012]	[0.001]
Widowed	0.011***	0.132***	0.054***	0.000
	[0.003]	[0.019]	[0.018]	[0.001]

No. of children aged 0–4 in household	−0.004 [0.003]	0.007*** [0.003]	0.000 [0.002]	0.001** [0.000]
No. of children aged 5–11 in household	−0.003 [0.002]	0.010*** [0.002]	−0.002 [0.001]	0.001*** [0.000]
No. of children aged 12–15 in household	0.007** [0.003]	0.006** [0.003]	0.000 [0.002]	0.000 [0.001]
No. of adults aged 65-plus in household	−0.018*** [0.003]	0.010*** [0.003]	−0.003 [0.002]	0.001 [0.001]
Household size	−0.013*** [0.001]	0.008*** [0.001]	0.005*** [0.001]	0.000 [0.000]
West Marmara	0.001** [0.000]	0.039*** [0.006]	−0.010*** [0.003]	0.005*** [0.002]
Aegean	0.000 [0.000]	0.006 [0.003]	0.000 [0.002]	0.003*** [0.001]
East Marmara	0.001*** [0.000]	0.003 [0.004]	0.001 [0.003]	−0.001 [0.000]
West Anatolia	0.000 [0.000]	0.009** [0.004]	−0.011*** [0.002]	0.001* [0.001]
Mediterranean	0.000 [0.000]	0.066*** [0.005]	0.027*** [0.003]	0.011*** [0.003]
Central Anatolia	−0.002*** [0.000]	0.000 [0.005]	−0.002 [0.004]	0.008*** [0.002]
West Black Sea	−0.001** [0.000]	0.056*** [0.005]	−0.021*** [0.002]	0.005*** [0.002]
East Black Sea	−0.002*** [0.000]	0.067*** [0.007]	−0.027*** [0.003]	−0.001 [0.000]
North-East Anatolia	−0.003*** [0.000]	0.071*** [0.007]	−0.016*** [0.003]	0.006*** [0.002]
Mid-East Anatolia	−0.004*** [0.000]	0.015*** [0.005]	0.001 [0.003]	0.008*** [0.002]
South-East Anatolia	−0.005*** [0.000]	0.009** [0.005]	−0.020*** [0.002]	0.022*** [0.005]
Rural	0.001*** [0.000]	0.097*** [0.003]	−0.004** [0.002]	0.001*** [0.000]
N	157,201			

Notes: Robust standard errors in brackets. Covers men aged 15–64 years. * significant at 10%; ** significant at 5%; *** significant at 1%. Reference categories are illiterates for schooling level; ages 15–19 for age categories; single for marital status; and Istanbul for regions. Base category is out-of-the-labour force.

Table 7.A4 Multinomial regression results for women in 2006 (Base category: out-of-labour force)

	Formal	Informal	Unemployed	Discouraged
	Marginal effect	Marginal effect	Marginal effect	Marginal effect
Functional Literate	0.006***	0.001	0.012***	0.001***
	[0.001]	[0.003]	[0.003]	[0.000]
Primary School	0.008***	−0.007***	0.013***	0.001***
	[0.001]	[0.002]	[0.003]	[0.000]
Secondary School	0.029***	−0.032***	0.018***	0.001***
	[0.004]	[0.002]	[0.004]	[0.000]
General High School	0.058***	−0.039***	0.041***	0.002***
	[0.007]	[0.002]	[0.006]	[0.000]
Vocational High School	0.099***	−0.033***	0.067***	0.002***
	[0.010]	[0.003]	[0.010]	[0.000]
Higher Education	0.280***	−0.037***	0.116***	0.001***
	[0.022]	[0.003]	[0.015]	[0.000]
Age 20–24	0.012***	0.058***	0.019***	0.001***
	[0.001]	[0.005]	[0.002]	[0.000]
Age 25–29	0.034***	0.068***	0.028***	0.002***
	[0.002]	[0.006]	[0.003]	[0.000]
Age 30–34	0.041***	0.079***	0.025***	0.003***
	[0.003]	[0.007]	[0.003]	[0.000]
Age 35–39	0.048***	0.097***	0.016***	0.003***
	[0.003]	[0.008]	[0.002]	[0.000]
Age 40–44	0.029***	0.104***	0.007***	0.002***
	[0.002]	[0.008]	[0.002]	[0.000]
Age 45–49	0.010***	0.092***	−0.003***	0.001***
	[0.001]	[0.008]	[0.001]	[0.000]
Age 50–54	0.003***	0.080***	−0.007***	0.000
	[0.001]	[0.007]	[0.001]	[0.000]
Age 55–59	−0.001***	0.052***	−0.008***	−0.000***
	[0.000]	[0.007]	[0.000]	[0.000]
Age 60–64	−0.002***	0.015**	−0.010***	−0.001***
	[0.000]	[0.006]	[0.000]	[0.000]
Married	−0.002***	−0.041***	−0.008***	−0.001***
	[0.000]	[0.002]	[0.000]	[0.000]
Divorced	0.000	0.010	0.009***	0.000
	[0.000]	[0.006]	[0.002]	[0.000]
Widowed	−0.001***	−0.046***	−0.004***	−0.001***
	[0.000]	[0.002]	[0.001]	[0.000]
No. of children aged 0–4 in household	−0.022***	−0.020***	−0.009***	−0.002***
	[0.002]	[0.002]	[0.001]	[0.001]

No. of children	−0.016***	0.000	−0.003***	−0.001
aged 5–11 in household	[0.001]	[0.001]	[0.001]	[0.000]
No. of children aged	−0.007***	0.005**	−0.001	0.001
12–15 in household	[0.002]	[0.002]	[0.001]	[0.001]
No. of adults aged	−0.004**	0.008***	−0.002*	0.000
65 plus in household	[0.002]	[0.002]	[0.001]	[0.001]
Household size	0.000	0.009***	0.001***	0.000
	[0.001]	[0.001]	[0.000]	[0.000]
West Marmara	0.000	0.055***	0.007***	0.015***
	[0.000]	[0.006]	[0.001]	[0.003]
Aegean	−0.000***	0.026***	0.002***	0.004***
	[0.000]	[0.004]	[0.001]	[0.001]
East Marmara	0.000**	0.016***	0.003***	0.000
	[0.000]	[0.004]	[0.001]	[0.000]
West Anatolia	−0.001***	−0.018***	0.003***	0.001**
	[0.000]	[0.004]	[0.001]	[0.001]
Mediterranean	−0.001***	0.034***	0.006***	0.015***
	[0.000]	[0.005]	[0.001]	[0.003]
Central Anatolia	−0.002***	−0.015***	0.001	0.008***
	[0.000]	[0.004]	[0.001]	[0.002]
West Black Sea	−0.001***	0.097***	0.000	0.003***
	[0.000]	[0.006]	[0.001]	[0.001]
East Black Sea	−0.001***	0.200***	0.004***	0.012***
	[0.000]	[0.010]	[0.001]	[0.003]
North-East Anatolia	−0.002***	0.043***	−0.006***	0.011***
	[0.000]	[0.006]	[0.000]	[0.002]
Mid-East Anatolia	−0.002***	−0.015***	−0.002**	0.015***
	[0.000]	[0.004]	[0.001]	[0.003]
South-East Anatolia	−0.002***	−0.073***	−0.007***	0.005***
	[0.000]	[0.001]	[0.000]	[0.001]
Rural	−0.001***	0.227***	−0.004***	0.000**
	[0.000]	[0.004]	[0.000]	[0.000]
N	167,033			

Notes: Robust standard errors in brackets. Covers women aged 15–64 years. * significant at 10%; ** significant at 5%; *** significant at 1%. Reference categories are illiterates for schooling level; ages 15–19 for age categories; single for marital status; and Istanbul for regions. Base category is out-of-the-labour force.

Table 7.A5 Multinomial regression results for women in 2009 (Base category: out-of-labour force)

	Formal	Informal	Unemployed	Discouraged
	Marginal effect	Marginal effect	Marginal effect	Marginal effect
Functional Literate	0.005***	0.005***	0.019***	0.000**
	[0.001]	[0.002]	[0.004]	[0.000]
Primary School	0.010***	0.001	0.012***	0.000***
	[0.001]	[0.001]	[0.003]	[0.000]
Secondary School	0.026***	−0.012***	0.019***	0.000***
	[0.003]	[0.001]	[0.004]	[0.000]
General High School	0.061***	−0.019***	0.043***	0.000***
	[0.006]	[0.001]	[0.006]	[0.000]
Vocational High School	0.096***	−0.015***	0.079***	0.000***
	[0.008]	[0.002]	[0.009]	[0.000]
Higher Education	0.286***	−0.020***	0.127***	0.000**
	[0.018]	[0.002]	[0.013]	[0.000]
Age 20–24	0.016***	0.045***	0.031***	0.001***
	[0.001]	[0.004]	[0.003]	[0.000]
Age 25–29	0.039***	0.046***	0.047***	0.001***
	[0.003]	[0.005]	[0.004]	[0.000]
Age 30–34	0.048***	0.057***	0.035***	0.001***
	[0.003]	[0.005]	[0.004]	[0.000]
Age 35–39	0.052***	0.060***	0.027***	0.001***
	[0.004]	[0.005]	[0.003]	[0.000]
Age 40–44	0.036***	0.065***	0.013***	0.001***
	[0.003]	[0.005]	[0.002]	[0.000]
Age 45–49	0.014***	0.059***	−0.002	0.001***
	[0.002]	[0.005]	[0.001]	[0.000]
Age 50–54	0.002***	0.051***	−0.009***	0.000*
	[0.001]	[0.005]	[0.001]	[0.000]
Age 55–59	−0.002***	0.035***	−0.013***	0.000
	[0.001]	[0.005]	[0.001]	[0.000]
Age 60–64	−0.005***	0.019***	−0.015***	−0.000***
	[0.000]	[0.004]	[0.000]	[0.000]
Married	−0.003***	−0.017***	−0.009***	−0.000***
	[0.000]	[0.001]	[0.000]	[0.000]
Divorced	0.003***	0.013***	0.022***	−0.000*
	[0.001]	[0.004]	[0.003]	[0.000]
Widowed	−0.002***	−0.019***	−0.003*	−0.000***
	[0.000]	[0.002]	[0.002]	[0.000]
No. of children aged 0–4 in household	−0.031***	−0.024***	−0.015***	−0.003***
	[0.002]	[0.002]	[0.002]	[0.001]
No. of children aged 5–11 in household	−0.018***	−0.003**	−0.006***	−0.001
	[0.001]	[0.001]	[0.001]	[0.000]

No. of children aged 12–15 in household	−0.008*** [0.002]	0.005** [0.002]	0.000 [0.001]	0.000 [0.001]
No. of adults aged 65 plus in household	−0.004** [0.002]	0.007*** [0.002]	−0.005*** [0.001]	−0.001 [0.001]
Household size	0.000 [0.001]	0.010*** [0.001]	0.001*** [0.000]	0.000 [0.000]
West Marmara	0.002*** [0.000]	0.040*** [0.004]	0.010*** [0.002]	0.009*** [0.002]
Aegean	0.001*** [0.000]	0.027*** [0.003]	0.007*** [0.001]	0.005*** [0.001]
East Marmara	0.001*** [0.000]	0.023*** [0.003]	0.005*** [0.001]	0.000 [0.000]
West Anatolia	−0.001*** [0.000]	0.025*** [0.003]	−0.002*** [0.001]	0.002*** [0.001]
Mediterranean	−0.001*** [0.000]	0.047*** [0.004]	0.012*** [0.001]	0.013*** [0.003]
Central Anatolia	−0.003*** [0.000]	−0.002 [0.003]	−0.005*** [0.001]	0.004*** [0.001]
West Black Sea	−0.001*** [0.000]	0.116*** [0.006]	0.000 [0.001]	0.004*** [0.001]
East Black Sea	0.000 [0.000]	0.146*** [0.008]	0.000 [0.002]	0.002** [0.001]
North-East Anatolia	−0.002*** [0.000]	0.055*** [0.005]	−0.009*** [0.001]	0.010*** [0.003]
Mid-East Anatolia	−0.003*** [0.000]	−0.010*** [0.002]	−0.004*** [0.001]	0.008*** [0.002]
South-East Anatolia	−0.003*** [0.000]	−0.027*** [0.001]	−0.009*** [0.000]	0.004*** [0.001]
Rural	−0.000* [0.000]	0.152*** [0.003]	−0.004*** [0.001]	0.000** [0.000]
N	168,751			

Notes: Robust standard errors in brackets. Covers women aged 15–64 years. * significant at 10%; ** significant at 5%; *** significant at 1%. Reference categories are illiterates for schooling level; ages 15–19 for age categories; single for marital status; and Istanbul for regions. Base category is out-of-the-labour force.

Notes

1. Discouraged workers are individuals who did not work in the reference period (one week) and have not looked for work in the past three months since they believe that work is not available but can take up work within two weeks should work become available.
2. The global financial crisis hit Turkey in the last quarter of 2008. Since the micro-data relating to 2008 is annual and not quarterly, we take 2009 as the crisis year.
3. Measured as five mutually exclusive categories: illiterates (no schooling); functional literates with no diploma; primary school graduates; general high school graduates; vocational high school graduates; and university graduates.

4. Although the predicted probability of participation for functional literates, primary and secondary school graduates are about the same as that for illiterates (at about 20 per cent).
5. All differences mentioned are statistically significant at conventional levels.
6. Note that the IIA (independence of irrelevant alternatives) assumption is not satisfied in any of the models.
7. This was probably due to composition effects such as the size of agriculture in that region and levels of female employment.
8. This would avoid a withdrawal of a draft Law, as happened in 2003 when proposing the establishment of a Severance Payment Fund.

References

Statistical resources

http://epp.eurostat.ec.europa.eu/portal/page/portal/eurostat/home, accessed on 2 October 2010.
www.hazine.gov.tr: Undersecretariat of the Treasury, accessed for information on crisis measures, accessed on 2 October 2010.
www.iskur.gov.tr: Turkish Employment Agency, accessed on various dates in September 2010 to January 2011.
www.tcmb.gov.tr: Central Bank website for balance of payments statistics. Accessed on 30 September 2010, accessed on 2 October 2010.
www.tuik.gov.tr: Turkstat for most statistics used in the report. Accessed on various dates September 2010 to January 2011, accessed on 2 October 2010.
OECD Employment and Labour Market Statistics (online database at www.oecd.org, accessed on 1 October 2010).

Articles and publications

Agénor, P.-R., A. Izquierdo and H. T. Jensen (eds) (2006) *Adjustment Policies, Poverty, and Unemployment: The IMPPA Framework* (Oxford: Blackwell).
Ercan, H. (2010) 'The Impact of the Global Financial Crisis on Employment in Turkey', in H. Ercan, E. Taymaz and E. Yeldan, *Crisis and Turkey: Impact Analysis of Crisis Response Measures* (Ankara: ILO Office).
Ercan, H., E. Taymaz and E. Yeldan (2010) *Crisis and Turkey: Impact Analysis of Crisis Response Measures* (Ankara: ILO Office).
European Commission (2010) *Self-Employment in Europe 2010. European Employment Observatory Review*, Belgium (September), available at: www.eu-employment-observatory.net/resources/reviews/EEOReview-Self-Employment2010.pdf
International Labour Office (ILO) (2009) *Protecting People, Promoting Jobs, a Survey of Country Employment and Social Protection Policy Responses to the Global Economic Crisis*, ILO report submitted to the G20 Leaders' summit in Pittsburgh (September).
International Labour Office (ILO) (2011) *Turkey's Response to the Crisis*, G20 Country Briefs. ILO, Geneva. Available at: www.ilo.org/public/libdoc/jobcrisis/download/g20_turkey_countrybrief.pdf
IŞKUR (2009a) *2008 Annual Activity Report*, at: www.iskur.gov.tr.

IŞKUR (2009b) *Report to the Vth General Assembly Undersecretariat of Turkey*, at: www.iskur.gov.tr

Organisation for Economic Cooperation and Development (OECD) (2010) *PISA 2009 Results: What Students Know and Can Do – Student Performance in Reading, Mathematics and Science, Volume I* (Paris: OECD). Available at: http://dx.doi.org/10.1787/9789264091450-en.

Taymaz, E. (2007) *Labour Taxes and Labour Demand in Turkey* (Ankara: Middle East Technical University).

Taymaz, E. (2009) *Informality and Productivity: Productivity Differentials between Formal and Informal Firms in Turkey* (Ankara: Middle East Technical University).

Taymaz, E. and Ş. Özler (2005) 'Labour Market Policies and EU Accession: Problems and Prospects for Turkey', METU ERC Working Paper No. 04/05 (Ankara: Middle East Technical University).

Tunalı, I. (2003) 'Background Study on the Labour Market and Employment in Turkey', paper prepared for the European Training Foundation, Turin, June.

Verick, S. and I. Islam (2009) 'The Great Recession of 2008–2009: Causes, Consequences, and Policy Responses', IZA Discussion Paper No. 4934 (May) (Bonn: IZA).

World Bank (2005) *Turkey: Education Sector Study. Sustainable Pathways to an Effective, Equitable and Efficient Education System for Pre-school through Secondary School Education*, Report No. 32450-TU, available at: www.worldbank.org.tr.

World Bank (2009) *From Crops to Jobs: A Report on Female Labor Force Participation in Turkey*. Draft.

World Bank (2010) *Turkey Country Economic Memorandum – Informality: Causes, Consequences, Policies*, Document of the World Bank, Report No. 48523-TR (March).

Yeldan, E. (2010) 'The Impact of the Global Financial Crisis on Employment in Turkey', in H. Ercan, E. Taymaz and E. Yeldan, *Crisis and Turkey: Impact Analysis of Crisis Response Measures* (Ankara: ILO Office for Turkey).

8
Conclusion

This book has traversed a broad range of labour market issues in emerging economies, with an in-depth focus on the situation in Brazil, Indonesia, South Africa and Turkey. Based on the empirical analysis of labour market indicators and a review of policies and institutions, the analyses identify a number of common trends and specific challenges.

The rapid economic growth in emerging economies has propelled the transformation of the global economy. In 1990, emerging economies together with developing countries represented just 30.8 per cent of world gross domestic product (adjusted for purchasing power parity). By 2012, this share had reached 50 per cent. The 2000s were a golden age of robust growth in all emerging economies, which was brought to an abrupt halt in 2008 as the global financial crisis sent shockwaves around the world. However, due to a range of factors, including robust domestic markets, large foreign currency reserves, low debt levels, and effective policy response to this deep downturn, the recovery in 2010 was swift in most middle-income countries, reflecting a further shift in the global economic balance.

Nonetheless, despite robust economic progress in emerging economies and, in most cases, falling rates of poverty, the labour markets of these countries have not always benefited to the same extent. In particular, informality, working poverty and vulnerable employment continue to be the norm for most workers. At the same time, women, youth and other segments of the population face hurdles to accessing the few good jobs in the formal economy.

For this reason, unemployment is typically not the best indicator of distress in the labour market. More importantly, the labour markets in emerging economies continue to be characterized by strong segmentation between a small formal sector and a large informal sector. Many people continue to live in rural areas and rely on small household plots and subsistence farming, while an increasing number have left for urban areas and to seek their fortunes in other countries. Another common feature is the presence of gender disparities as reflected by low female labour force participation in some countries (notably in India and Turkey), underrepresentation in industry and overrepresentation in informal employment in most economies. Other labour market inequalities exist for such groups as youth, as noted above, and some segments of society that have been excluded from benefiting from economic gains, such as the African population in South Africa and Brazil and the scheduled castes in India.

Altogether, the global financial crisis had a diverse impact on emerging economies with more severe outcomes in Central and Eastern Europe and the Commonwealth of Independent States (such as the Russian Federation) and milder effects in Asia (such as Indonesia). However, even for the harder-hit countries, economic recovery in emerging economies was strong in 2010 and has, subsequently, led to a fall in unemployment. Overall, these countries have demonstrated considerable resilience to the downturn of 2009, which contrasts with their experience in earlier periods of crisis. The milder impact on employment and wage outcomes in these emerging economies can be explained by a combination of factors including the continuing growth of China and its subsequent impact on commodity exporters, large domestic markets, lack of exposure to the financial calamities that hit the United States and Europe, and better policymaking. In terms of the last reason, the country chapters present specific examples of how policymakers responded to the downturn through stimulus packages and active labour market policies.

The country chapters reveal a number of commonalities and specific challenges in the labour market. Following decades of high inequality and poverty along with bouts of high inflation and crises, the performance of the Brazilian economy and labour market over the past decade has been, in some respects, a great success, notably in terms of falling unemployment and informality rates. However, inequalities remain, as reflected in poorer outcomes across regions and population segments and by educational attainment. Indonesia is another country that had suffered during the 1990s in the wake of the East Asian financial crisis but, this time around, the downturn was brief and conditions in the labour market have only improved. Nonetheless, as in most emerging economies, far less progress has been made on generating regular jobs in the formal economy; in fact, there has been a casualization of the labour market, particularly for the low-skilled. South Africa has exhibited fewer positive trends: the country has been battling with legacies of Apartheid since 1994, as captured by one of the world's highest unemployment rates, which is far higher for women, youth and the African population. During the first post-Apartheid recession in 2009, the labour market gains of previous years were wiped out: employment fell by almost 1 million, leading to a rise, in particular, in discouraged workers. Turkey is another country that has experienced many bouts of banking and currency crises. Despite a sharp contraction in 2009, the impact of the global financial crisis on the Turkish labour market proved to be more temporary.

The analysis of the unit-level data both confirms the insights provided by the aggregate data along with highlighting key issues. In this respect, the strongest common element to the analysis is the fundamental role education plays in determining labour outcomes. In Brazil, individuals with low levels of education have been less likely to move into formal employment, despite the strong gains in this dimension over the past decade. Indonesians with less than high school education are much more likely to be in casual jobs rather than in regular employment. In the South African case, those with poor levels of education have a much higher chance of being employed in the informal sector and giving up job search (that is, being discouraged). Finally, in Turkey, low educational attainment is associated with a greater likelihood of being unemployed or employed in the informal economy. Improving education and enhancing skills development, therefore, should be priorities of all emerging economies to ensure that future growth is more inclusive.

The comparative and detailed country-specific insights on labour market policies and institutions indicate that policymakers in emerging economies are, increasingly, turning to these interventions to shape and improve labour market outcomes. With regard to policies, countries are utilizing a range of measures to improve the match between labour demand and supply, while also trying to protect and create jobs, most notably during the global financial crisis. In emerging economies, training programmes are a common way of enhancing employability, while countries are running a range of entrepreneurship funds (typically targeting youth and women) and public employment programmes. Innovative schemes include the Indian Mahatma Gandhi National Rural Employment Guarantee Scheme, which is a rights-based approach. South Africa has also placed considerable emphasis on the Expanded Public Works Programme, and, more recently, the Community Works Programme. Like many advanced economies (most famously in Germany), Turkey relied on its work-sharing scheme to protect workers during the downturn in 2009. Countries such as Brazil (and others in Latin America) place more emphasis on conditional cash transfers, namely Bolsa Família, rather than interventions that directly target labour market outcomes.

Overall, the book confirms that labour market policies are increasingly being used and innovative schemes are being developed to tackle persistent labour market challenges. However, considerable gaps remain, for example, policies that target the low levels of job search among the poorly educated in South Africa. That said, it must also be remembered that labour market policies can only be part of the solution; ultimately, improvements in terms of employment and wages can only come about if the macroeconomic conditions are supportive. Hence, policymakers need to pursue complementarities and coherence with a broader set of macroeconomic and sectoral policies.

This book also examines the contentious issues that surround labour market issues, namely employment protection legislation and minimum wages. In Indonesian Manpower Law of 2003 (and the severance payments covered by this law) has been a highly controversial piece of legislation, but there is little evidence that it is a major hindrance to job creation in the country. Moreover, rather than having a negative impact on employment in the formal sector, minimum wages appear to, in fact, have had positive spill-over effects on wages in the economy. Also known in the literature as the 'lighthouse effect', this function of minimum wages has particularly helped improve workers' bargaining power in the informal sector and, thus, can make a serious contribution to poverty alleviation and a reduction in inequality, as has been evident in the case of Brazil.

In this context, this book goes beyond a narrow approach, with a focus only on flexibility, to the detrimental effects of labour market institutions, and argues that empirical evidence on the role of minimum wages and EPL, in particular, is facing serious measurement challenges. Moreover, it argues that research hitherto carried out in this field systematically assumed the direction of causality as going from institutions to economic performances without considering a possible reverse causality. The important message from this analysis is that policymakers should address security concerns in terms of employment and social protection more broadly. Ultimately, the aim should be to develop a comprehensive and integrated set of policies and institutions that promote effective worker protection, for job and income security, along with working conditions, while ensuring that employers have the necessary internal and external flexibility to cope with the demands of the globalized economy. This requires a sharing of the burden of protection between workers, employers and government, which can only be achieved through constructive and transparent social dialogue.

In summary, policymakers need to engage in social dialogue to focus on:

- Promoting the formalization of enterprises and workers through both stronger incentives (such as progressive taxation and access to social security) and improved labour inspection;
- Enhancing enforcement and relevance of labour market regulations, such as employment protection legislation and minimum wages in order to increase protection to workers, while not unduly hindering the flexibility of employers – here, the important issue is that governments and tripartite partners should strive to cultivate both flexibility and security which, in turn, reinforces positive outcomes in the labour market and the economy as a whole;
- Expanding coverage of social protection (in line with the recommendations of the ILO-initiated Social Protection Floor) to improve income security of workers and their families to help further reduce poverty and inequality, while supporting labour market participation;
- Improving access to and the quality of education and training, especially with the involvement of employers, to reduce the phenomenon of skills mismatch; and
- Enhancing (active) labour market policies that target both long-term structural problems and mitigate the impact of economic and natural shocks through both targeted interventions (such as interventions specifically targeted at youth and women) and universal schemes (such as public employment programmes).

Index

Italic page numbers indicate tables; bold indicate figures.

Printed and bound by CPI Group (UK) Ltd, Croydon, CR0 4YY